Y0-DEU-766

Berger, Louis S/Psychoanalytic theory an
RC506 .B38 1985 C.1 STACKS 1985

RC
506
B38
1985

Berger, Louis S.

Psychoanalytic
theory and clinical
relevance

DATE DUE

COLLEGE FOR HUMAN SERVICES
LIBRARY
345 HUDSON STREET
NEW YORK, N.Y. 10014

PSYCHOANALYTIC THEORY
AND
CLINICAL RELEVANCE

PSYCHOANALYTIC THEORY AND CLINICAL RELEVANCE

What Makes a Theory Consequential for Practice?

Louis S. Berger

THE ANALYTIC PRESS
1985

Distributed by
LAWRENCE ERLBAUM ASSOCIATES, PUBLISHERS
Hillsdale, New Jersey   London

Copyright © 1985 by The Analytic Press.
 All rights reserved. No part of this book may be reproduced in any form, by photostat, microform, retrieval system, or any other means, without the prior written permission of the publisher.

The Analytic Press

Distributed solely by

Lawrence Erlbaum Associates, Inc., Publishers
365 Broadway
Hillsdale, New Jersey 07642

Library of Congress Cataloging in Publication Data

Berger, Louis S.
 Psychoanalytic theory and clinical relevance.

 Bibliography: p.
 Includes index.
 1. Psychoanalysis—Philosophy. 2. Psychoanalysis—Methodology. 3. Psychotherapy I. Title. [DNLM:
1. Psychoanalytic theory. WM 460 B496p]
 RC506.B38   1985   150.19′5   85–9023
 ISBN 0–88163–042–X

Printed in the United States of America
10 9 8 7 6 5 4 3 2 1

Table of Contents

ACKNOWLEDGMENTS ... ix

CHAPTER 1. INTRODUCTION ... 1

CHAPTER 2. LOGICAL ENTAILMENT ... 9

  The Spectrum of Opinion
    Theory and Therapy Are Closely Tied
    Against Entailment or Relevance
    The Mainstream Moderate Range
  The Evidence
    Empirical Origins of Technique
    Questionable Counterexamples
    Curative Factors
    Technical Progress
    Therapeutic Effectiveness
    One-Many Relationships
    Many-One Relationships
    Overkill
  Actual Ties
    Observation, Description, and Explanation
    Diagnostics
    Models, Metaphors, and Technique
    Correlation
  The Matter of the "Clinical Theory"
  Comments

CHAPTER 3. SCIENCE, STATE PROCESS, AND THE LIFE WORLD ... 35

  Normal Science Frameworks
    Internal Domain
    Significant Fact
    Matching Facts with Theory
    Additional Aspects

State Process Formalisms
  State Spaces in the Natural Sciences
  State Spaces in the Behavioral Disciplines
  Emerging Difficulties
Mainstream Criticisms
  Logical Certainty: Indubitable Formal Foundations
  Objective Certainty: Indubitable Empirical Foundations
  Object Language and Theoretical Language
  Operationalization and Verification
  Translation, Commensurability
  Issues Raised by Contemporary Physics
Criticisms from Without: Science and the Life World
  The Cheshire Cat Phenomenon
  The Life World
  The Derivative Status of Science
Problem Areas, Undesirable Consequences
  Representational Defects
  Compartmentalization
  Motivations for Retaining Cartesianism and
     State Process Formalisms
Implications for Formalisms in Behavioral Disciplines

CHAPTER 4. THEORETICAL DISCOURSE　　　　　　　71

Scientific Views of Language
  Internal Features
  External Features
Traditional Psychoanalytic Views about Theoretical Discourse
  Internal Features
  External Features
Criticisms: Language, World, Person
  Wholeness
  Language as a Logical System
  Mechanization of the Person
  Ontology
  Reflexivity—the Remainder Problem, Again
  Explanation and Transparency
Implications: Representational Capacity
  and Theoretical Discourse

CHAPTER 5. THE FOCUS OF THEORIZING　　　　　　　100

The Pure Knowledge Medical Paradigm
  Pure versus Applied Knowledge
  A General Psychology

Table of Contents vii

 Theorizing in Medicine
 Psychotherapy and Medicine

CHAPTER 6. CLINICAL PRAGMATISM 111

 Levels and Models
  Ingredients of Cognitive Levels
  Hierarchies of Cognitive Levels
  Relationships across Levels

 Clinical Pragmatism as a Separate Cognitive Level
  Levels in Psychoanalytic Theory
  Advantages of a Clinical Cognitive Level

 Formalism: The Process Narrative
  The Requirements
  Specification by Proscription
  Specification by Example
  Salient Features

 Pragmatism: Background

 Pragmatism and the Process Narrative
  Legitimate Questions
  Thought Experiments

 A Critical Review of Past Proposals in Psychoanalysis
  Linguistic Proposals
  Proposals for "Clinically Useful" Theories
  Summary of Findings
  Some Possible Objections

CHAPTER 7. SPECULATIONS AND GENERALIZATIONS 154

 About Constructing Solutions
  Systematizing versus Edifying Traditions
  The Value of Generative Questions
  Looking before Leaping
  "Of Course"—the Obvious

 Speculations: The Clinically Relevant Framework
  Consensus: The State of the Art
  Oedipal Pathology and Classical Therapy
  Preoedipal Pathology and Expanded Analytic Therapy

 Generalization I: Other Clinical Frameworks

 Generalization II: Critics of Mainstream Behavioral Disciplines, and Backsliding
  Unorthodox Criticisms
  The Return of Disclaimed Practices—Formal Issues
  Focal Issues

Generalization III: First Language Acquisition
Bridging the Gulf
Trivialization of the Problem
Application of State Process Analysis
Generalization IV: Free Will, Determinism, Causality
Generalization V: Affects
Comment

REFERENCES   192

AUTHOR INDEX   205

SUBJECT INDEX   210

Acknowledgments

I am most grateful to Nicholas Cariello for his excellent line editing of the manuscript. His judicious pruning and weeding smoothed the discourse considerably. Furthermore, he raised some important substantive questions that needed to be, and were, addressed.

It is also a pleasure to acknowledge the help of two readers. Paul Stepansky, Ph.D., Editor-in-Chief of The Analytic Press, pointed out a number of problems that required attention, and suggested several recent references that enabled me to strengthen the discussion at key points. A publisher's reader offered comments and criticisms that prompted me to undertake certain organizational changes and to add elaborative material; the final version has profited from his input as well.

Ideas remain impractical when we have not grasped or been grasped by them. When we do not get an idea, we ask "how" to put it in practice, thereby trying to turn insights of the soul into actions of the ego. But when an insight or idea has sunk in, practice invisibly changes. The idea has opened the eye of the soul. By seeing differently, we do differently. Then "how" is implicitly taken care of. "How?" disappears as the idea sinks in—as one reflects upon *it* rather than on how to do something with it. This movement of grasping ideas is vertical or inward rather than horizontal or outward into the realm of doing something. The only legitimate "How?" in regard to these psychological insights is: "How can I grasp an idea?"

—James Hillman, *Re-Visioning Psychology*

ONE

Introduction

It is common knowledge that from its inception psychoanalysis has been plagued by difficulties and controversies, internal as well as external. The structure and content of its theory, diverse and sometimes conflicting recommendations concerning its technique, its status as a science, its effectiveness as therapy, its legitimacy as an investigative methodology, and its claim to being a general psychological theory are representative issues that remain largely unresolved today.

In the recent literature, for example, one finds general references to "the chaos pervading the entire area of psychotherapy and psychotherapy research to which several authors . . . have called attention" (Strupp, 1972, p. 76), or to "disarray in the theory and practice of psychoanalysis" (Levenson, 1972, p. 13). It has been said that "its theory and its method as science seem continuously to require justification" (Wallerstein, 1976, p. 198). Regarding its effectiveness as therapy, Strupp (1972) observes that "in the research literature . . . one finds a growing disenchantment with psychoanalysis and psychotherapy based on psychoanalytic principles" (p. 71); according to Gedo (1979), there is "a crisis of confidence on our own [psychoanalysts'] part concerning the effectiveness of psychoanalysis as therapy" (p. ix); Stein (1972) reports that "while the majority of patients—probably 60 to 80 percent—respond more or less favorably to psychoanalytic psychotherapy, a considerable number respond poorly or not at all. This is true even when the patients are carefully selected and the treatment is skillfully given" (p. 37).

The issues to which these comments broadly refer will be discussed in detail throughout this work. For the moment, I should like to single out one of them—the effectiveness of psychoanalysis as therapy—for some initial, quite general observations. Let me emphasize that the ensuing discussion is intended to provide no more than an informal introduction to problems I address with greater rigor in subsequent chapters.

As suggested by the remarks of Strupp, Gedo, and Stein, the effectiveness of psychoanalysis as therapy remains as controversial a subject today as it was at the turn of the century, for practitioners as well as observers, and in spite of considerable efforts to settle the matter. The persistence of the controversy supports the view of some (e.g., Greenson, 1967; Glover, 1972) that advances in clinical efficacy have been minimal since the essentials of psychoanalytic therapy were promulgated by Freud. Now, in a way, this is a quite curious situation. Here we have some ninety-odd years of psychoanalytic theorizing, and there are credible commentators within the field who agree that therapeutic effectiveness has failed to make corresponding significant advances, that the clinical yield of intense, concerted, continuing theorizing by a large number of workers has been disappointing.

Clinical relevance. Under these circumstances, it seems reasonable to wonder whether psychoanalytic theorizing is "clinically relevant." The record suggests that very possibly it is not; one could conclude, almost by definition, that if after so many years of considerable effort theorizing has failed to produce significant clinical progress, then it cannot be relevant theorizing.

I say "almost by definition" because the notion that clinically relevant theorizing simply is theorizing that somehow leads to improvements in clinical efficacy does not take us very far; at best it specifies an outcome measure, a necessary but not sufficient criterion. It does not describe the *kind* of relationship that ought to obtain between a relevant theory and its clinical products.

Let us try again. Could clinically relevant theorizing simply be theorizing about such clinical phenomena and ingredients as transference, resistance, or interpretation? About psychopathology (e.g., about genesis, nosology)? About the clinical material? About therapeutic action? There certainly has been a good deal of such theorizing in the past; but if we provisionally accept the premise that theorizing has failed to produce advances in clinical efficacy, and the necessary (but not sufficient) criterion that it should, then it becomes reasonable to reject definitions of clinical relevance based on these kinds of specifications and characterizations.

It is unlikely, then, that clinically relevant theorizing simply is equivalent to theorizing about matters that bear directly on the clinical situation. It begins to look as though when one attempts to pin down the meaning of "clinical relevance," one discovers that the notion itself is elusive and obscure; indeed, as we shall see, such attempts lead into deeper and deeper waters, and into more controversial realms.

It would seem that the meanings, the theoretical and empirical implications, of this notion could stand clarification and explication. It would therefore make sense first to seek an adequate understanding of just what kind of a theory one is searching for, what characteristics a clinically relevant theory should or should not have, before one attempts actually to construct that kind of a theory. To provide such clarification is one prominent goal of this monograph.

Logical entailment. Typically, discussions in the literature that take one or another position on issues concerning the clinical relevance of psychoanalytic theory do so on the basis of theoretical considerations and arguments. Perhaps the most familiar examples are provided by the innumerable discussions for or against the clinical usefulness, the epistemological legitimacy, or the necessity of the economic point of view (see, for example, Yankelovich and Barrett, 1970; Klein, 1973; Gill, 1976; Holt, 1981).

The literature also demonstrates, however, that these issues remain pretty much as they were, controversial and unresolved, in spite of the considerable theoretical attention they have received. The utility and role of notions concerning psychic energy, to cite only one instance, have yet to be settled conclusively. If, then, theoretical approaches have not been productive in resolving issues pertaining to the clinical relevance of psychoanalytic theory, are we not justified in seeking an alternative approach to the problem?

One such approach is suggested by the matter I alluded to earlier: the nature of the relationship between a relevant theory and its clinical products. In this regard, I propose that were psychoanalytic theory in fact clinically consequential, then advances in practices ought to be deductively derivable from that theory. It should lead one, by deductive steps, to more effective clinical practices; one might say that such advances would be "logically entailed" within a relevant theory.

This proposition suggests that the question of relevance could be illuminated by an examination of logical entailment. Furthermore, in the light of all the past failures of theoretical discussions to resolve the issue, it seems reasonable to begin with an empirical rather than a theoretical examination. Accordingly, I begin the study of clinical relevance by examining the literature to see whether therapeutic practice has in fact been logically inferred from mainstream psychoanalytic theory. The study of entailment in Chapter 2 examines representative examples drawn widely from past and current psychoanalytic literature.

Does a study of the literature support the premise that practice is now, or ever has been, logically entailed within theory? Can one substantiate the claim that technique is derivable from theory by logically valid inferential steps? My conclusion, based on several classes of indirect supporting evidence extracted from the literature, is a qualified no. Although theory and practice do exhibit certain kinds of relationships, these are not really inferential.

That conclusion naturally leads one to wonder next about the causes of the situation. It invites one to ask, Why is technique not logically entailed? After all, in the natural sciences it is commonplace to find that theory does harbor logical implications for technique; advances in theory routinely allow inferential deductions that lead to corresponding advances in technology and improved practices in general. Why should it not be the same in psychoanalysis?

I propose two different, yet ultimately intertwined, kinds of answers to these questions: (1) that theory has been circumscribed by the kinds of formalisms that have been employed (Chapters 3 and 4), and (2) that there is a cluster or constellation of what I shall be calling "focal" issues—themes, rationales, motives, perspectives, or goals that guide theorizing—that also contribute to the lack of entailment (Chapter 5). The proposed explanations, then, rest on two pillars—one formal-logical, the other focal.

Issues about formalisms. By "formalisms," I mean the languages, mathematical or other, that provide the vehicles for one's theorizing. In my view, the root issue pertaining to formalisms is the issue of *representability*. The fundamental question is (or should be), Is a given formalism able adequately to represent the phenomena that are central to one's enterprise? Is it an adequate vehicle, one that enables us to do the job at hand? In psychoanalysis specifically, can the formalisms one is using or proposing to use encompass the ingredients necessary for a clinically relevant theory?

This examination of formal issues grows out of a position I introduced earlier (Berger, 1978; see also 1974). It begins with a particular way of looking at and analyzing formalisms, a way of considerable generality that reveals basic formal-logical commonalities among apparently widely disparate scientific languages. This kind of formal analysis provides a framework within which one can pose and examine questions about representation in productive ways.

The formal issues addressed by the analyses in Chapters 3 and 4 are pertinent not only to recent proposals concerning formalisms and reformulations in psychoanalysis (e.g., Roy Schafer's [1976] for a "new language," George Klein's [1973] for "one theory"), but also to current discussions about how Freud used language in his theorizing. In these matters, a crucial question is, How formalized must the theoretical language of psychoanalysis be? Usually it is accepted as self-evident that a considerable degree of formalization is required (see, for example, Kubie, 1975; Schafer, 1978, Chapter 1). Recent work, however, strongly suggests that Freud's scientific practices deliberately and consistently eschewed scientific formalisms (see Bettelheim, 1983; Ornston, in press a,b); apparently, he steadily avoided formalistic practices that, as we shall see, are currently widely recommended and accepted without question, without further inquiry. Those standard presumptions reflect an arbitrary (and, in my view, inappropriate) picking and choosing among Freud's methodology; certain of his key positions are ignored, distorted, or rejected. To anticipate: The arguments and analyses of Chapters 3 and 4 return us, by way of explicit formal analysis, to less formalized conceptions of theoretical discourse.

The foci of theorizing. When I first mentioned formalisms and representability, the matter of adequacy also made an appearance. Asking about the representational adequacy of a given formalism almost automatically induces one also to introduce issues pertaining to use: One is impelled to ask, Adequate *for what tasks?* Formal issues almost inadvertently have brought pragmatic issues into the picture.

I shall label certain normative pragmatic issues "focal"—a term that is difficult to define simply, and whose sense will emerge, I trust, in the discussions of Chapters 5 and 6. An example of a focal assumption is the premise that one's understanding of a given disease necessarily will lead, sooner or later, to finding a cure. I shall propose that the foci of current psychoanalytic theorizing were tacitly accepted from the very start; they were already implicit in Freud's initial work. They have remained implicit rather than explicit, and so they easily have escaped notice, analysis, and evaluation. Furthermore, these focal assumptions also are consonant with focal assumptions in neighboring disciplines and sciences. At any rate, they tend to be perpetuated without much debate or question.

For reasons that should become apparent in Chapter 5, I call the applicable cluster of focal issues "the pure knowledge medical paradigm." I shall maintain that in a certain sense these foci have assigned a secondary status to clinical relevance, and that this policy had significant consequences for psychoanalytic theorizing. I will suggest that one's theorizing inevitably must bear the stamp of one's adopted foci. Consequently, if those were somehow ill-conceived, if the foci were somehow inappropriate to one's empirical goals and needs (in our case, to theorizing that could move clinical technique and overall methodology significantly forward), then that would constitute another kind of an impediment. In other words, I shall propose not only that certain formal practices could account for the inability of psychoanalytic theory to entail technique, but also that certain focal issues may have been getting in the way of clinically consequential theorizing as well. Furthermore, although it is convenient to treat formal and focal questions separately to some extent, as the analyses proceed it becomes increasingly clear that each class of questions has an impact on the other class. Issues are related in subtle, even obscure, ways: In the course of developing critiques about formal matters, focal issues insinuate themselves into the discussions, and vice versa. Eventually, the two types of analyses converge on common ground.

Implications and proposals. Chapters 3 through 5, then, primarily consist of analyses and criticisms. They draw on, and attempt to integrate, a great deal of available thought scattered throughout a variety of disciplines. As I explain in Chapter 7 (see the section "About Solutions"), I believe that careful critical analyses carry within them implications for future work; sound criticisms entail solutions. I also believe, however, that the analyses I shall present ought first to be examined, evaluated, and digested, before rushing into proposals and attempted solutions.

Nevertheless, there is the understandable expectation that a critic—especially an unorthodox critic—ought to give some indications of the implications of his criticisms. Chapters 6 and 7 are my guarded attempt to do so. In Chapter 6, I delineate general formal and focal guidelines for clinically relevant theorizing. These describe and specify various characteristics that I believe a relevant theory should exhibit.

Following these quite general considerations, the first part of Chapter 7 presents a more specific outline of how a clinically relevant theory might look. I here wish to state most emphatically some major qualifications (which will be repeated for further emphasis at various junctures in the last chapters). The sample theory that I shall eventually sketch will be just that—an example, intended to illuminate further the points developed in the earlier chapters. There are several reasons for being tentative at this time: The principal goal of this monograph is to clear away old impediments; my own thinking is still very much in flux, and I am not yet ready to offer a firm proposal; the scope of a clinical theory, as developed here, is very great, and may well be beyond the capacity and competence of a single worker; and, as I indicated above, before one would follow their implications, it would be beneficial, even necessary, to review and examine critically the analyses themselves. Thus, I would like to have this work judged principally on the basis of its contributions to critical analysis, that is, on the basis that it clarifies old and obscure issues, formulates productive and generative questions, and discourages the continuation of certain widely accepted, minimally analyzed practices. I would hope that, with this kind of a start, the criticisms and suggestions presented in this work would eventually stimulate others to pursue new directions; that eventually a clinically relevant theory would emerge from a process of orderly growth and "organic" evolution, strengthened by the assimilation of the additions I offer to mainstream thought. I also would hope in future work to join this kind of a sound effort with my own circumscribed clinical contributions.

Finally, there is the matter of generalizations of these ideas and proposals from psychoanalysis to neighboring disciplines. It will become evident just how large a debt this monograph owes to certain workers from a broad range of disciplines—psychology, philosophy, history, mathematics, physics, sociology, linguistics, biology, economics, and medicine. The book attempts to integrate contributions from these diverse sources by means of its main theme, clinical relevance of theorizing; at the same time, however, to the extent that it may have moved previous work forward, it could in turn have a contribution to make to some of the fields to which it is indebted.

The last sections of Chapter 7 consider that possibility. To illustrate the ways in which the material presented earlier might be generalizable to other areas, I present five sample topics for discussion: (1) another clinical framework—specifically, one school of family therapy; (2) certain difficulties that impede unorthodox critics of mainstream behavioral disciplines; (3) first language acquisition; (4) free will/determinism; and (5) affects. In these discussions, questions pertaining to formal issues and representability will predominate.

I am indirectly suggesting here that this monograph can be looked at in two different yet complementary ways. On the one hand, the work can be seen as one that seeks specifically to illuminate and advance clinical relevance of psychoanalytic theorizing. That is the more obvious aspect of the book; most of the offered opinions, discussions, premises, and arguments address clinical matters.

We may, however, invert that perspective, and look at the work in a wider context. From that second perspective, one could say that theorizing about psychoanalytic theory and clinical relevance, while important in its own right, has at the same time provided a suitable vehicle by means of which one can address basic formal issues, along with intertwined pragmatic issues. It is my firm conviction that for those disciplines that seek to deal with the subjective domain, the issues of adequate representability are crucial and central. I maintain that the kinds of questions I have raised about representability for psychoanalytic theory are equally salient for other disciplines that concern themselves with the person. In these disciplines, too, such issues are rarely addressed explicitly; standard views and approaches dominate, and typically are implemented without further ado. (As we shall eventually see, one can, however, find exceptions to the rule here and there; examples of exceptional approaches are provided by the work of Hexter and of Schumacher.)

If, then, my perceptions of these matters have merit and validity, it may be that the discussions of psychoanalytic theorizing that I am about to present could ultimately be useful in wider contexts as well. That possibility provided its share of motivation for writing the monograph.

TWO

Logical Entailment

> It seems to me desirable that the student of psycho-analysis, who is not only avid of authoritative direction but prone to believe that the technique is solidly based on a large body of accepted principle, should realize how far this pre-conception is from the truth.
> —Edward Glover, The Technique of Psychoanalysis

> The connection between metapsychology and practice has long been ambiguous and uncertain.
> —Merton M. Gill, "Metapsychology Is Not Psychology"

Questions about the relationships between psychoanalytic theory and therapy are neither new nor settled. Freud raised them at least as early as 1922 (Fenichel, 1941, p. 2; Eissler, 1953); they continue to remain controversial, unresolved, "pressing and difficult" (Gedo and Goldberg, 1973, p. 170).

THE SPECTRUM OF OPINION

Is theory relevant for clinical practice? The psychoanalytic literature displays a considerable range of opinions. At one end of the spectrum, there are claims that the ties are intimate; at the other end, theory is seen as irrelevant, or worse, for practice.

How is one to settle these kinds of questions? Although there have been many published works that claim to justify any given one of the various positions across the spectrum on the basis of theoretical supporting arguments, the issues continue to remain unresolved, suggesting that theoretical analyses may not be able to settle them. I have therefore proposed that these perennial disagreements could benefit from two shifts in the usual approaches: first, that rather than asking global questions concerning relevance, we ask specifically about logical entailment. Let us formulate the issues in terms of questions such as, Do theory and practice show inferential relationships? Can technique be logically derived from theory? Second, that we shift from theoretical discussions and arguments to empirical examinations of the literature that bears on these questions. Let us see what the literature actually shows or implies about entailment. To begin this empirical investigation, I present a brief survey of various positions within the spectrum of published opinions.

Theory and Therapy Are Closely Tied

Typical beliefs of the proponents of this position are that theory and therapy do display a vital reciprocal relationship; that each domain is necessary for advances in the other; that advances in theory lead to advances in therapeutic technique; or that therapeutic practice can be derived logically from theory.

Thus, according to Hartmann, Kris, and Loewenstein (1953), "few tend to object to the idea that the function of theory in psychoanalysis is not different from that of theory in any other science" (p. 13): "We know from experience that most scientific insights will, sooner or later, in one way or another, also gain practical significance" (p. 21, note 4). Freud (1910) remarks that "it is clear that every advance in our knowledge [the theoretical understanding of the unconscious minds of our patients] means an increase in our therapeutic power" (p. 141). Fairbairn (1958) claims that his theorizing does not "leave the technique of psychoanalysis unaffected"; "the fact . . . [is] that the practical implications of my views have seemed . . . far-reaching" (p. 374).

After noting that "historically analytic practice did not originate deductively from the theory of analytic therapy" (a matter to which we shall return shortly), Fenichel (1941) goes on to say that the latter theory "has today progressed so far that its practice can be made clear to the student in . . . [a] deductive way" (p. 14); he also speaks about showing "how freudian theory of neuroses is applied in psychoanalytic therapy" (p. 98).

It is "untenable", according to Thoma and Kachele (1975), to maintain the "thesis of the relative or absolute autonomy of practice from theory" (pp. 63–75). "Psychoanalysis does not just operate within a theoretical framework, it employs theory *per se* as an instrument of treatment" (L. Friedman, 1976, p. 259). Numerous other examples can be found—among them L. J. Friedman (1975), Kaplan

(1977, p. 208), Kohut (1979), Kovel (1978), Hartmann (1951, pp. 31, 42), and Modell (1976).

Against Entailment or Relevance

At the opposite pole of the spectrum one finds major reservations with regard to, if not outright rejection of, this first position. Glover (1955) implies the lack of clinical relevance in his observation that "it is well known that an analyst who is poorly oriented theoretically, can still be a good therapeutic analyst" (p. 373). Keat (1981), who has examined closely the logical dependence of clinical practices on theories in general and on psychoanalytic theory in particular, concludes that "therapeutic success, explanatory theories, and theories of technique, may display a high degree of logical independence from one another . . ." (p. 162).

According to Leavy (1980), at least some of the theoretical concepts "are not derivable from the psychoanalytic dialogue. . . . They may help to promote an agreeable sense of closure in the mind of the analyst and to the extent that this is desirable they may have some therapeutic usefulness. . . ." (pp. 50–51). Sutherland (1963) states that "most analysts have found the models put forward so far to have only limited relevance to their practice, and for those with more theoretical interests, the awareness of this gap between theory and practice has confirmed their lack of enthusiasm for them" (p. 110).

Guntrip (1961) mentions a specific case. He observes that once aggression is "at work," its analysis is done independently of theory (p. 396). Another specific instance is implicit in Winnicott's (1965) observation that although "fixing the date of the origin of the guilt feeling in the normal infant . . . is a matter of great interest . . . the actual work of analysis is not affected by this issue" (p. 24).

Those who maintain reservations about the usefulness or logical implications of theory for practice frequently voice particular objections about some specific portion of theory—usually its metapsychology. For example, we have George Klein's well-known view (as stated by Gill [1973, p. 99]) that metapsychology "is not only altogether irrelevant to the data of psychoanalysis but also *obstructs* the development of the clinical theory," that "there is much energy wasted in psychoanalytic journals on theoretical questions that have no fruitfulness for the psychoanalytic *clinical* situation" (Klein, 1973, p. 113).

Similar sentiments are expressed by Schafer (1976), namely, that there is a "large gap between metapsychological language and the assumptions that guide and inform the work of clinical psychoanalysis" (p. 20), and by Waelder (1962): "Metapsychology . . . is far less necessary [to the practice of analysis], and some of the best analysts I have known knew next to nothing about it" (p. 620). These remarks refer to presumably different segments or levels of psychoanalytic theory (e.g., metapsychology, clinical theory), a topic to which I shall return later in this and other chapters (especially Chapter 6).

Curiously, different authors use diametrically opposed rationales to explain why, in their view, theory is not clinically relevant. On the one hand, some believe this is so because theory is ahead of clinical practice: "The psychoanalytic view of psychopathology has far outdistanced our explicit rationales for the variety of interventions needed to deal with the broad range of problems we now treat. . ." (Gedo, 1979, p. 27; see also Hartmann, 1951, p. 42). On the other hand, there are those who see it in just the reverse way: There is " . . . a decided lag between modern innovative therapy and its peacock tail of theory, ornate, extravagant and trailing in the dust of tradition. . ." (Levenson, 1972, p. 19; see also p. 207; 1983, Chapter 1, especially pp. 6–7).

The Mainstream Moderate Range

The majority opinions seem to lean toward the orthodox position within "normal science" that theory sooner or later leads to "practical" benefits, but with some qualifications and reservations. Examples are Fenichel's (1941) claim that while "there exists between theory and practice an interesting and particularly important continual reciprocal action . . . it has not yet been studied in sufficient detail" (p. 2); Glover's (1955) remark that "theory and practice have a useful reciprocal relation but . . . both approaches must be carefully checked for possible errors" (p. 339); Sandler and Rosenblatt's (1962) reference to the "spiral of development, in which there is a progressive interaction of theory and observation" (p. 145); and, Matte Blanco's (1975) comment that "an increased knowledge is always a good thing and it paves the way for an increased power, but not necessarily in a direct way" (p. 386). Others who take this kind of moderate, qualified position include Bowlby (1979), Gill (1976, p. 102), Loewald (1960, p. 16), Modell (1976, p. 285), and Sutherland (1963, p. 110).

THE EVIDENCE

The major premise I wish to propose and examine is that clinical practice is *not* logically entailed in—that is, not logically deducible from—currently available theory. To support this premise, I shall cite indirect but extensive evidence from the literature; I shall use representative examples ranging from Freud's early work to the present, and organize these in terms of several themes. Inevitably, to some my hypothesis will seem self-evident, while to others it will equally obviously seem false. Such differences of opinion on this central issue suggest that the premise merits further exploration.

Some may object to my treatment on the ground that it lumps together all analytic theorizing, rather than dealing with each hierarchical level of theory as a separate case. One might maintain, then, that my premise, if true, would hold (or fail to hold) only for some particular subset or level of theory. It seems to me, however, that there are two good reasons why one may, for the present purposes, treat theorizing as a single process. First, as I shall discuss at the end of this chapter, there are circumstances particular to psychoanalysis that cast doubts on the notion that its theory can legitimately be hierarchically ordered. Second, the idea of such ordering is suspect also on more general, epistemological grounds to be examined in the chapters that deal with logical-formal issues.

Empirical Origins of Technique

The first theme to be examined is the empirical origin of clinical practices. Writers from Freud to the present have explicitly noted the empirical, trial-and-error roots of technique. As Needles (1962) observes, "Characteristically, he [Freud] proceeded from empirical clinical observation to the search for an explanatory hypothesis..." (p. 505). I have already quoted Fenichel's supporting view (1941, p. 14).

Freud (1912b) is explicit on the matter: "The technical rules which I am putting forward have been arrived at from my own experience in the course of many years, after unfortunate results had led me to abandon other methods" (p. 111). "Unfortunate results" imply, of course, a history of trial and error.

Let us consider some specifics, beginning with the origins of the technique of free association. Freud notes that for him it had a public as well as a private prehistory. That is, a number of earlier writers, poets, and physicians had recommended one or another form of free association for various purposes, such as stimulating artistic creativity. Precursors included Schiller and Wilkinson. On a more personal level, it seems probable that an essay by Boerne was influential in the discovery of free association as a therapeutic tool (Freud, 1920). In any case, its origins were empirical: Freud "found . . . a substitute [for suggestion or hypnosis]—and a completely satisfactory one—in the 'associations' of his patients. . ." (1904a, p. 251). Note "found," not "deduced."

Similarly, interpretation—the technique "at the heart of the Freudian doctrine" (Laplanche and Pontalis, 1973, p. 227)—also appears to have been "found" rather than deduced: "The rules [of the technique of interpretation were] reached empirically. . . . The details of this technique of interpretation or translation . . . comprise a number of rules, reached empirically, of how the unconscious material may be reconstructed from associations. . ." (Freud, 1904a, p. 252).

In speaking about more restricted, less general aspects of technique, Freud consistently refers to their empirical origins. He notes, for instance, the empirical roots of various specific recommendations: for dealing with problems in the first phase of analysis; for arrangements about the setting, including frequency and length of sessions; for patient selection criteria; concerning approaches to dream analysis (1904a,b; 1912a,b; 1913).

Let us next turn to more recent sources. Consider, for example, some of Kernberg's technical recommendations concerning the treatment of borderline disorders. Should the therapist be a "real" person to this category of patients? Kernberg (1975) notes that while some have argued for this position, "clinical experience has repeatedly demonstrated that the intervention of the psychotherapist as a particular individual, opening his own life, values, interests, and emotions to the patient, is of very little, if any, help" (p. 91).

Should one at first attend to the negative transference? "A repeated observation from the Psychotherapy Research Project at The Menninger Foundation about the psychotherapy of borderline patients, is that a high price was paid when the therapist tried to stay away from the latent negative transference" (Kernberg, 1975, p. 82).

How frequently should one see these patients at first? Kernberg recommends seeing most patients rather frequently: "Fears expressed in the early literature on the treatment of borderline conditions implying that excessive frequency of appointments fosters regression seem unfounded in the light of more recent experience" (p. 186).

Let us next consider some of Kohut's recommendations concerning the treatment of narcissistic disturbances. What is the main therapeutic task? "Experience teaches us . . . that the therapist's major effort must be concentrated on the task of keeping the old need mobilized." He has found that alternative approaches—e.g., blaming or "exhortations concerning realism and emotional maturity" will not work (Kohut and Wolf, 1978, p. 423).

What about handling transference phenomena in the early stages of treatment? Kohut's experience is that one should not "interfere with the unfolding idealization" (1979, p. 11). He has found it counterproductive to interpret phenomena such as rage or demandingness as defense manifestations. Clinical experience has led him to maintain that one should treat such phenomena with "respectful seriousness vis-à-vis important analytical material" (1979, p. 12).

It seems that many at least, if not all, important technical recommendations were reached empirically, often only after other, equally reasonable or appealing strategies had led to undesirable consequences in therapy. There is, as Hartmann (1951) has stated, "a continuous sequence of trials and errors, as we check our technical procedures by their immediate consequences and by their therapeutic results" (p. 33).

Questionable Counterexamples

The mere fact that trial-and-error procedures or intuitively implemented empirical techniques are used in a given discipline does not mean, of course, that its practices are necessarily logically independent from its theory. Examples of advances based on intuitively guided empirical trial-and-error procedures can be found in all sciences. In sciences such as physics, however, we find a two-way street. In those disciplines, not only is theorizing guided by empirical investigations and results, it is trivially obvious that there are also numerous important examples of material advances and techniques that were derived deductively from available theory. Well-known examples from physics of empirical consequences deduced from theory are relativistic phenomena such as the slowing of clocks, gravitational bending of light, or nuclear fission; or, from quantum theory, technologies such as lasers, transistors, or microchips.

Now, from the material presented earlier, it seems clear that in psychoanalysis empirical clinical experience has in fact allowed theory to be inductively constructed. Where, however, are the inferences that lead from theory to significant empirical practice? Were psychoanalytic technique truly logically entailed by theory, one might reasonably expect to find at least a few clear and explicit instances of significant technical recommendations or practices that had been logically deduced or derived from theoretical considerations. As far as I know, such examples do not exist in the psychoanalytic literature.

Some might object to this claim, citing counterexamples which supposedly demonstrate logical entailment. On closer examination, however, these supposed counterexamples turn out to be fallacious. They mask, and rely on, conjecture, dogmatic pronouncements, or non sequiturs. Let me give a few representative examples.

Consider Kohut and Wolf's (1978) treatment recommendations concerning the two major subcategories of narcissistic disturbances. Do these require two correspondingly distinct treatment approaches? "Since the psychopathology of both major types of analyzable disorders is identical, it follows that despite their divergent symptomatology—noisy demands and intense activity in the social field in the narcissistic behavior disorders; shame and social isolation in the narcissistic personality disorders—the process of treatment is identical in its essence" (p. 424). Does it follow? Although the reader can easily be left with the impression that a logical deduction has been presented ("since . . . , it follows that. . ."), a closer look reveals the questionable logic of the inference. Surely, given all the significant symptomatic differences between the two classes of pathology that Kohut and Wolf describe, one could equally plausibly argue that two correspondingly different sets of treatment approaches would be in order. I venture to say that had clinical experience indeed led to contrary findings (that is, that two such different approaches were in fact necessary), *those* empirical findings could have equally well, equally comfortably, been encompassed by theory.

Gedo (1979) states that "principles of psychoanalytic practice . . . [are] based on rational deductions from our most current conception of psychic functioning" (p. 16), and "my own outlook on the theory of therapy is a logical corollary of the epigenetic approach to psychological development" (p. 21). He then enunciates one of his basic principles, namely, "that the unfavorable outcome of any phase-specific developmental crisis can be reversed only by dealing with those results of all antecedent developmental vicissitudes that later gave rise to maladaptation" (p. 21).

But is that principle a "rational deduction," a "logical collorary" that follows from an epigenetic approach? I do not think so. It is one thing to assume that development follows an epigenetic scheme, quite another to assume that in therapy all the earlier vicissitudes must be dealt with. What inferential chain could lead one from the first to the second premise? Where is the supporting logical argument? Are the logical ties so obvious that they do not need to be demonstrated or explained?

It seems to me that Gedo's basic principle really is a hypothesis rather than a logical deduction. It is an assumption that is logically independent of the premise that development follows an epigenetic scheme. In fact, one can find in the literature a contradictory therapeutic principle that also seems to be based on an epigenetic framework. Kohut (1984) relies on a narcissistic developmental scheme drawn in terms of an epigenetic model, and yet recommends a therapeutic approach different from Gedo's, at least for some kinds of pathologies with borderline features. He explicitly tells therapists that under certain circumstances some kinds of developmental vicissitudes (the residues of certain kinds of narcissistic traumata) ought to be left alone (pp. 42–46). Evidently, epigenetic schema can be compatible with different, even mutually contradictory, therapeutic approaches, and that argues for my thesis. I submit that there is no logical deductive tie between the premise of an epigenetic scheme and the ways proposed to deal therapeutically with the synchronic residues (Gedo, 1979, p. 1) found in adult patients. I maintain that Gedo's claim that his principle is a logical corollary of theory is specious.

What kinds of phenomena should be interpreted in the early stages of therapy of borderline personality disorders? Kernberg (1976) recommends that one focus on the mechanism of splitting, rather than interpreting "directly" each of the alternating expressions of the defense. He notes that although "the analyst may try to interpret 'directly'" this will lead to failure: "Only the attempts to bridge these independently expressed, conflicting ego nuclei bring about severe anxiety, mobilize new defensive operations, and may bring about changes in the intrapsychic conflicts. In short, an important consequence of this formulation [the recognition, description, and theoretical explanation of the defense] for psychotherapeutic techniques is the active focus on the mechanism of splitting as a primary defensive operation to be overcome before any further changes can be achieved with such patients" (p. 46).

We see that in this example Kernberg claims that his recommendations are "an important consequence" of his theoretical formulations. Once again, however, an explicit articulation of an inferential or deductive chain does not seem to have been provided; Kernberg fails to demonstrate, even informally, the claimed deductive relationship. And once again, other, alternative clinical approaches seem equally compatible with Kernberg's formulations of borderline pathology. After all, others thought it the "consequence" of the pathology to interpret the alternating expressions of the defense "directly," and indeed, why should not interpreting those alternating expressions also lead to "severe anxiety?" Why would that not be an "attempt to bridge" conflicting ego nuclei? Kernberg does not say. One can deal with these borderline phenomena in yet a third way, delaying interpretations altogether for long periods, as some have suggested (see Kohut, 1984, pp. 176–184; see also Bettelheim, 1967; Schafer, 1983, pp. 165–180). Again, the existence of mutually contradictory therapeutic alternatives supports the conclusion that the theory of borderline phenomena presented here cannot be connected to any one particular therapeutic approach through readily discernible deductive steps. At least one can say that if indeed such an inferential chain did exist, it has so far failed to surface in the literature.

I submit that these examples are representative of a large number of equally spurious claims for theoretical grounding of recommended therapeutic techniques and principles. I shall discuss yet other examples of this practice in Chapters 6 and 7.

One other feature exhibited by several of the preceding examples is worth noticing. Recommendations, once they are said to have been based on theory, tend to become cloaked in an unwarranted mantle of authority and certainty. In the examples from Kernberg's and Gedo's work, note the "only": "Only the attempts to bridge..."; "the unfavorable outcome ... can only be reversed by...." Although these and other similar empirically discovered clinical principles may be highly effective, plausible, and compatible with theory, I can see no basis for presenting them as inferences that necessarily follow from theory, as I have said. To present such principles as theory-based inferences is misleading. Worse, it tends to close the door on further clinical exploration by fostering an illusion of theory-based certainty and authority. We now know how it "must" be, what the "only" effective procedure is; theory has told us; why look further?

Once one has become sensitized to these kinds of expressions of certainty, they seem to crop up everywhere. This is one way in which the myth of deductive ties between theory and practice tends to be fostered or perpetuated. Here are several more examples: "There is only one correct analytic attitude [in dealing with certain manifestations of an idealizing transference]..." (Kohut, 1971, p. 264). "Only narcissistic ... disorders are analyzable [among a certain class of pathologies]..." (Kohut and Wolf, 1978, p. 416). At times even Freud seems to succumb. For example, in a discussion concerning the need to give up hypnosis in favor of new techniques, he states that "there is no other way which leads to the desired goal. . ." (1904a, p. 252).

Some may object to my premise that practice is not logically entailed within psychoanalytic theory on another basis. We remember the position expressed in Fenichel's remark (1941, p. 14) cited earlier, namely, that one could now retrospectively furnish a deductive rationale; theory, so the argument goes, has advanced sufficiently. I would point out two difficulties with this position. The material presented above provides one kind of counterargument: On closer examination, it becomes apparent that presumed retrospective or retroactive "deductions" actually are spurious or fallacious.

A second kind of rejoinder concerns a wider epistemological issue. Graves (1971, pp. 34, 41) discusses and analyzes quite general considerations pertaining to the retroactive rationalizations of scientific theories. That is, he considers what is involved when one sets out to tidy up, to formalize, a given scientific theory that has evolved more or less informally. He calls the two processes needed for such programs "disinterpretation" and "reinterpretation." For the moment, let me merely note that Graves's analyses raise serious questions about the merits and legitimacy of this kind of retroactive formal reconstruction. These are issues to which I shall return in Chapter 5.

Curative Factors

Decades ago, it was generally held that an unambiguous rationale that would satisfactorily explain the therapeutic action of psychoanalysis was unavailable: "The Marienbad Symposium gives a clear picture of how far the opinions of analysts are still divergent concerning what really constitutes the effective factor in psychoanalytic therapy" (Fenichel, 1941, p. 111). "Whenever Freud speaks about therapy, he ascribes the main share in healing to the process of bringing into consciousness that which has previously been unconscious. All we know about therapy is actually comprised in this single sentence" (Nunberg, 1937, p. 161). Or, "What then, is interpretation? and how does it work? Extremely little seems to be known about it. . ." (Strachey, 1934, p. 141).

More recent statements echo this view: How analysis works "is not adequately understood" (Fairbairn, 1958, p. 385). "The fact is that nobody has, so far, succeeded in establishing with great precision what the other factors [other than understanding] are, and how they combine intimately with our understanding, to produce the cure" (Matte Blanco, 1975, p. 386). "The effectiveness of psychoanalysis as a clinical procedure has posed a continuing challenge for successive theories of mental life" (Gedo, 1979, p. 15). There is a "need for a new look at the actual process of interpretation, its underlying rationale and function" (Schimek, 1975, p. 864). Others who have expressed consonant views include L. Friedman (1978), Strupp (1972, p. 71), Stein (1972, p. 37), Storr (1967), Glover (1955, pp. 373, 266n; 1968, p. 115; 1972, pp. 131, 151), Kohut (1977, pp. 105ff), Modell (1976, p. 285), and Leites (1977).

In my view, the lack of an adequate understanding of the therapeutic action of psychoanalysis also supports the thesis that practice is not logically entailed in theory. If practices were logically entailed, we would be able to provide a clear theoretical explanation for their therapeutic action.

Technical Progress

Quite a few analysts maintain that little, if anything, that is really clinically significant has been added to psychoanalysis since the first crucial developments issuing from Freud's early work. Glover (1968) alludes to this view during his discussion of Brill's claim that psychoanalysis was "practically speaking a finished product" by 1907 (pp. 114–115).

Glover (1972) notes that in regard to progress in "treating mental disorders by psychological devices, the fact must be faced that apart from one revolutionary development now about 75 years old nothing psychologically new or advanced has been promoted" (p. 151). On another occasion (1968) he states, "For certainly and despite a multiplicity of articles on the subject of technique . . . no very radical advances have been made in the therapeutic field" (p. 115; see also 1955, p. 266n).

Greenson (1967) seems to agree: "It is an impressive fact that the fundamentals of psychoanalytic technique that Freud laid down in five short papers some fifty years ago still serve as the basis of psychoanalytic practice. . . . No acknowledged major changes or advances have taken hold in standard psychoanalytic technique" (p. 3). According to Gedo and Goldberg (1973), when Grinker was invited to discuss "the most important developments in psychoanalysis

Psychoanalytic Theory and Clinical Relevance

in the last thirty-odd years," his wry response was, "Have there been any?" (p. xiii).

As I mentioned in Chapter 1, the lack of significant progress in the clinical realm during an era of theoretical advances spanning some ninety-odd years of intensive effort lends considerable, although indirect, support to the premise that theory does not entail practice; the discrepancy in the two rates of progress is at least suggestive.

Therapeutic Effectiveness

For a significant number of practitioners and observers, the effectiveness of psychoanalysis as therapy has been, and continues to be, disappointing (see, for example, the remarks of Strupp, Gedo, and Stein quoted in Chapter 1). There is, of course, no logically necessary tie between therapeutic success and logical entailment; one could argue, for example, that theory may in fact entail practice, but that the existing ties have so far just not yet been discovered. Given the years of concerted effort, however, those kinds of arguments are not very convincing. In my view, shortcomings in therapeutic effectiveness can be explained more parsimoniously by the premise that practice is not entailed within theory.

Of course, not all would agree with the preceding opinions concerning the alleged shortcomings of psychoanalysis with regard to therapeutic efficacy. To quote Glover (1972) once more: "The topic of success and failure in psychoanalysis and psychotherapy is, I think, bound to stir a hornet's nest of controversial issues" (p. 131). The issue remains widely debated (e.g., Wolman, 1972; Horwitz, 1974; Chessick, 1977; Strupp, Hadley, and Gomez-Schwartz, 1977).

One-Many Relationships

This label refers to one particular kind of structural relationship (a "one-many mapping") between theory and related clinical practices. It means that the same theoretical framework may be associated with different, perhaps even mutually contradictory, therapeutic approaches. That is, either concurrently or at different times, proponents of the same theory may adhere to different, and in some instances logically incompatible, clinical principles and practices.

This kind of relationship can be noted in Freud's (1904a) observation that "the changes which [he] introduced in Breuer's cathartic method of treatment were at first changes in technique. . ." (p. 250).

"At first" implies a change in technique (in this case, over time) without a corresponding change in theory. Thus Freud provides an example of a one-many relationship.

Other examples can be found in the very divergence of techniques presumably based on a unitary theory. Fenichel (1941) writes, "We see from the few discussions about technique in the literature that opinion is extremely divergent" (p. 13). According to Glover (1955), there is "variation in technique within the framework of accepted analytical principles . . . *even in so-called classical analysis of the psychoneuroses, the approach of different analysts varies not only in numerous points of detail but also on many important points of policy*. . ." (p. 165); ". . . we discovered that a number of orientated and practicing analysts holding to the fundamental principles of psycho-analysis varied in their methods in every imaginable way" (p. 373); the results of his survey questionnaire to analysts (pp. 259–350) also demonstrate the existence (in this case, concurrently) of a one-many situation.

Another example is provided by Chessick (1977). He states that "although both authors [Zetzel and Kernberg] base their conclusions on what seem to be essentially similar metapsychological descriptions of the borderline patient," their views of treatment are quite different (p. 82; see also Guntrip, 1961, pp. 395–396).

Campbell (1982) has recently examined the approaches which eight major theorists follow in the treatment of borderline disorders. She shows that in spite of sharing a broad theoretical framework with only minor differences, these theorists disagree significantly about what constitutes the "correct" clinical approach. Campbell identifies three controversial themes: "(a) traditional psychoanalytic position of technical neutrality, (b) reality relationship in which the therapist shares thoughts and feelings with patients, and (c) establishment of a relationship to facilitate gratification of primitive developmental phases" (p. 166).

The presence of the subjective factor in technique is yet another example of a one-many relationship. Freud (1912b) explicitly states in the course of "bringing forward" technical rules, "I must however make it clear that what I am asserting is that this technique is the only one suited to my individuality; I do not venture to deny that a physician quite differently constituted might find himself driven to adopt a different attitude to his patients and to the task before him. . ." (p. 111). Of course, were technique in fact inferentially grounded in accepted theory, it would not exhibit this subjective cast: "Governing principles [of analytic practice] should after all be common to all analysts despite differences in personality" (Fenichel, 1941, p. 14).

Many-One Relationships

This label refers to the obverse logical structure, namely, that different theoretical positions can be associated with the same clinical practice. Levenson (1975) refers to this general state: "One certainly gets the impression that after a hasty genuflection in the direction of Rome, experienced and competent therapists settle down to dealing with the realities of the treatment situation in much the same way" (p. 2; see also his similar remarks in 1972, pp. 207–208). Kernberg (1976) notes that three very different theoretical frameworks—object relations, Sullivanian, and Kleinian—with very different conceptions of schizophrenia have come to essentially the same treatment approaches (pp. 127–128). The existence of one-many and many-one relationships obviously supports my premise that practices are not logically entailed within theory.

Overkill

Typically, one finds a considerable imbalance in the literature between the volume of theoretical discussion and the volume of technical principles or recommendations. The balance is greatly on the side of material pertaining to description of pathology—genesis, diagnosis, and the like. In other words, the yield of bulky theorizing for applications, for clinical technique, is disproportionately small. I believe this is true of the work of all major theorizers, from Freud to the present: When one examines the theoretical works of, say, Freud, Kernberg, Kohut, Guntrip, Fairbairn, Matte Blanco, Hartmann, or Rapaport with an eye to extracting specific technical recommendations, one must conclude that the great bulk of theorizing has generated comparatively few clinical principles or recommendations. This holds even in those works that specifically claim to consider the clinical implications of a particular body of theory, and further supports my premise that practice is not logically entailed in theory.

Here are some illustrations. In Kernberg's extensive writings (e.g., 1975, 1976) the greater part of his discussions, by far, pertains to (1) the metapsychological conceptualization of pathology (genesis, defensive aspects, quality of object relations, ties to symptomatology, etc.), (2) the ways in which theory is used to structure observation, and (3) related diagnostic applications. Ones sees that Kernberg's actual technical recommendations are relatively meager and quite general compared to the heavy and voluminous theorizing on which they presumably are based. For example, in a thirty-page paper (1979) whose title "Some Implications of Object Relations Theory for Psychoanalytic Technique" would lead one to expect a principal focus on technique, one finds instead the usual emphasis on the three areas outlined above. That paper examines, for instance, how unconscious intrapsychic conflicts are conceptualized within an object relations framework, how old internalizations are redissolved, and so on. Actual technical recommendations are brief (pp. 210–212) and general—for example, to maintain technical neutrality; to sharpen the process of interpretation; to explore various facets of transference.

Similarly, there is a great discrepancy in Levenson's (1972) book between theoretical discussion and treatment recommendations. He presents a complex and sophisticated systems-theoretical framework that ultimately yields but few general and, compared to the level of theorizing about pathology, simple recommendations: being a real person to the patient; extricating one's self "from the equifinality of systems" (p. 158) "not by interpreting . . . but by reporting one's *own* experience of the transaction" (p. 211); "like a continuous discordant note . . . [the therapist] shifts the melody" (p. 214).

Guntrip's (1969) extensive theoretical study of schizoid phenomena yields such technical recommendations as "to keep quietly on, sympathetically directing attention to the fears of the relationship, keeping them conscious so that the patient can repeatedly test them against the reality of his experience with the therapist. . ." (p. 328).

Hartmann (1951), in a paper whose title "Technical Implications of Ego Psychology" promises clinical relevance, devotes most of it to matters other than technique (fact finding, ordering of data and observation, etc.). When he does discuss technique, once more the discussion tends to be not only abstract but very general. Examples of his recommendations are "recognizing the resistance and making it conscious to the patient" (p. 37) and helping to strengthen the patient's ego by "redistributions of energy [not only] between the id and the ego, or between the superego and the ego . . . [but also by] shifts from certain spheres of the ego to other functional units within the ego" (pp. 34–35).

Finally, Matte Blanco (1975) presents a massive and elaborate scientific framework that conceptualizes pathology by means of "bilogic"—a peculiar, unorthodox logic that has a special, unconventional axiomatic basis. That ambitious theorizing produces disproportionately tame recommendations; basically, they amount to the suggestion that one should interpret to the patient the "bi-logical" features exhibited by the clinical material.

This completes the indirect evidence I offer in support of the contention that practice is not logically entailed in theory. The following themes were considered: (1) There are many references to the empirical origins of various clinical techniques, from Freud to the present. (2) There seem to be no logically valid counterexamples that would refute the premise. (3) The therapeutic action of psychoanalysis has not been adequately explicated by theory. (4) Important advances in theory have not been accompanied by corresponding significant changes in the fundamentals of technique; these fundamentals have remained the same in their essentials since their early formulation. (5) The therapeutic effectiveness of psychoanalysis has been disappointing. (6) There are numerous instances of a one-many relationship between theory and practice. (7) Similarly, there are examples of the obverse, the many-one relationship. (8) One routinely finds a great disparity between theoretical discussion and treatment recommendations. Although no one of these themes proves by itself the principal thesis of the chapter, I submit that the picture that emerges when one considers them as a group offers strong support for my major premise.

ACTUAL TIES

Although I have been arguing for the thesis that clinical practices are not logically entailed within theory, it would be untenable, I think, to claim that there are no ties at all between theory and practice. We know that most clinicians do feel that theory is useful, at least in some ways. In this section I shall consider three familiar ways in which theory bears on practice. I shall also call attention to one kind of formal or logical relationship—a correlational one—that does seem to hold between theory and technique; while it has occasionally been casually mentioned in the literature, it so far does not seem to have received much explicit study.

Observation, Description, and Explanation

Observation, description, and explanation are three interrelated aspects or functions of theorizing (see Chapters 3 and 4). Obviously, the psychoanalytic framework has brought with it a constellation of theoretical notions that provide, simultaneously, particular ways of observing, organizing, and explaining phenomena. These perceptions can then have an impact on technique, even though the relationships between theory and practice are not truly inferential.

A compelling example is provided by Kohut (1979). A patient was in analysis twice with Kohut, at two different stages of theoretical progress. The paper reports how changes in Kohut's theorizing affected his ways of perceiving and understanding the same patient's material (but see Schafer, 1983, p. 42 for a critical discussion).

Diagnostics

Diagnosis is a natural byproduct and application of the three interrelated functions of theorizing just mentioned (see, for example, Kernberg, 1977; also 1975, especially Chapters 4 and 5; 1976; Kohut, 1971; Horwitz, 1974; Chessick, 1977; Kwawer, Lerner, Lerner, and Sugarman, 1980). Theory can guide the construction and rationalization of nosologies, and thus the diagnostic organization of clinical data.

Models, Metaphors, and Technique

Various models, metaphors, or analogies have been used to rationalize and/or to suggest clinical techniques or principles; some examples have already been presented above in various contexts. Models certainly can be used to draw plausible (although not necessarily logically entailed) inferences concerning technical procedures or therapeutic interventions. Developmental frameworks, suggestive physical models, or models of the psychological apparatus and its pathology all have been used in this way. This seems to be one typical use of theory that writers have in mind when they refer to the beneficial effects that progress in theory has on practice, to increases in therapeutic potency brought about by "theoretical advances."

The use of analogies and commonsense arguments to arrive at technical recommendations seems to be attractive to clinicians, perhaps because the absence of logical ties makes few if any other alternative approaches available at present. The practice seems reasonable, has face validity, and can help perpetuate the illusion that therapy is tied deductively to theory. Fenichel (1945), for example, uses this kind of reasoning in his discussion of the ego and defenses: "Since we can therapeutically influence only the ego [tautologically, by definition?], there are in principle only two possibilities for such influence: we can try to strengthen the ego . . . or we can bring the ego to give up the defense or to replace it by a more suitable one" (p. 15). The rationale on which the technical recommendation is based appears to be a straightforward extrapolation from a physical model, such as a dam at risk. One can either shore it up, or defuse the danger by constructing some alternative outlet for the water. Similarly, in speaking of whether one "could and should" not reach the "early id-related layers" (rather than the ego) by interpretations, Fenichel (1941) uses "illuminating" analogies with biological organisms (p. 55). He also draws on the metaphor of a military commander separated from his allies by enemies at the front to rationalize technical recommendations (p. 71).

Greenson (1967) provides us with another example. In the section entitled "Rules of Technique Concerning Resistance" (pp. 136–150), he makes the usual recommendations concerning the need to analyze resistance before content, and to begin "with the surface." ("How otherwise? In what other way could we penetrate to the depths than by beginning at the surface?" [Fenichel, 1941, p. 44].) The underlying metaphor and guiding rationale again seems to be a physical picture. If something that we wish to reach is barricaded or encapsulated, it makes sense that we would have to begin by removing that barricade, the first accessible impediment. Likewise, we are led to believe on the basis of such metaphors that as one continues to work toward blocked material, most of the time one has no choice but to work from the surface inward, through successive layers of that barricade. The analogy is pressed even further by Fenichel (1941): The path may not always be orderly, through successive layers; "faulting" can occur (p. 62). These and similar metaphors may help to illuminate or enliven conclusions reached through clinical experience, or they can act as mnemonic devices, but they are not logically compelling.

I want to emphasize that I am not necessarily calling the efficacy or clinical wisdom of these recommendations into question. For now my only point is that while they may be plausible, or based on common sense, they are not based on logical inference. I have already pointed out that the practice of ex post facto pseudo-explanations may entail risks: It may mislead us into thinking that an empirically discovered recommendation is theory-based, and thus may discourage investigation of alternatives—perhaps even of radical alternative techniques.

Another important class of examples that illustrate the use of models, analogies, or metaphors consists of those based on extrapolations that transform childhood developmental needs into presumed corresponding therapeutic needs in work with adults. I have already mentioned Gedo and Goldberg's (1973) epigenetic framework and therapeutic modalities. Another example is the "translation" of Winnicott's (1965) views of child development and of the facilitating environment into parallel views about adult pathology and psychotherapy (see, for example, Modell, 1976). Yet another example is Kohut's extrapolation from childhood narcissistic developmental needs to corresponding issues in the treatment of adult narcissistic disturbances. In these kinds of procedures, a plausible rationale for a therapeutic approach to a given problem in adult psychopathology has been obtained by drawing analogies between two sets of corresponding issues: child pathology and adult pathology, and childhood environmental needs and therapeutic interventions in the treatment of adults. My earlier remarks about the metaphorical, non-inferential processes used to arrive at certain therapeutic techniques apply here as well. I shall return to these issues in Chapters 6 and 7.

Before I leave, for the moment, the subject of models, I should like to mention that their epistemological place and function within a given theory has been the subject of a good deal of discussion and controversy. In Chapter 6, when I come to locate clinical theory in a particular epistemological niche, I shall also discuss one way of conceptualizing the relationships between a theory's material aspects, formal characteristics, and models or metaphors.

Correlation

In addition to illustrating the use of informal reasoning, the last examples also illustrate one particular kind of formal-logical tie between theory and practice. That relationship is a correlational one. I see it as an important, ubiquitous, but scarcely discussed tie.

There are two major clinical areas where correlational relationships are invoked. First, there is the recognized, taken-for-granted tie between diagnosis and therapy. When one defines criteria that specify which kinds of patients are, or are not, suitable for a given therapeutic modality, one thereby has established a correlational relationship between classes of patients and therapeutic options. (As usual, the procedure, although originating in empirical clinical findings, may be "rationalized" retroactively by theory.) As one subdivides the patient population further in terms of more elaborate nosologies, and as one develops a more elaborate, complex spectrum of therapeutic options, correlational schemata—matching

Psychoanalytic Theory and Clinical Relevance

patient and therapies (or therapist)—become much more complex. Still, the basic logical feature of correlation remains unchanged. A goes with A', B with B', and so on.

The second realm in which theory and practice exhibit a correlational relationship is within therapy. That is, we have numerous correlative, actuarially linked clinical recipes: "In this clinical situation, when *this* happens, do (or don't do) *that*." The recipe is drawn from clinical trial and error, or from a reasonable extrapolation of childhood needs to the needs of adults, or from compelling metaphors and models, or from clinical intuition, and so on.

Most of the correlational relationships appear to be limited in scope. As L. Friedman (1976) has noted, it seems that "the days when analysts felt the need to build new large scale theoretical systems to discuss new clinical approaches are at an end. . ." (p. 145). Typically, the recipe connects some relatively circumscribed clinical phenomenon, say, a particular manifestation of a particular kind of resistance, to a specific recommended intervention.

There also exist, however, a few more encompassing frameworks. As far as I know, the most methodical and formalized of such larger-scale schemata is Gedo and Goldberg's (1973; also Gedo, 1979). These authors postulate five developmental eras within an epigenetic scheme, and five corresponding, correlated clinical modalities. For any given patient, the therapist needs to use more than just one of these approaches:

> We believe each of these modalities to be absolutely necessary to every psychoanalytic effort, even if in varying proportions, depending on how often the analysand functions in which mode. In other words, the use of the various modalities should be a routine feature of psychoanalytic treatment technique; it is *not* a departure from classical procedures, as Eissler (1953) seemed to suggest when he called any intervention on the part of the analyst other than verbal interpretation a "parameter" [Gedo, 1979, p. 6].

What Gedo and Goldberg have done, then, is formalize a general framework containing these two correlations: (1) A schema of child development, basically from birth to latency, and a correlated set of environmental requirements (e.g., the earliest, "reflex arc" developmental era goes with the environmental function of "pacification"); the child's intrapsychic world is correlated with perceived or actual environmental factors, favorable or pathogenic. (2) A conceptualization of adult psychopathology and a correlated set of therapeutic interventions, modalities, or settings; the adult patient's intrapsychic conditions and requirements are correlated with various kinds of assistance provided by the therapeutic environment.

We thus have a double translation: from child pathology to adult pathology, and from child environment to therapeutic environment. These translations provide the informal links between the two correlated pairs.

The logical relationship of correlation has not been extensively discussed in the psychoanalytic literature, as far as I know. These kinds of ties between theory and practice may have been muted or ignored in the literature because their explicit recognition and analysis would confront clinicians with the absence of the entailment relationship. As we have seen earlier, clinicians tend to cherish the illusion that theoretical advances will lead to derived clinical advances, much as theoretical advances in medicine or physics lead to better practices or technological advances: "It is the task of every theory in all of science to lead to better practice. . ." (Fenichel, 1941, p. 1). Psychoanalysis is a science, q.e.d.

The only explicit references to correlation with which I am familiar are by Kohut and Wolf (1978). These authors open their paper by saying, "It is the aim of this survey to provide a summary of the concepts and theories of the psychoanalytic psychology of the self and of the clinical (diagnostic and therapeutic) formulations that are correlated to them" (p. 413). Later they refer to "the therapeutic principles which we enunciated and the therapeutic strategy correlated to them. . ." (p. 424). In Chapter 7, I shall consider further the matter of correlational formats and their place in clinically relevant theorizing.

THE MATTER OF THE "CLINICAL THEORY"

I shall now return briefly to a subject introduced earlier, namely, the matter of hierarchical layers or branches of psychoanalytic theory. In this regard, it has frequently been argued that while there may be one branch of psychoanalytic theory—the high-level, experience-distant "metapsychology"—that lacks useful logical ties to clinical practice, there is at least one other level—bearing a label such as the "clinical theory"—that presumably is closely tied to the "data," and is clinically relevant, even indispensable.

The idea of a hierarchically layered theory (see Rapaport, 1960; Waelder, 1962; G. Klein, 1973; Rubinstein, 1976; McIntosh, 1979) has been adopted from the natural sciences and mathematics. In those fields, the domains of inanimate phenomena, it has an easy, commonsense appeal and face validity. Up to a point, one can legitimately maintain that there is a distinction to be made on the basis of

Psychoanalytic Theory and Clinical Relevance

distance from data, level of abstraction or generality, and so on. In psychoanalysis, however, the premise of hierarchical levels of theory seems to crumble under closer scrutiny; it becomes ambiguous and amorphous. Are there several layers? Is there (or should there be) only one kind of theory? Holt (1981) has identified three kinds of one-theory positions, two kinds of two-theory positions, as well as a whole range of concomitant epistemological issues and difficulties. The issues continue to be controversial and widely debated.

I said earlier in this chapter that in those disciplines that deal with the subjective, psychological realm the notion of hierarchical levels is suspect on general epistemological grounds, as well as for specific reasons particular to a given discipline. Here I shall consider only the latter kinds of reasons, those specific to psychoanalysis; discussions of more general difficulties, those stemming from wider epistemological considerations, will be postponed to the next two chapters.

In psychoanalysis, one of the difficulties that the notion of hierarchically ordered layers encounters is the matter of their "distance from data." A major rationale used to support the idea of a hierarchical order is the premise that different classes of psychoanalytic data are at different "distances" from "raw" data. Yet that distinction, the differentiation on the basis of levels of abstraction, seems to run into difficulties. It seems questionable, at least to some: "The fact [is] that psychoanalytic metapsychology, unlike the atomic theory of physics, for example, is still at the level of categorization of data" (Gedo and Goldberg, 1973, pp. 169–170; see also G. Klein, 1973).

What about logical ties between levels, say, between metapsychology and the clinical theory? Are various branches logically related? That seems to be another controversial, debatable issue. Gedo (1979) states that "clinical theories are derived from Freud's metapsychology" (p. 38). It would seem, though, that this claim goes directly against Freud's own position that the metapsychological points of view "are in no way the basis of psychoanalytic practice or clinical theory, but are . . . their 'speculative superstructure'. . ." (Thoma and Kachele, 1975, p. 71).

Let us next look at various labels, specifications, and definitions that have been proposed for the "experience-near" level of theory, the level that presumably is most directly relevant to clinical work.

Clinical theory. What is a (or the) "clinical theory?" Clinical theory is "designed to deal with psychopathology" (Gedo and Goldberg, 1973, p. 153). It "means the terms suitable for making interpretations to human beings about what they are doing" (Schafer, 1976, p. 210).

It is a general psychological theory whose terminology, while no less theoretical than metapsychological theory, is closer to experience (G. Klein, 1973). It "describes and explains neuroses" (Yankelovich and Barrett, 1970, p. 287). According to Rubinstein (1976), "the most unequivocal characteristic of clinical psychoanalytic statements is that they refer to persons. . ." (pp. 229–230). "Clinical psychoanalytic theory has two functions: (1) to explain our observations; and (2) to contribute to the confirmation of these explanations" (p. 247). (Note the striking omission: Rubinstein does not even mention technical or clinical consequentiality among the functions of a "clinical theory.") "Models of the mind are summarizing conventions which represent the clinical theory of psychoanalysis" (Gedo and Goldberg, 1973, p. 10).

Theory of technique. In Fenichel's (1941) view, the "theory of technique" is "an explanation of what the analyst does in psychoanalysis" (p. 98). It "attempts to sum up as general laws of human psychic activity, the facts which have been gathered by the psychoanalytic method in individual instances" (p. 3). "The *theory* of technique, and particularly its metapsychology, has lagged sadly behind [the knowledge of technique itself]" (Rapaport, 1967/1958, p. 734). (Apparently we now even have a "metapsychology of the theory of technique!")

Theory of therapy. Fenichel (1941) notes that some deny on logical grounds that a "theory of therapy" could even exist, but dismisses that argument as fallacious (p. 3). Glover (1955) implies that whatever else it might be, it is different from "our newer clinical understanding," since he suggests that therapeutic theory "should keep step" with that newer understanding (p. 368). L. Friedman (1978) says the theory of therapy is the "specification of the forces available to bring [the goals of treatment] . . . about" (p. 536).

On the basis of this brief survey, it seems safe to say that the entire matter of a "clinical theory" is highly problematic, to say the least. Specifications are vague, obscure, and conflicting, and so far I have been considering only problems particular to psychoanalysis. Studies in the philosophy of science reveal that in *any* theory there are certain other, more general difficulties that are raised by the notion of hierarchical layering; I shall consider them in the next chapters. These other difficulties become particularly salient in those disciplines that deal with the person as subject. The difficulties only compound those mentioned above that are specific to psychoanalysis; when these additional complications are taken into account, the notion of hierarchical ordering of branches of psychoanalytic theory becomes even less tenable and even less defensible.

Since the distinction between clinical and other psychoanalytic theories is so questionable and uncertain, since we cannot adequately specify what is meant by clinical theory, and since we aren't even sure that it exists, it has not seemed necessary to discuss the issue of entailment in this chapter separately for various levels of theorizing. I submit that the considerations that I have presented earlier about the absence of logical ties between technique and theory apply to psychoanalytic theory in general, and not just to some subset.

COMMENTS

We know that "pure" theorizing elsewhere—in mathematics, classical and quantum mechanics, thermodynamics, electrodynamics, relativity—has sooner or later always led to corresponding major technological advances; examples can be provided at will. This history of technological successes in the natural sciences has raised similar expectations in those disciplines, including psychoanalysis, that deal with human beings as "persons." Better theory should lead to better therapy. I have already cited several statements expressing this conviction. (This issue will be central to the discussions of Chapter 5.) According to this view, as Guntrip (1961) notes, "a revolutionary therapeutic technique . . . led to the most far-reaching changes in theory and it would be strange if this did not work the other way as well, especially at a time when this need for more effective therapeutic methods is so widely felt . . ." (p. 396). Guntrip is right—it would be strange. Yet I believe that this is exactly what history leads us to believe: On the whole, theoretical advances in psychoanalysis have failed to lead to corresponding significant advances in therapy. It *is* strange.

The absence of logical ties that I have examined throughout this chapter may be a symptom as well as a cause. It could be a symptom in the sense that the lack of ties suggests that for some reason, conventional theory may be unable to logically entail technique. At the same time, the absence of ties could also be a cause in the sense that it may account for the relatively stagnant status of therapy. In other words, the analyses suggest on the one hand that the theory may not be capable of yielding deductions concerning effective therapeutic techniques. On the other hand, the analyses suggest an explanation for the lack of progress: A therapeutic process that is not grounded in a generative theoretical base probably will not develop significantly.

At any rate, if there were indeed something about conventional theorizing in psychoanalysis that prevented it from being consequential for clinical practice, then would that not also raise the possibility that the usual scientific remedies and proposals may not be the answer? That is, if for psychoanalysis there were something wrong with the usual "normal science" approaches to theorizing, then they may not yield the hoped-for benefits. It may well be that as far as progress in therapeutic potency is concerned, it might not help to become more rigorous and more positivistic in one's research and theorizing, or to opt for more precise or operational definition of technical terms, or to adopt and adapt "better" approaches and models from information theory, structural analysis, linguistics, nontraditional logic, biology (e.g., synaptic models), or engineering physics (e.g., solid state devices, holography, cybernetics, masers), as recommended, for example, by Leites (1971), Kubie (1975), Steiner (1976), Levenson (1975), Peterfreund (1971), Wallerstein (1976), or Matte Blanco (1975).

That is the possibility that I shall investigate. Now, the suggestion that "normal science" may somehow fail to provide adequate means for our clinical ends and needs is not new; there is, for example, the continuing discussion about the "fusion of science and humanism." I do believe, however, that the approaches I am about to present and develop are different in important respects from apparently similar previous attempts, especially within psychoanalysis. The next three chapters are intended to support and explicate this claim. As I outlined in Chapter 1, my arguments will rest on two pillars of critical analyses. The first pertains to matters of form, logic, structure (Chapters 3 and 4); the second to focal, pragmatic considerations (Chapter 5).

Let me emphasize that the next three chapters primarily will present critical analyses, not proposals. Although some implications for reformulations will occasionally surface in these analyses, I shall delay any extended considerations of alternatives, proposals, revisions, or reformulations until the final two chapters.

THREE

Science, State Process, and the Life World

> *Misleading parallel: psychology treats of processes in the psychical sphere, as does physics in the physical.*
> —Ludwig Wittgenstein, Philosophical Investigations

> *Modern science has been on the scene now for three centuries, yet perhaps we still do not fully grasp its nature.*
> —William Barrett, The Illusion of Technique

> *What kind of understanding does one achieve through "controlled alienation"? Is it not likely to be an alienated understanding?*
> —Hans-Georg Gadamer, Philosophical Hermeneutics

Is psychoanalysis a natural science? A social or a behavioral science? One of the humanities? A hermeneutic discipline? A "fusion" of science and humanities? Furthermore, do questions such as these even matter to psychoanalysis?

There is no consensus. Some consider them irrelevant if not altogether meaningless indulgences in metaphysical nonsense. Take, for example, one important and representative issue that, sooner or later, surfaces during discussions of these kinds of questions, namely, the mind-body problem. It "is generally regarded as a philosophical rather than a scientific problem . . . [and one which] with few exceptions, psychologists, including psychoanalysts, have felt free to ignore. . ." (Rubinstein, 1965, p. 35); "most psychologists and psychoanalysts I have read and talked to give little thought to the mind-body problem and just can't take it very seriously, that's metaphysics; leave it to the philosophers, they say" (Holt, 1981, p. 132). That seems to be representative of the majority view about the relevance of these kinds of epistemological questions to psychoanalytic practice and theory. Meanwhile, a minority sees them as "the crux" of the matter (Leavy, 1980, p. x).

One may discern three clusters of concerns in discussions of these and allied questions. The first is that of the positivist, the hard-nosed researcher. Representative concerns are methodological: objectivity; verifiability; replication; prediction and control; terminological clarity; operationalization of concepts; internal structure; logical consistency; legitimacy of particular conceptual ingredients. The second cluster pertains to issues in the science/humanism dichotomy— to differences between the human and the inanimate realm, between person and organism. The third cluster are clinical concerns; typical issues are the legitimacy and clinical usefulness of certain kinds of theoretical models, e.g., reductionistic, energic, teleological. With regard to psychoanalysis specifically, comprehensive reviews, discussions, and summaries of these three clusters are presented by Yankelovich and Barrett (1970), G. Klein (1973), Matte Blanco (1975), Thoma and Kachele (1975), and Holt (1981); more general epistemological discussions can be found in Rorty (1979) and Barrett (1972, 1978).

I introduced my approach to these kinds of epistemological issues in an earlier paper (1978). In that paper I took the position that at this stage of theorizing the pertinent question is not so much whether psychoanalysis does or does not conform to the rigorous, standard criteria of "normal science," to use Thomas Kuhn's evocative term, as whether or not normal science methodology necessarily imposes some "innate constraints"—that is, certain very general restrictions that, from the beginning and in some fundamental way, will exclude crucially important phenomena and manifestations from the domain of psychoanalytic theorizing. Let me briefly review what I mean by that concern.

Suppose one sought to deal systematically with some given aspect or domain of the world. Suppose, furthermore, that one were to select just those particular methodological and conceptual tools that were bound to exclude, to filter out, those very phenomena that are the most vitally important features of the domain of interest. Suppose, in short, that one had in the preliminaries chosen inappropriate tools, ones that could not deal adequately with the phenomena that matter. In that case, the investigative enterprise would obviously be severely flawed from the very start. If, for example, you were interested in studying the use of color in painting, and if you had confined yourself to studying the subject by means of black-and-white photographs, you wouldn't—or at least shouldn't—be surprised to find the progress of your investigation to be severely limited, to say the least; you could obtain only trivial results. Or, if you wanted to catch fish, you may have difficulties if you were to choose wrenches, screwdrivers, and other tools from a standard tool kit. These may be extreme or overstated examples, but they illustrate the point I made in 1978, and which I seek to amplify in this and the next chapter.

I begin by reviewing the conceptual frameworks employed by normal science. I shall pay particular attention to those aspects that one injects at the very start when one elects to adopt traditional scientific methods and frameworks.

NORMAL SCIENCE FRAMEWORKS

Science is "concerned with providing descriptions of phenomena under which significant regularities emerge and with explaining these regularities" (Danto, 1968, p. 297); it achieves this goal by combining "the rigor of mathematical logic with the experimental method" (Hacking, 1975, p. 95). What are the components science employs to these ends?

There are, of course, numerous alternative ways of classifying "philosophical-ontological viewpoints" (Hoffman and Nead, 1983, p. 510); the various schemes differ from one another in their selection of particular epistemological dimensions and characterizations. Graves's (1981, Chapters 1–4) lucid and comprehensive organizational scheme is well suited to the needs of my discussions, and I shall draw on it frequently in the material that follows.

In general, as Kuhn (1970) puts it, ". . . three classes of problems—determination of significant fact, matching facts with theory, and articulation of theory—exhaust . . . the literature of normal science, both empirical and theoretical" (p. 34). "Articulation" could be called the *internal* component of the framework; it is that self-contained, circumscribed domain that exists in its own right, without necessarily referring to the empirical domain. The "determination of significant fact" of course refers to the *external* component, to identifying "raw data" in the empirical world. Observation, measurement, or other means of translation between these two realms are the various procedures for *matching* "facts with theory," for shuttling back and forth between the two principal regions. Let us look at these three constituents more closely, one at a time.

Internal Domain

Invariably, the basic conceptual realm within which theorizing occurs is some variety of "logical space" called a "state space." For our purposes, we can imagine state spaces as some version of a coordinate space. The familiar spaces used in plane and solid geometry are representative examples.

The state space, then, is an abstract logical region. It is structured and specified in terms of some formal descriptive scheme (such as a coordinate system), an "alphabet." By means of that alphabet or state space "descriptor" scheme, one can specify any and all of the locations within a given state space, any one of the "points" within that logical space.

There is another component of the internal system, namely, its laws. One needs to specify a set of rules—the "transition" or "translation rules"—that will describe or define how the system changes from one state to the next. A given set of rules, defined for any one given state space framework, will govern the movement, the path, of points within that state space; they will specify how, for this particular system, changes in state (represented as changes in the location of a point in the state space) are to take place.

Significant Fact

One begins by excising some particular portion or aspect of the empirical realm and identifying it as the target of one's theorizing. A fact, then, is some observable (measurable) aspect of the excised system; it is some particular feature or characteristic of the system in the external realm.

"Determination" of significant fact then means measuring, observing, or otherwise acquiring "data." One extracts from the empirical, external domain those elements to which we routinely refer as facts or events or processes. They are what we observe and measure, and what we try to understand, predict, control, by means of the internal component of the scientific framework, by the theory. Let us note that the typical scientific realist's position implicitly harbors value judgments about this state of affairs; the empirical realm and its data are viewed as veridical, objective, atheoretical, value-free, "presuppositionless"—or at least, to paraphrase Orwell, "more veridical" than "theory." (The quotation marks around "theory" here refer to an epistemological misconception, namely, to the fallacious idea that "theory" and "data" can be rigorously separated.)

Matching Facts with Theory

Here is the key move. Much of the power of natural science comes from one apparently innocuous move that actually has very great, yet often hidden consequences and implications. This basic move consists of positing *two* basic isomorphisms. The first is an isomorphism between fact (observation, measurement, empirical aspect of the framework) and a corresponding point or location in state space; in other words, an empirical fact is conceptualized as (representable by, matched with, correlated to) a particular specified state or location within the state space. From the point of view of "state process" theories, facts are considered to be logically equivalent to, and representable as, points or locations in some particular state space. "Initial conditions" then are a special case of facts; they are facts that are found at the start of observation, say, those that obtain at time t_0; they are represented by some specific initial location of a point in the state space.

(Conversely, we can and do "interpret" the state space: Its formal characteristics and features are readily ascribed to the empirical domain. Consequently, everything in the external world begins to look to us like a physical embodiment of an abstract state space. Eventually, we reach a point where the state space perspective has become second nature for us. We cannot even imagine that any aspect of our experience—for example, the subatomic world, the world of everyday objects, the subjective domain of a person—might have some properties that could not be adequately represented as positions and motions in a state space.)

The second isomorphism is one between a particular "law of nature" (which presumably governs the behavior, the "processes," exhibited by the particular real-world system one is observing) and a corresponding transition rule (the logical rule that specifies, often in terms of a mathematical function, the paths that points must take in the state space). In other words, laws of nature governing particular systems are conceptualized as (representable by, matched with, correlated to) abstract mathematical transition or translation rules.

Additional Aspects

The preceding bare-bones outline of the ingredients of scientific theories has been simplified in at least two respects, for the time being. I have set aside two sets of considerations. The first set pertains to what Graves (1971) calls the "levels hypothesis." As we shall see in Chapter 6, it concerns such matters as the division of theories into groups, and various issues concerning the relationships, hierarchical and other, that hold within and between levels.

The second cluster of issues concerns the epistemological place or role of models in theories. The term "model" is ambiguous; it has been used in a variety of ways by different scientists and philosophers, and all too often its status within a given theory is obscure.

For my present purposes, the simplified schema of scientific theories that I have developed will be adequate; moreover, to introduce new matters pertaining to levels or to models would obscure the principal points I wish to develop here. I shall draw on these more complicated aspects of theorizing only later (particularly in Chapter 6).

STATE PROCESS FORMALISMS

State Spaces in the Natural Sciences

Wigner (1982) tells us that much of this "invented" picture of the world is due to Newton: "The initial conditions describe the original state of a system, the laws of nature should describe only its development in time, i.e., its state at any later time, assuming the initial condition is given" (p. 119).

From its early simple beginnings this approach has been refined and elaborated over centuries (see, for example, Goldstein, 1980). Its development is associated with such names as Lagrange, Laplace, Hamilton, Jacobi, Hertz. According to Janik and Toulmin (1973), the ultimate, advanced version was hailed as "a stroke of genius . . . [by which means] one could eliminate finally all subjective references . . . and replace them with rigorous mathematical descriptions" (p. 144). These authors tell us that

> Boltzmann took Hertz's account of mechanics as defining a system of "possible sequences of observed events," and made it the starting point for a general method of theoretical analysis *in physics itself.* He did so, by treating each independent property of a physical system as defining a separate coordinate in a multidimensional system of geometrical coordinates. All the possible locations of each separate body in the physical system, for instance, were ordered along three spatial "axes of reference"; all values of, say, temperature along another axis; all values of, say, pressure along a fifth; and so on. The totality of theoretical "points" in the resulting multidimensional coordinate system gave one a representation of the "ensemble of possible states" of the physical system in question; and any actual state could be defined, by specifying the particular point in this "multidimensional space" whose coordinates corresponded to the actual values of all the variables [p. 143].

Psychoanalytic Theory and Clinical Relevance

We have a system, then, that is fundamentally referential, with its two domains (logical-formal and empirical) and the two isomorphic correspondences (between fact and state; between natural laws and transition rules). The empirical world has become the referent of the state process.

Let us be quite clear about the centrality of this framework for the natural sciences (and other disciplines too, as I shall shortly discuss). "The facts in logical space are the world. . ." (Wittgenstein, quoted by Janik and Toulmin, 1973, p. 144). In mathematics, the distinctions reemerge as those between "proof theory" (which concerns itself with "internal" mathematical issues) and "model theory" (which pertains to the "interpretation," the referential use, of mathematics; see, for example, Hunter, 1971; Davis and Hersh, 1981, p. 139). It is *the* common ground found in all scientific conceptualizations—classical or statistical mechanics, electrodynamics, hydraulics, acoustics, and thermodynamics, for example. It does not matter whether our theory is deterministic or probabilistic; whether it assumes a Euclidean or non-Euclidean space; whether it assumes a continuous or discrete universe; or whether it pictures events in terms of one, two, three, or more dimensions (see Janik and Toulmin, pp. 180–185, 215; Bunge, 1976, p. 147; Weizenbaum, 1976, pp. 39–46; Bronowski, 1978, p. 85, Dreyfus, 1979, p. 71ff; Rorty, 1979, pp. 104, 328, for further discussions). A fact, an empirical datum, is conceptualized as a state—as a point in a state space; events, processes, and the like are then conceptualized as corresponding changes and motions of that point in the state space. Laws of nature become equivalent to transition rules. The "outside" world is mirrored in terms of a state process formalism.

All phenomena that are to be treated scientifically must be accommodated within this grand formal scheme. Knowledge, for instance, becomes equated with knowledge of the state: "To know [in normal science] is to represent accurately what is outside the mind" (Rorty, 1979, p. 3).

Likewise, the scheme tells us what causality is: "We can never, by our utmost scrutiny, discover anything but one event following another. . . . We never can observe any tie between them" (Hume, quoted by Wolman, 1971, p. 897). Laplace's often quoted version is even more explicit:

> We ought to regard the present state of the universe as the effect of its antecedent state and as the cause of the state that is to follow. An intelligence knowing all the forces acting in nature at a given instant, as well as the momentary positions of all things in the universe, would be able to comprehend in one single formula the motions of the largest

bodies as well as of the lightest atoms in the world, provided that its intellect were sufficiently powerful to subject all data to analysis; to it nothing would be uncertain, the future as well as the past would be present to its eyes [quoted by Wolman, 1971, p. 879].

State Spaces in the Behavioral Disciplines

Enough has been said to demonstrate the role of state process notions in the natural sciences. What about other disciplines, particularly those whose subject matter is the psychological realm? I submit that the situation is no different there: State process formalisms continue to be the underlying basis for theorizing in the behavioral or social sciences. The trouble is that much of the time their presence is veiled if not invisible. Nevertheless, they are there.

I have already demonstrated (Berger, 1974) that state process notions implicitly underlie observational schemes used in psychotherapy research, and in Chapter 4 I shall demonstrate that they also underlie conceptualizations of scientific discourse, including the discourse of psychoanalytic theorizing. Let us now briefly look at some other examples to illustrate my point.

When a "phenomenon" in, say, psychology, is treated "scientifically," that invariably means it is conceptualized in exactly the same way as any other "external" fact or datum in any other "science." Aristotle's notion that "mind is itself thinkable in exactly the same way as its objects are" (Wartofsky, 1968, p. 372) is perpetuated. Typically, it is assumed that mental phenomena have the "attributes of an object" (L. Friedman, 1976, p. 263). Rorty (1979) speaks of "raw feels, mental images, and thoughts" as "states of things" (pp. 66–67); for Locke, according to Rorty, Newtonian mechanics was a model for the mechanics of 'inner space'. . ." (p. 328, note 13). Harman's (1973) "conception of a person takes him to be a functional system of states and processes that possess representational characteristics by virtue of their role in the functional system" (p. vii).

The ingredients of this psychological realm have posed continual difficulties for philosophy and psychology. A bewildering variety of candidates for the "objects" and "attributes" of the psychological state space have been proposed and used over the centuries. At one time or another, each of the following has had its day as a valid object or attribute of the mind: ideas, images, imageless thought, motor representations, form qualities, phenomena, sense data, feelings, emotions, impalpable consciousness (*unanschauliche Bewusstheit*), memories, phenomenologically reduced observations, attributes, perceptions, Gestalten, structures, trains of thought, impressions, patterns, schemata, faculties, active constructive functions, associations, cognitive processes, modes, and attention, among others (Boring, 1950; Langer, 1967, p. 58; Wolman, 1971, p. 878; Hacking, 1975; Malcolm, 1977; Horowitz, 1979; Rorty, 1979).

Once we become alert to the use of these representations in the behavioral or social disciplines, we recognize their presence and role literally everywhere, from obvious spaces such as Osgood's "semantic differential" (Osgood, 1952; Osgood, Suci, and Tannenbaum, 1957) to less obvious, taken-for-granted, unexamined representations—for example, the standard conceptualization of emotions as "states."

We can come to this same realization from another direction. Consider the use of computer or other mathematical models in the behavioral and social sciences. It has been shown that any such model is logically equivalent to a rudimentary version of so-called "Turing machines" (von Wright, 1971, pp. 43–48; Weizenbaum, 1976, pp. 46–72, 97–98, 158, 170; Dreyfus, 1979, pp. 72–79, 192). The prototypical, root form or version of this class of logical "machines" is a conceptual system that has a very simple logical structure. A simple Turing machine consists of (1) a two-symbol alphabet, (2) a set of elementary "read," "write," "move tape" computer operations, and (3) simple transition rules that dictate how one is to move from one state to the other. It is "a machine that shuttles a tape back and forth, reading and changing marks on a square of tape at a time and going from one state into another. . ." (Weizenbaum, 1976, p. 60). What Turing proved was that in principle—conceptually—this rudimentary system can do anything that any other computer can do. (Needless to say, this primitive version would not be practical as an actual, embodied machine.)

There is an obvious resemblance between Weizenbaum's description of a Turing machine and a state process framework, and this resemblance does, in fact, turn out to be more than superficial: "All science is a Turing machine which is the model of any machine that we can conceive" (Bronowski, 1978, p. 85; see also Weizenbaum, 1976, pp. 39–64). State process formalisms and Turing machines are logically equivalent. Therefore, *any* application of computer or mathematical modeling in the behavioral sciences is really only a thinly disguised instance of yet another application of state process notions. We can now see that the widespread employment of computer models in the behavioral sciences (see, for example, Rapoport, 1983; also Abelson, 1984) attests to the ubiquitous presence of state process notions in the behavioral or social sciences.

From the point of view of logical structure, then, the psychological realm is divided into the same kind of dichotomy as is the realm of the natural sciences. On the one hand, we have a theoretical framework consisting of state spaces, representations, and transition rules. On the other hand, we have psychological phenomena, the "data" or "processes," viewed as objects and their attributes. Then we assign correspondences: Attributes are conceptualized and represented as points in a state space; "processes" are represented as movements of a point in a state space; psychological laws are represented by means of transition rules.

Emerging Difficulties

I trust that I have demonstrated convincingly that state process frameworks dominate "normal sciences." Whether explicit or tacit, they are *the* omnipresent formalisms and thus structure one's conceptualizations of the formal and the material aspects of scientific theories. The arguments I present next are intended to cast doubt on the legitimacy of using such formalisms as vehicles for theorizing about certain domains and in certain applications. Specifically, I shall argue for the hypothesis that state process formalisms are inappropriate formalisms for clinical theorizing in psychoanalysis.

Two streams of critical analyses have arisen to cast severe doubts on the legitimacy of using state process pictures as representational vehicles in every scientific endeavor. One broad stream comes from within orthodox science itself; the Cartesian state process picture ultimately has led to a series of significant problems within disciplines like physics or mathematics. The other critical analyses come from various "outside" critics—sometimes not only outside the natural sciences, but outside the mainstream of their own particular disciplines as well. They include "figures . . . on the periphery of the history of modern philosophy. . ." (Rorty, 1979, p. 367). Rorty's illustrative list includes Goethe, Kierkegaard, Santayana, William James, Dewey, the later Wittgenstein, and the later Heidegger. We shall meet yet others.

My purpose in introducing these general criticisms of the frameworks of orthodox science is to prepare a way for understanding parallel criticisms levelled specifically at orthodox state process conceptions of scientific language. That is, if indeed there are some cogent reasons against using state process formalisms in certain situations, and, if furthermore we were to find that scientific discourse typically is conceptualized and used as a state process formalism (as

I plan to show in Chapter 4), then the use of such discourse will become open to the same kinds of criticisms that can be levelled at state process formalisms in general.

MAINSTREAM CRITICISMS

Logical Positivism—roughly, Humean empiricism plus mathematical logic—expected to put science on an indubitably certain, "hard-nosed" foundation. The quest was for certainty, completeness, rigor, logical necessity, and similar "solid" ground (Austin, 1962, pp. 104–105; Kaufmann, 1980, p. 55). The approach assumed that "all problems were either questions of fact or questions of logic" (Barrett, 1978, p. 7). All "soft" questions of metaphysics, ontology, or cosmology would either be translated into scientific equivalents or ruled out as meaningless.

The positivists' early expectations ran into difficulties no sooner than the program was outlined. These difficulties can be conveniently divided into two groups corresponding to the two divisions of theorizing (internal, regarding "questions of logic," and external, or referential, regarding "questions of fact"). That is, basic difficulties appeared both within the representational frameworks themselves and in the process of relating the internal branch of theory to its external referents—the "objects," events, phenomena, data, and similar features of the "real world."

Both sets of difficulties pertaining to the logical positivists' and similar programs have been extensively discussed and reviewed in the literature (see, for example, Pepper, 1961; Bronowski, 1966, 1978; Nagel, Bromberger, and Grunbaum, 1969; Yankelovich and Barrett, 1970; Turner, 1971; Janik and Toulmin, 1973, especially Chapter V; Hacking, 1975; Settle, 1976; Shea, 1976; Barrett, 1978; Rorty, 1979). I shall only outline them here. Some of the problems of positivist science will, however, be examined further in Chapter 4 in the course of discussions pertaining specifically to discourse.

Logical Certainty: Indubitable Formal Foundations

As I have said, the internal difficulties pertain to the logical, formal, symbolizing, mathematical branch of natural science theories. Just as logical positivists believed they could, by following certain principles, construct a science free from metaphysical aspects, so at one time did mathematicians and logicians such as Russell, Frege,

Peano, and Whitehead believe they could set mathematics on a secure logical foundation built from first principles. Eventually, it became obvious that this goal could not be reached. In discussing these issues of foundations, of certainty and infallibility, Davis and Hersh (1981) refer to an important paper by Lakatos that

> starts out with an impressive collection of quotations, from a dozen or so eminent mathematicians and logicians, of both the logicist and formalist stripe, all showing that the search for secure foundations has been given up. All agree that there is no reason to believe in mathematics, except that it seems to work. Von Neumann says that at least it is no worse than modern physics, in which many people also seem to believe [p. 351; see also pp. 330–338, 345–359].

It seems that the ideal of a complete, fully axiomatizable, self-consistent formalization of logic and mathematics has come to be seen as unreachable in principle.

One particular set of difficulties and paradoxes that surfaced in mathematics is the group of so-called "limitative theorems" associated with the names Gödel, Tarski, Church, Turing, and Post. These deal with questions concerning decidability of mathematical systems, their consistency, and their self-referential features. From the perspective of the behavioral disciplines, the last issue is particularly interesting and suggestive. Questions concerning what a formal logical system can say about itself begin to approach the problems of subjectivity, awareness, and human self-reference (which, as Bronowski (1978) says, "like self-consciousness, is in fact the glory of the human mind. . . ." [p. 98].

Objective Certainty: Indubitable Empirical Foundations

Just as the internal characteristics of theory exhibited fundamental difficulties, so did the empirical aspects. The empirical ties between the representational system and its laws and the "outside" "real world" were shown to encounter basic major problems.

One initial hope was that empirical ("raw") data could be considered as indubitable, reliably "objective," free from theoretical prejudice or contamination. This solid base was then supposed to provide a veridical foundation for theorizing. However, the disarmingly simple, apparently transparent notions of "objective" ("presuppositionless") observation or description, separable and distinct from "theoretical" explanation, have turned out to be untenable and fallacious, and an epistemologist's nightmare to boot (see, for example,

Pepper, 1961; Louch, 1966; Fodor, 1968; Nagel et al., 1969; Hanson, 1971; von Wright, 1971; Wolman, 1971; Gadamer, 1976; Rorty, 1979; Nozick, 1981).

The hope that data would provide incorruptible foundations, that they would put you "at the basement," at a level where you couldn't doubt, turned out to be "one of the most venerable bugbears" (Austin, 1962, p. 104). It very much looks as though theory and observation must always, necessarily, be interwoven. There simply does not seem to be an unassailable, solid "very beginning" on which one could build: On closer examination, what initially appear to be "pure" observational data are shown to be "theory-laden," to use Hanson's (1971) familiar term. The "innate constraints" begin to come into view; the seemingly certain empirical foundations of theory, the supposedly irrefutable status of "raw data," are shown by careful analysis to be "a matter of social consent rather than proof" (Settle, 1976, p. 15). Classification schemes (e.g., nosologies) turn out to be *de facto* theories (Kohut, 1984, p. 204). The apparently self-evident notion of "pure," theoretically uncontaminated fact eventually "spreads into argument over all the issues of logic" (Pepper, 1961, p. 35).

These findings in the natural sciences were extended to the behavioral and social sciences as well. (See Ingleby's brief review "The Myth of Objectivity" [1980, pp. 29–34].) Freud, for example, seems to have been aware of this aspect of "objective" observation:

> Even at the stage of description it is not possible to avoid applying certain abstract ideas to the material in hand, ideas derived from somewhere or other but certainly not from the new observations alone. . . . We come to an understanding about [the meaning of new ideas] . . . by making repeated reference to the material of observation from which they appear to have been derived, but upon which, in fact, they have been imposed [quoted by Loewald, 1960, p. 21].

In the same paper, Loewald develops a conceptually closely allied notion. He makes a persuasive case for the premise that no personal experience can be meaningful without transference (used in its broad sense). He shows that the idea that one could perceive current reality "objectively," without the necessary contribution from one's own primitive psychological realm and one's own developmental history, is untenable. There is no such thing as pure objectivity without subjectivity. Yankelovich and Barrett's (1970) telling label, one can never perceive *just* the "really real."

Langer (1967) has also commented on the perennial quest for presuppositionless, certain, objective "inner data":

> The methods of introspection which were used by Wundt, Tichener, Kulpe, Brentano, James and some other great nineteenth-century psychologists showed that direct observation without any conceptual frame is impossible; some schema is bound to impose itself on the findings in the very process of seeking them, and the data reflect the expectation of the observer to whom they are supposed to be purely "given" [p. 58].

As Schafer (1983) says, "The introspectible world reflects the purposes for which one is introspecting" (p. 123); there "can be no theory-free, method-free analytic facts" (p. 188).

Basic difficulties have also been revealed by various linguistic analyses of behavioral concepts. Examples are Rorty's (1967, 1979) exploration of the search for presuppositionless bases of linguistics, Austin's (1962) criticisms of the idea of sense data, and Malcolm's (1971, 1977) critique of the concept of memory. An even more fundamental, extensive, and unconventional examination of mainstream psychology's assumptions and methods was undertaken by Merleau-Ponty (1962, 1963). The targets of his sympathetic but devastating analyses were such basic notions as stimulus, response, and behavior.

The status of objective observation has been clarified in yet another context. There has been a good deal of work in the behavioral disciplines pertaining to the influence of the observer. As early as 1885, Ebbinghaus expressed concerns about "observer error." Contemporary workers such as Postman, Strupp, Rosenthal, Orne, and Holt have examined extensively the observer effects associated with formal methods (see Rosenthal, 1966; Rosenthal and Rosnow, 1969; Wolman, 1971, p. 883).

Object Language and Theoretical Language

Closely related to the premise of objectivity was the program for separating the ingredients of theory into notation "close" to data— "observation language"—and more distant, abstract levels—"theoretical language." The former, in keeping with the search for veridical, presuppositionless bases, was not to be open to question. It would be grounded in an unchallengeable bedrock; some advocated that this base be "sense data," others "physicalist data" (e.g., the everyday objects one observes), but in either case the advocates were sure of the veridical nature of their chosen basis. So-called "correspondence rules" were to provide the logical linkages between the two languages.

The notions that data can be entirely objective and veridical, that there is an atheoretical "object language" that describes "directly perceivable" entities or events, and that this object language can be logically distinct from a supposedly higher-level theoretical language constitute what Graves (1971) calls the "empiricist error" and the "logicist error" (Chapters 2 and 3). Graves's review and analysis extends the arguments of earlier critics such as Sellars (p. 16) and Putnam (p. 26). He shows, for example, that so-called observational terms in fact have theoretical aspects, that so-called theoretical terms actually harbor observational aspects, and that the class of theoretical and the class of nonobservational terms do not coincide. Graves concludes that "the observational-theoretical distinction has no profound ontological significance" (p. 28).

As Barker (1969) puts it, "unfortunately, this way [of dichotomizing the vocabulary and processes of science] raises more difficulties than it settles" (p. 9; see also Rorty, 1979, especially Chapter VI). I shall return to this linguistic issue in the next chapter.

Operationalization and Verification

Another major positivist goal was to define meaning in terms of operations. To begin with, it was assumed that statements that presumably referred to the external world could be categorized into two major groups. The first class comprised all those statements that were "meaningful." It contained two subcategories: those statements that dealt with logic, and those that dealt with questions of fact (Barrett, 1978, p. 7). (Note again the internal/external polarity.) The former were either tautological (true by internal logic) or internally contradictory. The latter statements had to be either true or false; the decision could be made by translating the question or statement about "facts" into corresponding physical operations (measurement, observation, etc.). Thus, factual statements about the world would, in principle, take on meaning only in terms of operational processes, actual or imagined.

The second major class of statements, propositions, or questions were simply all those that remained, all those not in the first class. These would be statements that could neither be operationalized nor answered by mathematical or logical analysis. By fiat, statements in this second, remainder class were declared as metaphysical and meaningless, by definition outside the domain of science.

A cornerstone of this operationalist program was the so-called verification principle—roughly: "The meaning of a statement is its method of verification." It was meant to adjudicate among statements that presumably were telling us, or asking us, something about the outside world; it was to be used to discern whether or not a given statement about the world was "legitimate." The verification principle presumably could classify supposed statements about facts into those that were meaningful (operationalizable) and those that were meaningless (not operationalizable). Simultaneously (tautologically?) it would tell us what a given meaningful statement actually did mean: It meant its operationalized verification.

The verification principle was unable to withstand a succession of critical analyses that identified a chain of fatal flaws. Hacking (1975) gives a detailed history that follows the twists and turns of unsuccessful attempts to save the verification principle from this sequence of devastating criticisms (pp. 94–112; see also Powers, 1982, pp. 6–12). To meet the earliest criticisms, the idea of "meaningful" statements was changed to the idea of "cognitively meaningful" statements; subsequently, "verifiable in fact" became "verifiable in principle"; similarly, "conclusive" verification became that apparent contradiction "inconclusive verification"; when that approach in turn ran into difficulties, the principle was modified to refer to "falsifiable" statements; then came "indirect" rather than "direct" verification, an approach that also failed.

Translation, Commensurability

Another set of controversial difficulties concerned the matter of alternative theories. When theories change (for example, from classical mechanics to relativity theory), or when competing theories are offered to account for the same "data," complex questions arise. There are questions about "reference"—for instance, to what entity does a theoretical term "really" refer, and what happens to that referent when the theory changes? (Specifically, when theory changes, do terms such as "gravity" or "electron" still refer to the same phenomena?) There are also intricate questions concerning translatability between alternative theories, issues of "commensurability." Commensurability of different statements about the same "facts" would imply either that one could translate all these statements into a "neutral" language, or that there would be a formal way, a set of rules, that would tell us how to translate between alternative versions of theoretical statements. Hacking (1975) discusses these issues in terms of "three philosophical fantasies [of

Psychoanalytic Theory and Clinical Relevance 51

translation methodologies] that we could label 'too much', 'too little', and 'just right'. . ." (p. 151); Rorty (1979) discusses them in terms of Quine's "two dogmas of empiricism" (Chapter V, especially pp. 268–269, Chapter VI, pp. 322–332; see also Powers, 1982).

Issues Raised by Contemporary Physics

The difficulties posed by these kinds of issues pale before the epistemological problems raised by the post-classical developments of relativity theory and, particularly, quantum theory. Their impact on our conceptions of theorizing and our our ontologies has been widely discussed. I shall report some of the principal concerns, using the perspective offered by one well-known worker in quantum theory, David Bohm (1976, 1980; also Wilber, 1982).

Bohm (1980) critically examines the way that new phenomena have been dealt with throughout the history of physics. From ancient times through the eras of Ptolemy, Copernicus, Newton, and up to the present, new phenomena have been incorporated adaptively into theory by a process of accommodation. It has been a matter of forcing new findings into old frameworks by adding "epicycles"—cumbersome, convoluted, increasingly unsatisfactory, stopgap adaptations (p. 140). (Yankelovich and Barrett [1970] use the same term and the same general ideas in their discussions of the increasingly convoluted, ad hoc practices within psychoanalysis.)

Bohm comes to reject that epicycle-generated patchwork, and, what is particularly relevant to the thesis of this chapter, comes to reject the automatic, uncritical use of state process models and frameworks. As any physicist would, he recognizes and deeply appreciates their use within the domains of their proper application; he also is acutely aware, however, of the drastic limitations of state process forms, and thus of their inappropriate use otuside a particular domain. He comes to a radical reconceptualization of the world (1980, pp. 142–150; see also Weber, 1982, p. 40). It is based on a new notion of order, the "implicate, enfolded" order. That is a domain whose characteristics cannot be represented adequately by Cartesian frameworks. Hierarchies, states, Aristotelian logic—a logic "proper to things" (p. 60)—no longer suffice.

His argument starts from the familiar principal characteristics of quantum theory:

(1) The mathematical description of nature is statistical. Systems are conceptualized in terms of wave functions. These are thought of

as descriptions of the potentialities of the system rather than as "actual" descriptions, that is, descriptions of the way "things really are."

(2) Observation cannot be properly conceptualized as in principle separable from an observed: "The description of the experimental conditions does not drop out as a mere intermediary link of inference, but remains inseparable from the description of what is called the observed object" (1980, p. 133).

(3) A closely associated aspect is that one cannot properly retain apparently unassailable notions of a "signal" (pp. 136–137).

(4) Matter exhibits a "wave-particle" duality, at times behaving more like a particle, at other times more like a wave, "but always, in certain ways, like both together" (p. 128).

(5) Causal explanations cannot account for correlations that seem to exist between spatially separated events. Some other domain of explanations must be invoked (p. 129).

Obviously, I cannot explain or even summarize Bohm's notions here, although I should indicate that they are becoming fashionable (but, as I see it, trivialized and misunderstood) in the behavioral disciplines (Levenson, 1975; Wilber, 1982). The following extended quotations may suggest the direction of his thought, but the interested reader must go to the cited literature for a satisfactory presentation.

> The Cartesian order is suitable for analysis of the world into separately existent parts (e.g., particles or field elements). . . . We look into the nature of order with greater generality and depth, and discover that both in relativity and in quantum theory the Cartesian order [read, roughly: state process framework] is leading to serious contradictions and confusion. This is because both theories imply that the actual state of affairs is unbroken wholeness of the universe, rather than analysis into independent parts. Nevertheless, the two theories differ radically in their detailed notions of order. Thus, in relativity, movement is continuous, causally determinate and well defined, while in quantum mechanics it is discontinuous, not causally determinate and not well defined. Each theory is committed to its own notions of essentially static and fragmentary modes of existence (relativity to that of separate events, connectable by signals, and quantum mechanics to a well-defined quantum state). One thus sees that a new kind of theory is needed which drops these basic commitments and at most recovers some essential features of the older theories as abstract forms derived from a deeper reality in which what prevails is unbroken wholeness [1980, p. xv].

> This sort of ability of man to separate himself from his environment and to divide and apportion things ultimately led to a wide range of

negative and destructive results, because man lost awareness of what he was doing and thus extended the process of division beyond the limits within which it works properly. In essence, the process of division is a way of *thinking about things* that is evidently convenient and useful mainly in the domain of practical, technical and functional activities (e.g., to divide up an area of land into different fields where various crops are to be grown). However, when this mode of thought is applied more broadly to man's notion of himself and the whole world in which he lives (i.e. to his self-world view), then man ceases to regard the resulting divisions as merely useful or convenient and begins to see and experience himself and his world as actually constituted of separately existent fragments. Being guided by a fragmentary self-world view, man then acts in such a way as to try to break himself and the world up, so that all seems to correspond to his way of thinking. Man thus obtains an apparent proof of the correctness of his fragmentary self-world view though, of course, he overlooks the fact that it is he himself, acting according to his mode of thought, who has brought about the fragmentation that now seems to have an autonomous existence, independent of his will and of his desire [1976, p. 2].

Bohm is speaking about drastically alternative ways of conceptualizing order, structure. One of his principal themes is a special kind of structural "wholeness"—what he terms the "implicate, enfolded" order. This conception excludes the standard structural notions implied by traditional logic. Such commonsense notions as the linear succession of events (their sequential structure) or their hierarchical structure are seen to hold only in a very limited sense. Thus, it is not always legitimate to think of theory, or of the world for that matter, in terms of layered levels of abstraction. Neither is it always legitimate to proceed in terms of the usual Cartesian procedures that divide the scientific situation into two separate parts: an "objective" domain under study and an independent subjective observer. Furthermore, another typically Cartesian, scientific division also should be limited to certain classes of situations: One cannot always casually separate one portion (the system to be studied) from the rest of the "objective" domain; one cannot simply assume that one can, without major consequences and costs, excise some part of the world for study and represent the rest adequately by boundary conditions, by the "surround." These basic Cartesian procedures do, of course, have their legitimate uses; the point is that there are domains of application in which the procedures necessarily will lead to basic error. One must be very careful, therefore, when one applies the traditional approaches in areas outside the usual ones covered by classical physics.

It is interesting and pertinent that Bronowski (1978) comes to a similar conclusion:

> The world is totally connected: that is to say, that there are no events anywhere in the universe which are not tied to every other event in the universe....
>
> We make a cut. We put the experiment, if you like, in a box. Now the moment we do that, we do violence to the connections in the world [pp. 58–59].

Bronowski uses an example from biology to illustrate this point: You "falsify the whole procedure . . . [when] you think of the brain as receiving the information, processing it, and then giving an instruction to the muscle. . . . There is no nerve without the muscle and no muscle without the nerve in the total animal. . ." (p. 99). Incidentally, Bronowski's view is very close to Merleau-Ponty's notion that the typical results of experimental psychology are, in a particular sense, "artifactual": Results of experiments typically are seriously skewed by the unnatural excision of a subject, and the replacement of the subject's actual complex, integrated surroundings by a highly restricted set of "stimuli" (which formally serve the function of boundary conditions); putting a subject in the extremely unnatural situation of an experiment produces a "pathological" case, and will yield pathological artifacts (Pollio, 1972); in many cases, these artifactual results obscure and mislead.

Whereas these conclusions are not readily apparent from commonsense considerations, they do follow from careful and deeper analyses. Formally, these issues raise questions pertaining to mathematical linearity, a topic to be considered further in Chapter 4.

That is not to say, of course, that one can or must treat the whole universe in every bit of theorizing one undertakes. One does, however, need to be much more aware of what one is doing when one excises something from its surround for the purpose of scientific analysis. Typically, that step is implemented in much too casual a manner, without sufficiently appreciating all that it involves.

As Weil (1983) has said, "Physics has gone totally soft by the nineteenth-century standards doctors still use. . ." (p. 268). For the moment, let us leave it at that. I shall return to further consequences of Bohm's thought when I discuss applicable issues in linguistics. What counts for now is that rigorous work has led science itself to a stage where it questions the application of Cartesian, state process representational frameworks outside some carefully delimited domains. Furthermore, unlike the previous criticisms that arose within a more or less conventional, classical Cartesian context, this latter class of criticisms has brought us very close to ontological questions that lie outside the province of traditional normal science.

CRITICISMS FROM WITHOUT: SCIENCE AND THE LIFE WORLD

The second major group of criticisms that call the Cartesian, state process formalistic frameworks into question come from disciplines that lie outside normal science. Let us now consider these.

The Cheshire Cat Phenomenon

Cartesian state formalisms structure for us a lifeless, arid moonscape, a wasteland where all that is visible is the state space within which events occur and which the representational notation specifies. All signs of life have been carefully removed, except to the extent that they can be represented, exactly like any other "scientific" events or processes, as points and paths in a state space. "All semantic considerations (appeal to meanings) [have been reduced] to the techniques of syntactic (formal) manipulation" (Dreyfus, 1979, p. 69).

This has led to a situation I like to call the "Cheshire Cat" phenomenon: One is left only with a dehumanized, lifeless remainder of the Cartesian/state process legacy in which the person is nowhere to be seen. Science either forgets, or ignores, or laments its origins. The curious result, with far-reaching implications, is that in mathematics, physics, history, psychology, and all other disciplines that have "scientific" ambitions or pretensions, there has arisen an overwhelming tendency to view the remnants sifted out by state process frameworks as the totality, as "all there is." The origins of science are no longer seen—worse, cannot be seen: "It is ironical that such scientists cannot see the way they see with their way of seeing. . ." (Laing, 1982, p. 15). "Nothing is more subjective than objectivity blind to its subjectivity" (p. 17). Scientists when pressed might admit that indeed there might have been a person in the picture at one time—an unfortunate necessity perhaps—but now that that's over with, one can deal tidily with the autonomous domain, purified of its suspiciously subjective origins. Let us look at some comments about this state of affairs.

Dreyfus (1979) writes extensively about the practice to which I am calling attention in his explorations of the limits of computer science, *What Computers Can't Do*. He notes, for instance, how easy it is to remove the programmer from the computer situation and look only at the program, creating the illusion of "a third-person process in which the involvement of the processor plays no essential role" (p. 117). We perform a "sleight of hand" in which we totally cover over a fact that should be obvious: that any "insight" displayed by the computer was, of course, "*introduced by the programmers before the actual programming begins*" (p. 116). We now have put ourselves in a position where we can readily and glibly speak about what computers *can* do, forgetting where they and their "doing" came from in the first instance.

A similar idea is expressed by Rabil (1967) in his comments on the "perversion of geometry" by Galileo: "His perversion was due to the fact that as time passed the realization that geometry was based on an idealization of nature *produced by the human mind* was forgotten, and it came to be regarded as something true *in itself,* having no relation at all to the men who created it. In other words, the thinking mind and the object thought about were divorced from one another" (pp. 55–56).

This seems to be generally true within mathematical thought (see, for example, Davis and Hersh's [1981] survey). Mathematicians apparently tend to view their subject matter as an "object" in and of itself, with a separate, autonomous existence; the persons who created it had at best only a midwife's role that is now irrelevant. Surely this is a basic and drastic epistemological move.

Gadamer (1976) makes related observations about the role of "objectivity" in history. He frames his comments in the context of the "dogmatism" which separates and places into opposition "the ongoing, natural 'tradition' and the reflective appropriation [i.e., the objectivization] of it. . . . In this objectivism the understander is seen . . . in such a way that his own consciousness does not enter into the event" (p. 28).

The Cheshire Cat phenomenon has sprung up. Even a casual contemplation of the move that conceals or casts aside the origins of "objectivity" would lead one to anticipate that drastic consequences would necessarily follow from the severing of ties between person and object of thought.

The Life World

The criticisms that I am about to present are all based on the recognition of the removal of subjective origins from the scientific disciplines and the exploration of the consequences of the basic bifurcation. They cover an extensive range of topics, but their common point of departure and their common target is the initial "Cartesian move." That is, the criticisms focus on that first step of splitting a preexisting totality into two independent parts: the knower-subjective-internal and the known-objective-external. (The latter, objective realm is then always conceptualized in terms of some state process formalistic framework, as I have pointed out.)

The critical analyses are broadly based, not the objections of some few isolated, unorthodox dissenters. They come from diverse disciplines. In philosophy, comprehensive reviews and discussions can be found in Rorty (1979) (whose principal sources are Sellars, Quine, Davidson, Ryle, Malcolm, Kuhn, and Putnam), Barrett (1978) (Wittgenstein, Heidegger, and Dewey), Grene (1948, 1969), Janik and Toulmin (1973), Merleau-Ponty (1962, 1963), and Gadamer (1976). More mathematically oriented considerations are presented by Bronowski (1966, 1978), Bellman (1967), Dreyfus (1979), and Weizenbaum (1976). In psychiatry, relevant material can be found in Ingleby (1980), Laing (1982), Deikman (1982), and Weil (1972, 1983). In economics, these issues are extensively discussed by Schumacher (1973, especially pp. 72–94; see also Schumacher, 1977, and Kumar, 1980). Additional sources that pertain primarily to linguistic issues will be considered later.

It is obvious that the Cartesian strategy has been very useful when it has been applied to the inanimate domains of the natural sciences, at least if success is defined or judged according to materialistic or technological criteria and accomplishments. (All the same, we have seen in the discussions pertaining to modern physics that even in that discipline one finds warnings that the strategy may ultimately be untenable [see also Bronowski, 1966, 1978; Bellman, 1967; Holton, 1968, pp. 664–665, note 12; Robinson, 1975, p. 169, note 1; d'Espagnat, 1979; Hughes, 1981].) It is when one applies the same state process framework and approaches to the domains traditionally served by the behavioral "sciences" that intractable difficulties are bound to arise, as the critics see it. In their view, these difficulties must follow automatically because the Cartesian wrenching of the observer from the matrix destroys a relationship that is (or should be) a basic aspect of any discipline that concerns itself with subjective, behavioral, humanistic issues. The Cartesian move does violence to a preexisting unity, often referred to as the "life world," which is the bedrock, the ground of all our experience.

As we shall see, the critics point out certain kinds of losses that seem to be inherent in the undoing of that integration. Furthermore, they believe that once incurred those losses cannot be recovered as long as one remains within the Cartesian framework. Before going on to these criticisms, let us first look at how some of the critics have attempted to describe that prior integrated state. The life world,

> this total context, with its interlinked meanings, is the world in which we live, the human world and not the abstract world depicted by the physical sciences... [Yankelovich and Barrett, 1970, p. 245].

> [The life world] has, in some way or another, to do with common everyday prescientific experience. This version of reality is what Wittgenstein means when he states that the facts which concern us lie spread out before us; it is what William James means by radical empiricism, what John Dewey means by his emphasis on common experience, what G. E. Moore means by his particular concept of "common sense," what Husserl means by the *Lebenswelt*, and it is what, with some qualifications, Heidegger means by his concept of being-in-the-world [p. 254].

It is "the world in which we are immersed in the natural attitude that never becomes for us an object as such, but that constitutes the pregiven basis of all experience..." (Gadamer, 1982, p. 281); it is the realm of the "bicameral mind" (Jaynes, 1976); it is "the region of our ordinary experience out of which all meanings, scientific or other, must emerge.... The life world is the concrete totality in which any individual bit of consciousness unfolds..." (Barrett, 1978, pp. 122–123).

Phenomenologists such as Merleau-Ponty point to this unified realm when they make the distinction between "unreflected" and "reflected" modes of consciousness—when they make distinctions between "thinking" and "thinking about thinking" (or some elaboration such as "thinking about 'thinking about thinking'"). The former, unreflected thinking, occurs *within* the life world; the latter, thinking about thinking, is self-conscious, and grounded in a thinker/object-of-thinking bifurcation (Pollio, 1972).

The Derivative Status of Science

Obviously, if one does not reject out of hand what is being said here, one must be prepared to question drastically the privileged status usually granted to science. As the critics see it, the usual position within science is to belittle, ignore, or deny its derivative nature. Typically, the obvious—namely, that science must be parasitic on the life world, and thus necessarily derivative in nature—is set aside. For instance, logic is usually considered the ultimate court of appeal in matters concerning the life world; yet "where else would logic come from than from the everyday world?" (Mehan and Wood, 1975, p. 68).

Thus, a very basic misperception is injected by the Cheshire Cat mentality when it grants science a privileged status, when, for example, the "scientific" view of the person is taken as veridical and when "unscientific" views are scornfully rejected out of hand. Ontological priorities have been turned topsy-turvy. This practice shows a blatant disregard of the insight that many thinkers consider to be "the principal philosophical development of the twentieth century" (Linge, 1976, p. xli), namely, that

> all scientific abstractions are developed and assume their ultimate meaning within this concrete life-world. . . . These abstractions can never be used to substitute for the concrete world of human life. The mistake of scientific materialism is to confuse what is derivative with what is basic, i.e., to take the abstractions of physics as the ultimately concrete—the really real—realities behind the everyday world rather than the other way around [Yankelovich and Barrett, p. 254].

In psychoanalysis, one consequence of the erroneous position that is being criticized here comes to light in the course of the numerous explorations of the issue of the two realms, the science/humanism duality (see, for example, Guntrip, 1961, 1969; Grene, 1969; Stoller, 1971, p. 18; G. Klein, 1973; Gedo and Pollock, 1976; Rubinstein, 1976; Schafer, 1976; Wallerstein, 1976; Bowlby, 1979; McIntosh, 1979). Invariably, the assumption is that these two aspects, science and humanism, are somehow coordinate, of equal rank. If that were the case, then it would be reasonable to consider their "fusion."

The preceding general criticisms, however, strongly suggest that viewing psychoanalysis in terms of two branches of equal ontological rank is fallacious; the humanistic branch is not a branch at all—it is the foundation. Science and the life world are not cognates. Yet invariably the premise is that psychoanalysis is somehow capable of being erected on these two corresponding and complementary pillars, that it would somehow bring about a "fusion" of these two supposedly cognate branches. Worse still, if one "branch" is to be given preferential treatment, a reading of the standard literature reveals that usually it is the "scientific branch" that is selected for privileged status. Plainly, these mainstream views, approaches, and practices could profit from a basic review.

PROBLEM AREAS, UNDESIRABLE CONSEQUENCES

Representational Defects

According to the critics, all sorts of undesirable consequences are bound to follow from the distorted state process view which grants the life world only secondary status. Major consequences are trivialization of subject matter, loss of significance, depersonalization, alienation, and fragmentation. These consequences in turn follow from certain basic restricting characteristics inherent in any and all logical-formal systems. One of these characteristics is a circumscribed representational system that must render state process formalisms incapable of adequately representing certain aspects of the life world.

What logical systems can encompass. What does it mean to say that a state process formalism is necessarily incapable of representing the central phenomena, the key subject matter, of a given discipline? The general idea, of course, is that since a state process formalism is based on strictly circumscribed conceptual ingredients, it must necessarily be limited by those logical ingredients. In other words, the premise is that Cartesian formalisms necessarily impoverish the life world by screening out certain domains right from the start.

As an example of ingredients that impose unavoidable representational limitations, consider the formal means that are available for representing such unruly and unpredictable phenomena as freedom, choice, creativity, or will. Because of the nature of mathematical representational systems and transition rules, state process formalisms can represent any phenomenon only by means of either deterministic or statistical mathematical models. Familiar examples of the former are algebraic functions; of the latter, random variables. That is all that mathematics or logic can offer, all that is "in" them. Within those frameworks, phenomena such as those just mentioned must therefore be handled either by a deterministic system which views them as illusions, consequences of incomplete or unavailable knowledge, or by blind statistical rules.

Weizenbaum (1976) makes this point in terms of the kinds of limitations one has automatically imposed when one has chosen to theorize within computer model frameworks. These provide a system that "permits the asking of only certain kinds of questions, that accepts only certain kinds of data, and that . . . has effectively closed many doors that were open before it was installed" (p. 38). (Recall the formal equivalence of computer models, Turing machines, and state process representations.)

Schumacher (1977) also undertakes a thorough examination of the limits that mathematical-formal representations necessarily exhibit (pp. 50–60). He presents compelling arguments and discussions in support of the position that formal representational systems such as mathematics must rule out adequate representation of crucial sectors, phenomena, or experiences pertaining to the life world. He shows that numerous highly undesirable consequences follow when one bases economics on those classes of formalisms.

The same point can be made about psychoanalytic theorizing: If one initially selects, deliberately or unwittingly, a schema incapable of representing the domain of interest, then one necessarily will have screened out phenomena in that domain from the yield of theorizing. Matte Blanco (1975) discusses this issue in terms of the notion of "thinking-logic," a system whose elements are "something" (S), "something else" (SE), and logico-formal "relations" (R). He observes that "the conclusions of modern physics reflect the structure of thinking and of logic; one might even say that they could have been anticipated, in their general outline; because if we use thinking-logic to understand nature, it is not surprising that we find in it the same elements out of which thinking-logic is made or which it can know" (p. 389).

Dreyfus (1979) considers this consequence in an examination of the place of "rules" in the modeling of "expert performance, judgement." He shows how the thinking of those who assume that such performances must follow from a set of internalized (although perhaps unconscious) rules must perpetually be circumscribed by that assumption: "If there is a limit to what can be understood by rules . . . [the investigator] would never see it" (p. 29). An extended discussion is presented by Thoma and Kachele (1975) in a section entitled "Circularity and Self-Fulfilling Prophecy" (pp. 102–113).

We find in the world the logical structure that we impose on it. Furthermore, as long as one remains within the usual framework, its practices tend to be hidden and consequently to be self-perpetuating; thought applied within a certain framework tends to become trapped reflexively within that domain. The representation usurps the place of life-world events.

Consider Wittgenstein's early analytical work. It usually is seen as a logician's striving to put scientific language on a firm formal foundation, to "clean up" language-induced fallacies, and the like. As Janik and Toulmin (1973) convincingly show, however, his motivation actually was quite different. A major purpose of Wittgenstein's work in formal logic and analysis was to contribute, albeit indirectly, to the specification of those things that are really important. In his view, these are things that lie outside language; they are things that "cannot be said"—in my terms, things that cannot be represented by state process formalisms or their logical equivalent, the Turing machine. Wittgenstein thought that since they "could not be said," these important things could only be specified indirectly by first making clear just what *can* be said. As Engelmann (1967) puts it,

> positivism holds—and this is its essence—that what we can speak about is all that matters in life. *Whereas Wittgenstein passionately believes that all that really matters in human life is precisely what, in his view, we must be silent about.* When he nevertheless takes immense pains to delimit the unimportant (i.e., the scope and limits of ordinary language), it is not the coastline of that island which he is bent on surveying with such meticulous accuracy, but the boundary of the ocean [p. 167].

Janik and Toulmin devote much of their book to demonstrating that this position was very much part of the Viennese tradition in Wittgenstein's era.

These introductory remarks concerning the limitations inherent in state process representations will be amplified in Chapter 4, when I consider the issues further in the context of discursive language.

Impoverishment, trivialization, alienation. As I have indicated, because they cannot be adequately represented, life world aspects subsumed under such terms as meaning, understanding, knowledge, freedom, and creativity are either ruled out of bounds for the behavioral disciplines or trivialized. Criticisms along these lines of thought have a long history: "The notion that social facts are 'things' which can be described like any other natural objects has been the target of continual criticism since Durkheim first articulated it in 1895" (Ingleby, 1980, p. 29). To certain thinkers, it has seemed self-evident that an adequate treatment of such phenomena becomes a "theoretical impossibility" in a logical positivist's world (Barrett, 1978; see also Bergson, 1946; Jordan, 1968, pp. 78–79; Kohut, 1977, pp. 70–71; Furlong, 1981). "Mathematical methods we now possess are not adapted to study significant decision-making processes" (Bellman, 1967, p. 301). As I see it, this is a deplorable instance of scientism: "the view that [normal] science alone represents a genuine form of human knowledge. . . . the conviction that we can no longer understand science as *one* form of possible knowledge, but rather must identify [all] knowledge with science" (Keat, 1981, p. 16;

see also Hexter, 1971, Chapter 10, especially pp. 272ff.). Knowledge becomes, can only be conceptualized as, "accurate representation of facts" (Rorty, 1979) or mere "logicality" (Weizenbaum, 1976, p. 13).

To represent experience in terms of "spatio-temporally locatable sense-data [one variety of state process formalisms] that logic or mathematics works on . . . [removes] the subject matter of philosophy from any relevance to the felt reality of the individual consciousness" (Grene, 1948, p. 11). What Grene says about philosophy applies equally well, as I see it, to the behavioral disciplines. Science can represent only an "impoverished version" of direct experience (Weizenbaum, 1976, p. 25). Before one makes the Cartesian move, persons may contain "a hidden dimension" that may not be "abstractable into organismic terms. . ." (Kovel, 1978, p. 40; also pp. 50–51). These considerations reflect the issue Rorty (1979) calls "the problem of personhood . . . what more a human being is than flesh. . ." (p. 34).

"Disciplines that proceed according to these rules [of logic, mathematics, positivist methodology] lose their significance. . ." (Habermas, quoted by Kaplan, 1977, p. 220). Perhaps this abuse of logic, this compartmentalization of the life world, is what Loewald (1975) had in mind in his reference to "that disease of the age and especially of official science—the disruption between fantasy and rationality—which it [psychoanalysis] is intended to cure or ameliorate. . ." (p. 291). In Goethe's *Faust* Mephistopheles caustically points out to a student that when you argue according to a strict logical system, you have never "learned to weave"; you may know everything and lack nothing—except the vital element, "the spirit's connections. . ." (quoted by Kaufmann, 1980, p. 34). Man, when conceived as a scientific system, becomes alienated man (Barrett, 1972, 1978), mechanical man (Weizenbaum, 1976, p. 6).

According to Schumacher (1977), when we represent the world in terms of the results of "pointer readings made by a single color-blind eye," then it should not be surprising that "the world picture resulting from this method of observation [and, I would add, representation] is 'the abomination of desolation,' a wasteland in which man is a quaint cosmic accident signifying nothing" (pp. 52–53). Laing (1982) refers several times to this impoverishing aspect of scientific representation:

> There is no experience or meaning *in* the objective order because the objective order is the way the world appears, subtracted of meaningful experience [p. 33].

> Science finds time for our ordinary world only to find more and more subtle and effective ways to exclude it. Its testimony is not heard

in the discourse of science. . . . And so, ordinary experience . . . is consigned by science to its slop bucket. . . [p. 69].

When we turn to experience and learn what it may have to teach us, we cannot do so by a method constructed to exclude it [p. 12].

Compartmentalization

Up to this point, I have emphasized the limitations introduced by the formal characteristics inherent in state process notation. It has been a matter of considering the kinds of representational limits that logical systems must exhibit and introduce. State process representations bring about other kinds of limitations as well, namely, ones introduced by various kinds of compartmentalizations that state process frameworks require.

The knower as the known. One kind of limitation follows from the basic Cartesian dichotomy between the knower and the known. When one attempts to encompass the person within a Cartesian, state process framework, that is, when one makes the person an object of scientific study, one really should expect that such attempts would automatically and necessarily create certain logical difficulties.

The expectation that paradoxes and conundrums would surely follow for any discipline whose subject matter is the person, the knower, arises from the following considerations. The Cartesian framework begins with—indeed, is predicated on—the distinction between a knower (observer, consciousness, objective scientist) and the outside "known objects" that are the targets of study. That is the basic Cartesian dualism that resonates throughout our scientific views in the form of various other analogous dualisms: mind/body, word ("predicate")/thing, science/humanism, person/organism, idiographic/nomothetic, analytic/synthetic, a priori/a posteriori, proof theory/model theory, theoretical/empirical, representation/reality, mathematical/observational.

We start by placing the knower on one side of an equation, and the object on the other. That is basic to the framework—the knower and the known are distinct and separate. So far so good, at least for classical physics, chemistry, biology, and so on. Next, if we wish to study persons scientifically, we must of course place the person—or at least a "part" of that knower—on the other side as well, on the side of objective object. In the Cartesian framework, that is the only side that one can study.

Here is where the troubles come. We want to have our cake and eat it too. The basic distinction becomes blurred; we now want to have the knower on both sides of the equation. The knower has become part of the known, and the known, part of the knower. Should not that move be logically suspect? Have we not initiated a circular, infinitely regressive process? Have we not created a mirrored labyrinth? Are we not necessarily asking for trouble? That is, should we not expect that such a peculiar strategy is bound to run into logical, if not other, difficulties?

Obviously, such a move must always leave a remainder—a remaining "part" of the knower—on the subjective side. That "part," separated from the objects that we wish to study, then remains inaccessible to study; one might say it must always remain on the wrong side (the subjective side) of the Cartesian equation. (If we were to remove "all" of the knower to the side of the object, who would be left to do the studying?) How is one to deal with that remainder? That is, how is one supposed to go about understanding or studying it? Remove yet another piece of the subjective knower to the other side? Introduce another observer? The situation must lead to an endless regressive process. The specter of infinity comes into view. There always will be a remainder, one part of the knower that does the knowing and that cannot and must not be removed to the other side; some part of the knower—perhaps, for psychology, *the* essential part?—remains away from the side of the object, away from the domain that the knower can study. In other words, it is a logical necessity that there always will be some remaining part of the knower that must elude the behavioral disciplines, that will be unavailable as an object of study. As Deikman (1982) puts it, "the observing self is an anomaly—not an object, like everything else" (p. 11).

One example of this infinite regress and the elusive remainder will be considered further in the next chapter: the remainder that emerges in the course of studying language. Since one always must use *some* language, artificial or otherwise, in one's study of language and discourse, that "theoretical" language (or one of its infinite successors) ultimately must remain beyond the reach of one's efforts.

The remainder seems to be implicated in all the paradoxes of self-reference, reflexivity, "knots," that are a principal preoccupation of logicians, physicians, sociologists, and others who are involved in making the study of the person "scientific." It is implicated in, for example, Bronowski's previously cited work concerning limitative theorems and logical paradoxes; Mehan and Wood's ethnomethodological studies of reflexivity; Laing's writings on knots, or infinite linguistic regressions; and Wittgenstein's reference to linguistic analysis: It is like an Indian rope trick, "like trying to climb up an unsupported ladder and hold it up at the same time" (Janik and Toulmin, 1973, p. 189).

This fact of the remainder may also account for the situation discussed by such critics of artificial intelligence or "person" computer models as Matson, Dreyfus, or Weizenbaum. A representative example is Matson's (1976) discussion of the failures, after early promise, of machine translation, chess playing, pattern recognition, or control of artificial limbs. After each failure, it was thought that only "a little bit extra" would be needed to achieve success; yet that "little bit extra"—perhaps a manifestation of the remainder I have been considering?—"never was forthcoming despite the efforts of teams of ingenious and dedicated workers. . ." (p. 103). We still hear the same promises made today: These kinds of successes (e.g., computer simulation of high-level decision processes) are just around the corner.

The subject/object dyad. I have said that one set of difficulties with the Cartesian dichotomies is the problem of the elusive remainder. Another, related cluster of difficulties pertains to traversals of the boundaries between the observing, knowing person and the "external world." When we create the knower/known, internal domain/external world dichotomies, we inevitably also create the need to explain the commerce between these two domains. If there is a knower/known dichotomy, there inevitably also arise questions as to how it is that one can get the domain of the known "inside" the knower. How does one conceptualize the traversals across the boundary, the commerce between knower and known? For example, what do you observe? Sense data, or material objects? Who is it that does the observation? (Here we encounter the remainder problem again.) What do observations imply ontologically? Thus arise all the issues about perception, "direct" perception, contentions between sense data and physicalist versions of perception, idealism versus realism, and so on.

In a slightly different vein, there is a cluster of logical problems identified and studied in a recent book by Feffer (1982). His thesis is that because of the "Cartesian view of the relationship between the subject and object of knowledge and, because of the explanatory limits which are thus given" (p. 42), any attempted explanations of the nature of human development must ultimately run up against inherent logical paradoxes. Feffer shows that certain paradoxes must arise, no matter whether one pursues some variety of instinct theory or of behavioral theory. He labels the consequence of this general Cartesian entrapment the "immutability-discontinuity problem." I shall return briefly to his approach in Chapter 7. In any case, what his work demonstrates, among other things, is that the Cartesian premise of a subject/object dichotomy ultimately returns us to significant difficulties—in Feffer's work, to ones concerning developmental issues. The difficulties again pertain to the "subject" side of the dichotomy; the concept of the knower as distinct from the known leads once more to basic and important difficulties for psychology.

Decoupled systems: The object/surround dyad. Yet another kind of Cartesian dichotomy ultimately leads to difficulties. This time, the dichotomy of interest lies entirely on the "object" side of the subject/object, inside/outside equation. Typically, normal science assumes that the subject matter under scrutiny can be "decoupled" from the rest of its surroundings, and studied as an independent system. On the objective side of the equation, then, we have an excised system under study, with the rest of the objective universe conceptualized, incorporated, and represented in terms of boundary conditions.

This picture is highly misleading. According to Lewontin, Rose, and Kamin (1984), organisms are not simply alienated respondents that react to, or interact with, an autonomous environment. Organism and environment interpenetrate; are open to one another; are both cause and effect for each other. Their relationship is dialectical (pp. 265–277).

I have already mentioned the similar views of other scientists on these matters in the section "Issues Raised by Contemporary Physics." Some humanistic critics arrive at the same objections, although from other perspectives (see, for example, Barrett's comprehensive review and studies, 1972, 1978; Kovel, 1981). Their objections stem from various subjective consequences (e.g., alienation) that are brought about by such a fragmented, compartmentalized world view.

Motivations for Retaining Cartesianism and State Process Formalisms

How important for those disciplines concerned with the study of persons are the losses and undesirable consequences of using Cartesian state process schemata? Does the perpetual remainder contain domains that should be central to psychology? Is the representational system adequate to encompass the phenomena that properly ought to be encompassed by such disciplines? If one is looking toward generating a nontrivial discipline, are these losses tolerable?

Logic cannot provide authoritative answers, since it is itself derivative. Using formalisms to disprove the importance of the life world would be to engage in circular thinking.

These and similar issues seem to divide people into opposing factions. As Bronowski (1978) points out, "The world is pretty well divided into people who are proud of being machines and people who are outraged at the thought of being machines" (p. 55). To some, the views of critics such as Barrett, Rorty, Malcolm, Austin, Searle, Wittgenstein, Grene, Merleau-Ponty, Gadamer, Robinson, Bronowski, Jameson, Rommetveit, Hexter, Weizenbaum, Goodman, Abelson, Quine, Mehan, Wood, and others whom we shall encounter in the next chapters seem quite obvious, certainly congenial. To others, they are incomprehensible, or naive, or even revolting; positivists "have regarded these approaches with a mixture of contempt and bewilderment—for [within their framework of thought] . . . they cannot think that their thought is wrong. . ." (Ingleby, 1980, p. 46). They take the position, for example, that "obviously, any rational person will favor rigorous analysis and careful experiment" (Chomsky, 1972, p. xi). At any rate, we might as well recognize that criticisms of the machine view of persons routinely encounter negative reactions ranging from skepticism to outright hostile reflexive rejection.

Why should this occur? Obviously, a study of the motivational aspects, fascinating as it may be, would require a separate undertaking. Here I will only mention some of the explanations advanced in the literature. The principal clusters of motives seem to be (1) a yearning for certainty, objectivity, presuppositionless thought, absolute truth, veridical knowledge, prediction, control; (2) equivalently, needs to avoid the anxieties that uncertainty and lack of closure might bring about; (3) a bias toward the unity of all the sciences; (4) a fear of introducing "ghosts in the machine" or similar anthropomorphisms and reifications; (5) a wish to be accepted by the scientific community; for example, in psychoanalysis, we find a plea for orthodox conformity "if we are to have an impact, scientifically, beyond our profession. . ." (Dorpat, 1973, p. 171); (6) social/political: the motives for "rationalizing and universalizing thought. . . [are] ultimately political in inspiration. . . . It would not be difficult . . . to show how such thinking is characterized by a turning away of the eyes, a preference for segments and isolated objects, as a means to avoid observation of those larger wholes and totalities which if they had to be seen would force the mind in the long run into uncomfortable social and political conclusions" (Jameson, 1972, pp. 23–24); (7) needs for godlike perfection, for an idealized world (see the mathematicians' needs discussed by Davis and Hersh [1981, pp. 108–112]). A provocative, wide-ranging motive is suggested by Jaynes (1976), who proposes that the veneration of science is just one among many other functionally equivalent attempts to use a "mythological" belief system to recover the lost "bicameral mind" (pp. 441–443). Further discussions of motivational issues can be found in Austin (1962, p. 104), Bettelheim (1983), Braginsky and Braginsky (1974, pp. 8–9), Dreyfus (1979, pp. 87–88), Hexter (1971, pp. 43–45), Jaynes (1966), Lewontin, Rose, and Kamin (1984, Chapters 1–3), Loewald (1960, p. 21), Mehan and Wood (1975, p. 208), Milner (1973, pp. 161ff), Pepper (1961), Rorty (1968, 1978), Wolman (1971, p. 883), and Weizenbaum (1976, p. 280).

IMPLICATIONS FOR FORMALISMS IN BEHAVIORAL DISCIPLINES

I have presented general arguments designed to show the severe limitations that Cartesianism imposes on one's theorizing capabilities. While they may be quite adequate for the many important applications pertaining to the inanimate world, Cartesian approaches—assumptions, methodologies, or practices—create too many persistent, intractable difficulties and limitations for dealing with the person, the domain of therapy. A state process view or representation of a given domain stringently limits what can be said about, or accomplished within, that domain.

If we accept this premise at least provisionally, then we must rethink issues pertaining to formalisms. I have sought to demonstrate that state process formalisms are *the* expressions of a Cartesian perspective. They embody Cartesianism's formal and material premises.

In that event, the limitations that these formalisms bring with them cannot be circumvented merely by switching from one state process version to another; the use of a state process formalism in any of its embodiments will retain the standard features and therefore the standard stringent limitations. That is why I mentioned in Chapter 2 that various alternative models proposed for use in psychoanalytic theorizing (e.g., cybernetic, informational, structural linguistic, synaptic) just would not do. In an important sense, these would be pseudochanges; they would not bring about any basic changes in the formal structure of the theoretical language.

If one cannot adequately represent the phenomena in one's domain of interest, it follows that one cannot think adequately about one's subject matter. It also follows, then, that one needs to cast about for some genuinely alternative system of representation, meaning an alternative that will not just return us to a state process framework by the back door, so to speak.

I am suggesting that it might be useful to accept, as a provisional hypothesis to be carefully explored, the premise that theorizing about technique in psychoanalysis ought to be done by means of some vehicle or formalism other than a state process framework. This is not exactly an entirely new thought:

> For some years now the chief problem confronting psychoanalytic theoreticians has been the need to develop a new language in which to speak of their methods and findings and conduct their debates with one another and with members of other disciplines [Schafer, 1978, p. 5].

Discursive language comes to mind immediately. As I shall show in the next chapter, however, there are concealed complexities and pitfalls in the standard conceptions and usages of theoretical discourse. I submit that unless one has identified the fundamental formal issues, unless one has them clearly in view, one will run a very large risk of offering solutions that in fact are not solutions at all. If one does not thoroughly understand state process issues, if one cannot identify the presence and use of a state process representation, then one is likely to retain, unwittingly, the very kind of a representational framework from which one seeks to escape.

FOUR

Theoretical Discourse

> *We grow up, and we become acquainted with men and in the last analysis with ourselves when we learn to speak. Learning to speak does not mean learning to use a preexistent tool for designating a world already familiar to us; it means acquiring a familiarity and acquaintance with the world itself and how it confronts us. An enigmatic and profoundly veiled process!*
> —Hans-Georg Gadamer, *Philosophical Hermeneutics*

> *And right here, at the beginning, one sniffs something peculiar about language; it is not a thing quite like other specific things whose nature we can dissect; and yet it is the medium within which other things are brought into the open and become clear and evident.*
> —William Barrett, *The Illusion of Technique*

The "inextricable meshing of language and psychoanalysis" (Steiner, 1976, p. 256) is widely recognized within the field. Almost every discussion, be it theoretical, clinical, didactic, or epistemological, at least touches on one or another aspect of language.

Let us remind ourselves why and how language matters in psychoanalysis. It plays three familiar major roles. First, spoken language is of course one, if not *the*, basic constituent of the clinical situation; it embodies the patient's material and the analyst's interventions. Second, language may become an object of metapsychological analysis, in the sense that it can be conceptualized from the perspective of the psychological apparatus; verbal material can be viewed as a manifestation of the secondary process, or as one component element of an underlying entity, and so on (see, for example, Fenichel, 1945, pp. 46–51; Fliess, 1949; Loewenstein, 1956; Laplanche and Pontalis, 1973, pp. 447–449; Kovel, 1978). Finally, language is the principal vehicle for theorizing, at all levels of abstraction, It is the tool for "treating" (describing, analyzing, discussing, explaining, organizing) raw clinical data, and the means by which higher-order discussions—discussions about discussions—are conducted.

In this chapter I shall focus on this last role. The argument I shall develop can be stated quite simply. In skeletal form, it is this: (1) Traditionally, formal scientific discourse serves as a state process descriptive system. (2) The assumptions and arguments presented in Chapter 3 suggest that all state process conceptualizations necessarily display certain fundamental limitations. (3) Therefore, when theoretical discourse is used in a state process fashion, it, too, may be inadequate as a vehicle for theorizing in certain applications. A corollary is that if one advocates this critical view, one then has the burden of developing some adequate alternative vehicle with which to theorize. My initial discussion will seek to demonstrate that theoretical discourse—including psychoanalytic theoretical discourse—normally is viewed, and used, as a state process descriptor.

SCIENTIFIC VIEWS OF LANGUAGE

As does any other scientific study of some "object," the scientific examination of language also begins with an excision. In this case, it is a "piece" of language, a "corpus," that is lifted out from extended spoken or written language. ("The vice of Anglo-American empiricism lies indeed in its stubborn will to isolate the object in question from everything else, whether it be a material thing, an 'event' in Wittgenstein's sense, a word, a sentence, or a 'meaning'" [Jameson, 1972, p. 23].)

That excised segment then becomes the object of one or both of two types of analyses. It is analyzed either in terms of *logical syntax* or in terms of *interpretation*. Syntactical analysis is "internal" (Holt, 1961), intralinguistic; the segment (its composition, logical features, and so on) is considered in and of itself. Interpretive analysis is "external" (Holt, 1961), and pertains to the relationship between the example under study and some "real world referent" of that linguistic piece. The referent is usually some physical or psychological "object," but it also may be some other linguistic corpus, or worse yet, the excised corpus itself.

Here we meet another version of the internal/external, proof theory/model theory dichotomy that characterizes Cartesian state process frameworks in general. We might note, however, that we can already see some peculiarities here. Unlike the objects that are usu-

Psychoanalytic Theory and Clinical Relevance 73

ally decoupled for analysis in the natural sciences, this particular kind of decoupled "object" can *say something* about something else, or even about itself. That means that in the case of language the excised object becomes, at one and the same time, an object *of* state process analysis and also *itself* a state process descriptor (as we shall soon see). Thus, a fundamental ambiguity is injected into formal linguistic analysis from the very start. Let us first consider the internal characteristics of language as these are seen by science.

Internal Features

For science, the interesting internal properties of language are "the formal devices of language . . . studied independently of their use" (Chomsky, 1972, p. 198). This is particularly true of "formal" languages. According to Weizenbaum (1976),

> a formal language is a game. That is not a mere metaphor but a statement asserting a formal correspondence. But if that statement is true, we should, when talking about a language, be able to easily move back and forth between a game-like vocabulary and a corresponding language-like vocabulary. Precisely that can be done [p. 50].

Weizenbaum goes on to show that in the way he uses the term a "game" is logically equivalent to, isomorphic with, a Turing machine and thus with a state space representational system (pp. 39–62). It displays all the necessary and sufficient characteristics. Language is seen as composed of "units"—its alphabet, "what things there are in language" (Chao, 1968, p. 57), the elementary particles or building blocks; these are usually categorized (e.g., into parts of speech). Then there is a set of formal rules that defines what is admissible as a "well-formed formula" (Hunter, 1971), that is, "what goes with what, and how, in the language" (Chao, 1968, p. 57); these rules define, and enable one to construct, those basic assemblages of building blocks deemed, by fiat, to be "correct." Finally, to the alphabet and the formation rules one adds the "deductive apparatus," the logical procedures that provide an axiomatic base and license the derivation of new well-formed formulas from the axiomatic base set. These procedures and rules are analogous to what in the context of state processes are called transition or translation rules; we recall that these latter rules prescribe how one moves from one state description to another.

An important aspect of logical analysis applied to language is grammatical analysis, a special case of formation and transformation rules. Typically, the excised corpus is the sentence, its units are words, and the grammatical form displayed by the "string" is the subject-predicate, propositional form. More generally, in grammatical analyses one studies the rules of organization (e.g., morphology and syntax) at the level of morphemes, words, phrases, or sentences. Other representative topics of logical analyses are transformations (e.g., Chomsky), levels of abstraction (e.g., "observational" versus "theoretical" language), or grammatical versus "logical" form (Russell—see Hacking, 1975, p. 74). A limiting case of this kind of approach is exemplified by the work of Russell and Whitehead. Their *Principia Mathematica* studies language by means of an elaborate system of symbolic logic that is presumed to express "the logical core of all languages" (Barrett, 1978, p. 5).

Analogous approaches are followed in acoustic studies of speech. In phonemics, one studies the logical organization of sound patterns at the level of the phoneme, an "object" conceptualized in terms of some mathematico-logical scheme (e.g., coordinates in some "hyperspace," a set of "distinctive features"; see, for example, Chao, 1968; Dreyfus, 1979, p. 239).

An important characteristic of all these logical analyses is their "atomistic" perspective. That is, logical analysis of language always is predicated on the presence of elements or building blocks; it studies their categories, rules of combination, transformations, hierarchical aspects, and so on.

From the standpoint of standard scientific analysis, then, from the point of view of what Rommetveit (1974) calls "the Harvard-MIT school's approach" (pp. 2–18), language is seen internally as a logical system of notation—although perhaps one that is imperfect and flawed when measured against the standards of mathematics. (These "flaws" motivate the ideal language movements in linguistics; see Rorty, 1967; Chappell, 1964). To complete the standard view of language we still need to consider its "external," referential aspects.

External Features

Propositions. In the traditional view, language, especially formal, propositional language, serves the same function as any other state process descriptor in normal science. This is what we learn from various theoreticians. Take Wittgenstein's formal views, for example: "A proposition determines a place in logical space. . . . A proposition can determine only one place in logical space. . . . [For Wittgenstein] a 'logical space' is similar to a coordinate system in theoretical physics" (Janik and Toulmin, 1973, p. 144; see also p. 185).

"Any concept and relationship that can be clearly stated in ordinary language can be translated into computer model language" (Forrester, quoted by Weizenbaum, 1976, p. 250). If we remember the formal equivalence between computer (Turing) representations and state process formalisms, we recognize that what Forrester is saying about translation into computer language also necessarily would apply to state process forms; thus, his claim also amounts to saying that intelligible statements in ordinary language are equivalent to state process descriptions.

That, in turn, is equivalent to saying that a proposition somehow is "an image of a fact. A proposition is a description of a state of things, an image of an element of the world" (Engelmann, 1967, p. 101). (To anticipate: Engelmann goes on to say that a proposition—a picture, an image—"can represent anything except its own representational relationship to the depicted subject" (p. 101), surely a limitation with ominous implications for those who would seek to use this framework to analyze language itself.)

How does language become a specification of a coordinate? Barrett (1978) explains the process in considerable detail. Here is the crux of the matter:

> In the older tradition of logic of Aristotle, when we say that A is B, we wish to exhibit what kind of thing A is, and specifically that it is of the kind B. A proposition, in Aristotle, is a *logos*, a saying or sentence. But not every sentence is a proposition: a prayer, entreaty, and question are sentences but make no statement of fact. . . . The first step in transforming logic [and language] into a mathematical calculus was to change our understanding of its fundamental element: the statement or proposition. . . . Thus to transform logic into a calculus we must take a giant step at the very beginning. . . . *The proposition states a certain distribution of facts within logical space* [p. 37].

In that way, language—or at least language of interest to the linguistic analyst—comes to be equated with "proposition." That means that nonpropositional forms—"performance utterances" (Searle, 1969; Black, 1970, pp. 209–221) such as curses, promises, announcements, prayers, bits of incomplete or nongrammatical discourse—all are excluded. Language that isn't formal (i.e., propositional in structure), utterances that are "degenerate," do not interest the scientific analyst (Robinson, 1975, p. 37).

That, then, is how language, and most particularly scientific language, has come to be conceptualized as a reflection, an isomorphism, that by means of its logical structure mirrors the world of "facts." And since propositions are now viewed as state process descriptors, that means in turn that from a formal perspective any real world phenomenon one describes by formal scientific discourse comes to be seen as analogous to a point or a path in state space. That of course includes all phenomena in the realm of subjective experience: meaning, knowledge, causality, will, truth, "emotional states," "processes," actions, or any other phenomena that pertain to persons rather than things (see, for example, Engelmann, 1967, pp. 96, 102; Erickson, 1970, p. 118; Quine, 1970; Janik and Toulmin, 1973, pp. 144–146; Robinson, 1975, pp. 118–119; Barrett, 1978; Rorty, 1979).

Logical atomism. One theoretically and historically important example of formal, propositional language treated as a state process representational system is the conceptualization, associated primarily with Russell, Whitehead, and Wittgenstein, called "logical atomism" (Janik and Toulmin, 1973, pp. 167–201; Hacking, 1975, pp. 82–92; Barrett, 1978, pp. 32–50). The specifics are as follows. The "world" exhibits facts, and "language" (particularly scientific discourse) exhibits the propositional form. In turn, each of these two bifurcates; we then are dealing with two dyads. On the one hand, in a state process view of the "external world," empirical events or phenomena are seen as exhibiting a dual nature. They have two components: There are "objects"—things, entities, systems, thoughts, affects, images, ideas, organisms—that possess "attributes"—qualities, properties, contents, shapes, characteristics. In this perspective, a "fact" is presented to us by the world if and when the empirical realm "fills in . . . the line" (Hacking, 1975, p. 87) between object and attribute, connecting them. The first dyad, then, is the object/attribute pair; it exists in the empirical realm.

On the other hand, propositions also exhibit a dual structure; the second dyad is the subject/predicate logical pair. One might say that the formal sentence, the proposition, also "fills in the line" but in the linguistic realm—it connects the two linguistic constituents.

Thus, facts have a dual nature (object/attribute), and so do propositions (subject/predicate). Settle (1976) puts it this way: "Each of us seems to have a mental trick of classifying objects and incidents which is mirrored in ordinary language. Verbs name types of action and nouns name classes of objects . . . [This takes] for granted a theory of the world as divided into kinds of objects and of properties" (p. 23). It is a basic premise of logical atomism that propositions mirror facts, which means that one therefore can place these pairs of dyads into correspondence. This yields a "correspondence," or "picture," or "referential" theory of language. Propositions and "facts" are presumed to reflect one another's formal structure: The grammatical subject of the proposition refers to and is paired with a real-world object; the predicate is paired with the object's attribute

(Bergson, 1946, p. 32; Black, 1970; Erickson, 1970; Wiggins, 1971; Janik and Toulmin, 1973, pp. 144–146; Hacking, 1975; Engelmann, 1967, pp. 96, 101; O'Manique, 1976; Barrett, 1978; Rorty, 1979).

To give a simple example, when we say that the grass is green, the "object" grass has a certain "attribute," greenness; then the proposition "The grass is green" mirrors the "fact." The real-world connection between grass and green is mirrored by the proposition that connects the subject and predicate. Furthermore, explicitly or implicitly the proposition defines a certain location of the object, grass, in some logical space, say, one particular coordinate (the attribute "greenness") in the abstract space of color. "Processes" are represented in the same general way. They may be mirrored, for example, by a single proposition (e.g., "The grass is growing") or by a sequence of propositions (e.g., "The grass is 1/4" high. . . . The grass is 1/2" high. . . . The grass is. . . ."). In either case, the process is described and represented as a path in state space.

Parenthetically, I should like to recall one other aspect, mentioned in Chapter 3, of the view of formal language that we have been considering. In the earlier discussion of operationalization and verification, I noted that formalists classify propositions in terms of two principal groups. The first is the class of "meaningful" propositions. It comprises three subcategories: (1) necessary truths (tautological statements, e.g., "A widow has at least one dead husband"); (2) contradictions in logic (e.g., "It is and it is not raining"); (3) "empirical" propositions that are made true or false by "facts," by the extensional state of affairs. For logicians, this "artificial language of truth functions was the skeleton of the language of ordinary discourse" (Urmson, 1956, p. 12). The second large class of propositions are the remainder—the "meaningless" statements, sentences, and propositions, which is to say, any and all that do not belong to the first category.

TRADITIONAL PSYCHOANALYTIC VIEWS ABOUT THEORETICAL DISCOURSE

I submit that psychoanalytic thinkers have, by and large, adopted as an ideal the views of formal discourse just presented. Internally, such discourse should exhibit the characteristics of a properly formalized logical system; the idealized model is mathematics. Consequently, there is the usual concern with component elements, logic, structure, hierarchy of levels, and the like. Externally, theoretical discourse should be systematically and unambiguously referential.

Adequate theoretical discourse is discourse that can be placed into clear correspondence with external data (including psychological data); it should provide an orderly, rigorous, operationalizable, verifiable logical picture of the "external facts."

Internal Features

Although the bulk of psychoanalytic theorizing about discourse pertains to external issues, there are some indications that theorists have a vision of theoretical discourse whose internal characteristics are those of a traditionally conceived formal notational system. The emulation of standard contemporary linguistic theoretical frameworks and practices is widely recommended. The assumption is that the injection of such logically based, rigorous formalisms will elevate psychoanalytic discourse to the desired level of scientific standards. For example, during a discussion of the "hypothetical deep syntactic structures" of linguistic theory, Edelson (1975) suggests that "the psychoanalysts, using linguistic tools, may study transformations through a series of utterances" (p. 94). Steiner (1976) supports Lacan's belief that "psychoanalysis must establish its foundations in an adequate linguistics" (p. 255), which for him means a linguistics based on such rigorous, logic-based approaches as Frege's symbolic logic, Saussure's and Chomsky's grammatical analyses, or Levi-Strauss's structural approaches in anthropology.

Consequently, the emphasis is on logic, rules, and the like: "Language consists of a set of rules. . . . The analysts must . . . have some internalized knowledge . . . of the rules of language" (Edelson, 1975, p. 99). "A psychoanalyst . . . may be permitted to choose, if he wishes, between structural linguistics [e.g., Lacan] and transformational-generative linguistics [e.g., Chomsky] as a theoretical model of language" (p. 8). "It is only by means of sets of language rules that we are ever able to achieve a systematic approach to knowing anything, including knowing anything psychoanalytically" (Schafer, 1976, p. 4). "Most psychoanalytic propositions . . . fall into another class of 'truth statements' known to logicians as 'entailment propositions'" (Rosen, 1974, p. 203). Holt (1961) speaks of verbal "discursive symbols" and the various operations on these (pp. 370–371).

Technical/scientific psychoanalytic discourse is to be differentiated stringently from "ordinary" discourse, "the utterly unsystematic discourse of everyday life" (Schafer, 1972, pp. 420–421). That kind of second-class discourse is disparaged and should be replaced by "a completely intelligible mathematical lan-

Psychoanalytic Theory and Clinical Relevance 79

guage . . . [by] a formal signification system . . . which we can intellectually dominate . . . [and which will serve to replace] ordinary language (with its brute and chaotic associations) by a completely mathematical language" (L. Friedman, 1976, p. 262). "The appeal of metapsychology stems [in part] . . . from its being a formalized language" (Schafer, 1976, p. 5).

External Features

As far as the "interpretation" of discourse is concerned, it can readily be seen that psychoanalytic theorists adopt the standard positivist positions. One finds the typical atomistic concern with terms, their referents, hierarchical levels of abstraction (see Chapter 2), operationalization, removal of redundancies, verification, and so on.

An unambiguous, methodical referential theoretical language is the ideal. Shortcomings in the present language of psychoanalysis are to be overcome by theoretical progress that will "bridge this gap between the verbal tools of the 'hard' and of the psychological sciences" (Kubie, 1975, p. 11), by developing scientific verbal tools that can and will provide "conceptual precision" (p. 12); "glossaries of technical terms . . . must identify and weed out redundancies and the multiplication and overlapping use of terms" (pp. 12–13). We seek "referential clarity" and must separate "the term into its several meanings" (Rosen, 1974, p. 201). "What a terms means, precisely . . . is the test for any science" (Stoller, 1971, p. 10). We want to know what "splitting" means (Pruyser, 1975), or words like "anger" or "self" (Schafer, 1976, pp. 165–169). Terms that must be "exorcized" in the name of scientific purity and rigor are instances of "metaphorical language" such as sublimation, censor, incorporation, levels, libido, cathexis, structural terms ("structural parables"), and the like (Kubie, 1975, pp. 12–20). Spence (1982) observes that "the bulk of putative observation sentences in our literature can never be checked because the utterances giving rise to these sentences have disappeared. . ." (pp. 55). We need to eschew the use of "hybrid concepts," that is, concepts that mix levels of abstraction (Slap and Levine, 1978).

Thoma and Kachele (1975) present a very clear instance of these traditional referential views and standards:

> It could be said in general that metapsychological assumptions have an empirical scientific significance only if they can be linked to observations by rules of correspondence (Carnap). Such rules do not furnish

a complete definition of the theoretical concepts through the language of observation, but they give an empirical content that is good enough for applicability and examination [p. 72; see also pp. 92–101].

I trust these quotations demonstrate that the goal of mainstream psychoanalytic theorists is to acquire a vehicle for theoretical discourse that will be as close as possible to a state descriptor; ideally, it should be applicable within a rigorous state process formalism.

CRITICISMS: LANGUAGE, WORLD, PERSON

The specific criticisms of the "scientific" view of language that I am about to describe parallel the criticisms presented in Chapter 3 of state process formalisms in general. Their point of departure is basically the same, namely, the casual, uncritical, and often unwitting implementation of the Cartesian compartmentalization of the unified life world. In the case of language, what is being carelessly fragmented by this opening move is the integrated complex of being, life world, and language.

Wholeness

What do the critics mean when they speak of this triad as an integrated whole? Let us look at some metaphors used by various critics of the orthodox approaches in their attempts to describe and comment on this unified domain: "Language, world, and human being are co-ordinate terms. . ." (Barrett, 1978, p. 43). "My language is a region of Being I inhabit. . ." (p. 173). "Only where there is language, is there world" (Heidegger, quoted by Danto, 1968, p. xiii). "By being spoken, they [words] establish a mode of existence. . ." (Buber, 1970, p. 53). "The sentence detached from use is . . . an experimenter-centered fallacy" (Rommetveit, 1974, p. 14). "To understand a sentence means to understand a language" (Wittgenstein, quoted by Black, 1970, p. 258). "One cannot study language without studying human nature" (Robinson, 1975, p. 185).

> We are already at home in language just as much as we are in the world. . . . It is part of the nature of language that it has a completely unfathomable unconsciousness of itself. . . . No individual has a real consciousness of his speaking when he speaks. Only in exceptional situations does one become conscious of the language in which he is speaking. . . . In all our knowledge of ourselves and in all knowledge

of the world, we are always encompassed by the language that is our own [Gadamer, 1976, pp. 62–64].

Actual talk does not occur like a travelogue, with the scene and the narrative separate. In everyday life, scene and action are not discrete but mutually determinative [Mehan and Wood, 1975, p. 140]. An utterance not only delivers some particular information, it also creates a world in which information itself can appear [p. 12].

A historian's viewpoint:

The rhetoric of history . . . is ordinarily deemed icing on the cake of history; but our investigations indicate that it is mixed right into the batter [Hexter, 1971, pp. 246–247].

According to these kinds of approaches, then, language cannot be considered in a compartmentalized fashion, as something external to the person, as a tool that one picks up when it is needed to do a certain job and puts down when the task is finished, at least not without significant loss and distortion. As Gadamer (1976) puts it, in the life world "we never find ourselves as consciousness over against the world and, as it were, grasp after a tool of understanding in a wordless condition" (p. 62). That is, we never have three separate, independently existing domains—person, world, and language. When we do treat language in that way, when we separate it from the person and the "external" world and make it into a logical state process notational system, all sorts of undesirable consequences are sure to follow. Ultimately, the strategy of compartmentalization leads to fundamental difficulties in all three areas; our understandings of the person, of language, and of the world all will suffer.

In principle, the difficulties one creates will include at least all those general consequences of using state process frameworks considered in Chapter 3: impoverishment of representational capacity, introduction of logical paradoxes, creation of the elusive remainder, trivialization, alienation, fragmentation. Let us consider the linguistic situation in terms of several major themes—issues pertaining to logical analysis, the mechanization of the person, ontology, reflexivity or self-reference, and explanation and transparency.

Language as a Logical System

The elementarist view. "Formalisms inevitably introduce an elementarism into a holistically understood system" (Overton, 1975, pp. 67–68). One difficulty with seeing language in terms of atomistic elements or building blocks is that this perception fosters a linear view of language. I am using "linear" in its mathematical sense, a usage I mentioned briefly in Chapter 3. Roughly, linearity in that sense implies that elements can be considered independently of one another, while nonlinearity means that an interaction exists between terms. In a linear world or system, "any one fact can either be the case, or not be the case, and everything else remains the same" (Wittgenstein, quoted by Barrett, 1978, p. 33; see also Janik and Toulmin, 1973, p. 144).

Graves (1971) describes nonlinearity in relativity theory:

> The field equations are nonlinear, a situation unprecedented in either classical or quantum physics. This means that we cannot take the sum of the individual effects from two sources to get a total effect. Conversely, given a total effect we cannot break it down uniquely into the contributions from individual sources. This rules out atomism [p. 314].

Nonlinearity, then, introduces new, qualitatively different phenomena into a conceptualization.

In the standard formal-logical conceptions and analyses of language (e.g., Wittgenstein's *Tractatus*), language is treated in a linear fashion: Each constituent building block, each "atomic" element, is "absolutely self-contained and independent of all the others. It could be true or false whatever the truth value of any others [might be]. . ." (Graves, 1971, p. 37). Terms, or sentences, or even larger units are considered and analyzed individually, in isolation from one another (e.g., one defines the "operational meaning" of a term). The nonlinear aspects of language are ignored. That means that a major feature of meaningful discourse is inadequately treated by current formal analyses; traditional logic does not deal with the heavily interactional characteristics of language, the fact that a sentence is much more than the sum of its parts, that it cannot be "broken down uniquely into the contributions from individual sources."

There have been attempts within orthodox, formalistic linguistics to remedy the usual linear focus on isolated, excised portions of language. Rommetveit (1974) discusses work concerning "the expansion of scope of propositional analysis from the sentence *in vacuo* to the sentence in a context described in terms of presuppositions and propositional content" (p. 15). Specifically, he cites the recent introduction by the Harvard-MIT school of the formal pair (F,P), focus and presupposition. According to Rommetveit, however, in spite of this and similar formalistic attempts to include the role of context in linguistic analysis, "what remains unchanged and shared across all recently developed expansions and ramifications [of the standard approaches in linguistics] . . . is a primary concern with propositional form and content of what is said" (p. 15). This retention of logical frameworks seems to be the typical practice within contextual approaches in general (see Hoffman and Nead, 1983). Thus, contextualism does not really avoid an essentially linear, atomistic conception of language. It attempts to bolster the shortcomings of a linear methodology with formalistic expansions that, on further analysis, are seen to retain the basic linear and atomistic characteristics.

Another consequence of standard formal-logical analyses is that they tend to convince us that language "really is" a logical system. When we superpose a logical net over language in formal analyses, it becomes first "a set of sentences" (with each conceived as rule-bound, exhibiting the grammatical structure of simple declarative sentences or their tranforms), then slides into "sequences," and then becomes "grammatical utterances," propositions (Robinson, 1975, p. 36). Thus, language comes to be viewed as being intrinsically atomistic; it is then seen as composed of, and decomposable into, collections of constituent elements and various associated logical rules.

Is language "really" a rule-bound concatenation of elements? It is easy to think so. The Cheshire Cat phenomenon insinuates itself: Logical analysis easily misleads one into taking the "invented" logical properties of language as ontologically prior. When language is viewed as a logical system long enough, eventually it seems peculiar, if not downright silly, to question the orthodox picture; no one doubts that language really is comprised of elements, determined by rules of formation and transformation, and so on. One comes to forget or ignore the obvious, namely, that logical analysis finds, can only find, what it has cast over its "object" (Matte Blanco, 1975, p. 4), in this case, over language. It thus becomes easy to be misled into viewing the logical structure of language as basic—in Yankelovich and Barrett's (1970) term, as the "really real"—instead of recognizing and remembering steadfastly the imposed, derivative nature of logic and analysis; reasoning has been turned upside down. If we recall the discussions in Chapter 3 about the effects of imposing formal-logical systems and analyses on phenomena, we see that here we have a special case of the more general situation and practice.

The "obvious," usually taken-for-granted presence of logical features is questioned by the critics to whose work I have been alluding.

These see language elements in a different light; they question the tradition that language is composed of words, especially nouns and verbs; indeed, they see that tradition, so highly developed in the Harvard-MIT school, as a handicap. It misleads us into taking as somehow basic and "real," logical features that, from the critics' point of view, are artifacts that reflect the nature of the analysis imposed on the phenomena. Mehan and Wood (1975) put it this way:

> To claim that any reality, including the researcher's own, exhibits a coherent body of knowledge is but to claim that coherence can be found *upon analysis*. The coherence located in a reality is found there by the ethnomethodologist's interactional work. The coherence feature, like all features of realities, operates as an incorrigible proposition, reflexively sustained.
>
> Consider the analogous work of linguists. . . . Within language-using communities, linguists discover the "rules of grammar." . . . Rules can be located in their [the speakers'] talk, upon analysis. . . [p. 18; see also p. 68].

"The unit of linguistic communication is not, as has been generally supposed, the symbol, word, or sentence, or even the token of the symbol, word, or sentence, but rather the production or issuance of the symbol or word or sentence in the performance of the speech act" (Searle, 1969, p. 16). "Words do not 'mean' something in isolation; they obtain their meanings by being part of a theoretical system" (Feyerabend, 1975, p. 7). "A word like 'self' naturally knows more than we do; it uses us, and can command us" (Winnicott, 1965, p. 158). "The actual operation of language lets grammar vanish entirely behind what is said in it at a given time" (Gadamer, 1976, p. 65; see also pp. 76, 93).

> Both linguists and philosophers . . . are full of the miracle that we can arrange words in different ways. But all of them overlook the central problem and point of interest, which is that before you can arrange words in different ways something else must happen. You have got to ask yourself, "How did the words come to fall out of the sentence in the first place?" And that is the real miracle [Bronowski, 1978, p. 38].

Others who have discussed the "invented" nature of sentences, propositions, terms, words, phonemes, grammatical rules, and so on include Robinson (1975, p. 175), Dreyfus (1979, p. 239), Malcolm (1971, p. 392), and Goodman (1972, pp. 76–79).

Hierarchies. The analyses that cast doubt on the premise that language "is" in fact a logical system also are relevant to the notion that language can properly be separated into hierarchically ordered levels or layers. This premise has been critically analyzed from several points of view. One of these pertains to the supposed distinctions that can be made between "theoretical language"—language that supposedly is experience-distant, abstract—and "object language"—presumably a level of language closer to experience, closer to empirical phenomena.

I have already mentioned in Chapter 3 that although such distinctions between a certain, veridical "observational language" (basic sentences") and higher-level, theoretical levels of discourse ("protocol sentences") are widely held, they nevertheless are shown to be highly suspect by careful analysis: "It emerges that contrary to what we were once told by logical positivists and others, no natural language and no scientific language of any richness can be regarded as organized into logical levels such that all terms are reducible to, or definable upon, a common (and usually, as the story goes, extremely restricted) definition base" (Koch, 1961, p. 638).

Jaynes (1966) makes a general observation that seems relevant here as well. He compares the overall formal characteristics of the natural sciences with those of the psychological sciences. In the former disciplines, work and progress are cumulative. The ascent, in Jaynes's metaphor, is like climbing a mountain—each step builds on the previous ones. In their histories as well as in the structures of their theories, these disciplines exhibit all sorts of hierarchical features, synchronic as well as diachronic. By contrast, disciplines such as psychology may be rich, but they are somehow structurally "flat." By and large, work is not cumulative; rather, it spreads out horizontally, with different workers staking out different and not well-connected parts of a dense, rich, "huge entangled forest" (p. 94). Concomitantly, theories in this realm tend to be "horizontal" as well. Again, there is evidence of basic structural differences that suggest that the notion of hierarchies may somehow be out of place in the behavioral disciplines.

Let us approach the issue of hierarchical structure from another perspective. Bohm's (1980) notions of order (roughly, formal structure) were introduced in Chapter 3. He presents a conception of an implicate or enfolded order that goes beyond formal logic. In general, "it seems clear . . . that the implicate order is particularly suitable for the understanding of such unbroken wholeness in flowing movement, for in the implicate order the totality of existence is enfolded within each region of space (and time)" (p. 172). Speaking specifically about the order of language, Bohm observes that "this order is more like that of a symphony in which each aspect and movement has to be understood in the light of its relationship to the whole, rather than like the simple sequential order of a clock or a ruler" (p. 41). Capra (1982), commenting on this view, notes: "These various levels that we observe are not separate but are all mutually interconnected and are all interdependent. Although we have systems within systems, as we should say in modern language, this is not a hierarchy" (p. 235).

Hierarchies in psychoanalysis. The usual assumption is that theoretical discourse in psychoanalysis can be hierarchically ordered. (I have already given several standard references in Chapters 2 and 3. Others who have written about this issue include Gedo and Goldberg [1973], G. Klein [1973], Rapaport and Gill [1959], Thoma and Kachele [1975], Spence [1982], and Kohut [1982].) In Chapter 2, I briefly criticized this notion for reasons specific to psychoanalysis; the critique pointed out specific ambiguities, contradictions, and lack of agreement concerning the notion of a clinical theory. In Chapter 3, I mentioned more general epistemological difficulties pertaining to the notion of layering (see the section "Object Language and Theoretical Language"). Now we see that a hierarchical, stratified view of psychoanalytic theory also can be questioned on the basis of linguistic considerations. That is, if the hierarchical properties of theoretical language in general are in doubt, if one can seriously question the legitimacy of conceptualizing theories in this fashion, then these same questions must apply also to the specific case of psychoanalytic theoretical discourse. This means that the usual basic distinctions drawn in psychoanalytic theorizing—for example, the distinctions between metapsychology and clinical theory, or the layering of theory within metapsychology, or the separation of theories on the basis of "experience-near" and "experience-distant" characteristics—must be critically reevaluated.

An example of the enfolded order of language in clinical situations comes from a detailed study of a five-minute segment excised from a psychotherapy session (Pittenger, Hockett, and Danehy, 1960). The analyses of that corpus are performed from linguistic and paralinguistic perspectives, at various levels. It then becomes evident just how tightly interwoven and interdependent these supposedly independent levels really are. "Information" cannot be related in any simple fashion to discrete levels or units of analysis. According to the general critique of the hierarchical structure of language, this would also be the case for analyses of that same corpus performed from the perspectives of metapsychological and clinical theoretical discourse. Levenson (1975), borrowing Bohm's notions of an implicate or enfolded order and his metaphor of the hologram, indirectly supports that critique with regard to psychoanalysis: "Any small piece of the clinical material contains the total configuration. Both past and future. . . . Thus, a virtuoso performer can take almost any small piece of material and explicate a huge amount of information about the patternings and style of the patient" (p. 10).

The assumption that psychoanalytic theory can be hierarchically ordered according to some self-evident principle seems to be another fundamental misconception that follows from adhering to orthodox perspectives that conceptualize theoretical discourse in terms of logical systems. I shall complete the discussion of this issue in Chapter 6, when I use Graves's "levels hypothesis" to propose an alternative way of structuring the branches of psychoanalytic theory.

Mechanization of the Person

We have already met the argument that when phenomena in the subjective realm are represented by state space formalisms, that realm is depersonalized, alienated, mechanized, fragmented. In short, because of what I have called "representational defects," the use of these formalisms to represent phenomena causes us to lose those very aspects that should be the domain of study of disciplines such as psychology. An example from language would be "meaning," certainly a widely discussed, problematic feature of discourse. There are those who believe it is meaningful to speak about the "meaning" of discourse. All that any state process formalism can express of this meaning, however, are logical features such as contiguity, relationships defined by mathematical functions, statistical correlations, and the like. Another, similar problematic feature of discourse is its capacity to provide explanations in terms of "causes," explanations that many feel are not at all like explanations given in terms of "reasons." I shall elaborate on this issue in Chapter 7, when I subject the notion of determinism to a brief state process analysis.

Let us now consider another depersonalizing aspect introduced by orientations that view language as a formal-logical system. When one perceives language according to this perspective, that tends to bring about a corresponding view of the person. The language user comes to be seen in a way that matches the "logical system" view of language. That is, when language comes to be seen as a set of generated propositions, when it is transformed into a formalized logical system, it is then also natural to conceptualize a depersonalized "generator" of strings or symbols. There is thus a concomitant urge to transform the speaker or writer into a corresponding "disembodied processor" (Dreyfus, 1979, p. 254).

Malcolm (1971) quotes Lenneberg: "We know that the mechanism [of internalized linguistic rules] must exist for the simple reason that every speaker knows and generally agrees with fellow speakers whether a sentence is grammatical or not" (p. 392). Malcolm goes on to demonstrate that "a mistaken metaphysics lies in this 'must'. . .".

By falsely equating language and logical system, the standard analyses tend to obscure that in important ways language and logic are poorly matched (Goodman, 1972, pp. 76–79; Rommetveit, 1974, pp. 39, 107; Méhan and Wood, (1975), p. 75). Propositions, syllogisms, and similar logical formats are "very foreign to human language" (Bronowski, 1978, p. 46); the brain does not take sentences apart in that fashion, "otherwise it would be a printing [Turing] machine" (p. 103). Even formal analyses performed by prominent mathematicians strongly suggest that the psychological characteristics of persons cannot be adequately represented by available ("normal") mathematical concepts and methods (see von Neumann, 1958; Bellman, 1967).

Furthermore, linguistic "speech acts" (Searle, 1969; Robinson, 1975) such as "illocutionary" acts (e.g., asserting, questioning, commanding, apologizing) or "perlocutionary" acts (e.g., persuading, convincing, alarming) all escape propositional analysis, as do fragments of language or "ungrammatical" language. Propositional or formal analysis cannot deal with these supposed anomalies, and therefore sets them aside.

The view of language as a formal system strongly encourages the corresponding view of the person as an empty producer, a language-generating Turing machine, rule-bound, depersonalized, alienated, mechanized, trivialized, dehumanized. Even though Wittgenstein warned us that "propositions can express nothing that is *higher*" (Janik and Toulmin, 1973, p. 190), we become dedicated to analyses of such trivia or anomalies as "a pretty little girls' school" and "They are flying planes," presumably gateways to understanding language (Robinson, 1975, p. xiii). We study structural transformations of "The man hit the ball," expecting that these will illuminate more meaningful discourse in some significant ways. For logical analysis the person necessarily becomes a generator of propositions, since these are the sole "objects" of formal logic (see Church, 1981). Weizenbaum (1976) sadly notes, "No wonder, given this view of language, that the distinction between the living and the lifeless, between man and machine, has become something less than real, at most a matter of nuance!" (p. 250).

The ontological sequence again becomes inverted: The formal-logical model of man as rule-bound language generator is now seen as basic rather than derivative. The Cheshire cat phenomenon arises once again. By this route, we are brought to "a world from which nature as such has been eliminated. . . . [There is] a profound consonance between linguistics as a method and that systematized and disembodied nightmare which is our culture today. . . ." (Jameson, 1972, p. ix). The focus on logic has deprived language and the language user of *meaning*: "There is no further appeal in language beyond meaning, and until we get to meaning we are not studying language. So the decision of structural linguistics to postpone the study of meaning was a quite stupendous refusal to pay attention to language. . ." (Robinson, 1975, p. 173).

Thus, seeing language as a logical structure, and, for that reason, as one that can be considered independently of the user and of the life world, ultimately brings about an impoverished and inadequate view of the whole situation: language, user, world. Valid linguistic analysis should appropriately reflect the logic of genesis and the genesis of logic; the life world comes first, logic, one of its derivatives, second. If we wish to enlarge our understanding of the person, we shall have to invert the process of analysis: "I suspect that if there can be anything called 'psycholinguistics' it will have to work by meditating on the psychology built into our language, the ways in which the psyche makes itself in speech. . ." (Robinson, 1975, p. 160). "One cannot study language without studying human nature. . ." (p. 185).

Again, positions seem sharply divided. To some, these kinds of criticisms of orthodox views seem self-evident, perhaps even bordering on the trivially obvious. To others, these kinds of statements seem absurd, false, antiscientific; some in this latter group just cannot understand what those in the former are talking about. For example, Wittgenstein's views were and still are widely misunderstood. In Wittgenstein's day, they seem to have been seriously misunderstood by Russell (Engelman, 1967; Bartley, 1973, pp. 136–140, 168; Janik and Toulmin, 1973). They seem to remain misunderstood by some today; Robinson (1975) argues that Chomsky "simply can't understand Wittgenstein's objections to the idea of 'science'. . . ." (p. 152; see also Chomsky's statement concerning scientific methodology quoted in Chapter 3, and Goodman, 1972, pp. 76–79).

Ontology

Another considerable body of criticisms of referential-logical conceptions of language pertains to ontological issues. Just as the standard views of language tend to lead to distorted notions about the person, so do they tend to lead to distorted notions about the "outside" world.

Some of the most general logical difficulties entailed in the standard referential conceptions have been examined by Quine (1970) in an extensive critical analysis. Examples of logical difficulties and issues that he explores include: "distributing sensory evidence over sentences"; "generalizations" about sentences; defining equivalence between sentences; oblique "semantic ascent"; and the referents of theoretical terms. Quine's analyses show that attempts to explain and clarify these and related referential notions tend to leave us in a situation "exactly as obscure as the notions . . . that we are in the end trying to justify. . ." (p. 9; see also Weizenbaum, 1976, p. 199).

The inanimate domain. There are also other, more homely, less esoteric difficulties with referential notions. We saw earlier that picture theories of language predicate an isomorphism between the "structure of a fact" (e.g., the object/attribute dyad) and the corresponding "structure of language" (e.g., the subject/predicate dyad of the propositional form). In the view of certain critics, however, "nature is not a gigantic formalizable system. . ." (Bronowski, 1978, p. 80). It seems that a careful examination of the referential view of even as simple an "object language" sentence as "The snow is white" will lead to a whole group of serious ontological difficulties (Quine, 1970, Chapter 1).

Hacking (1975) discusses this issue at length. He examines criticisms by logicians such as Russell, Quine, and Davidson. Russell, for example, has said that an "ontology of substances (for which subjects stand) possessing attributes (designated by predicates) . . . is a strange ontology, for the substance becomes a sort of pin-cushion into which the pins of attributes are stuck. . . . [Russell firmly suggests] that both the [subject/predicate] logic and the [substance/attribute] metaphysics are artefacts of language, not reality" (p. 80).

Take Hacking's example of an orange marigold. As the history of the philosophy of science demonstrates, conceptualizing such an entity in terms of the object "flower" and the attribute "orangeness" raises considerable epistemological and ontological difficulties; it apparently also raises a host of pseudoproblems, such as questions about ideal properties ("orangeness"). In general, it is "not so clear that we see a thing, on the one hand, and a property on the other. . ." (p. 87). If we insist on this picture, we inherit pseudoquestions and pseudoproblems. For example, it becomes necessary to "explain how articulated language effects the representation of a nonarticulated part of the world. . ." (p. 87); we are led to ask questions about constituents, individual terms—their operationalization, their "meaning"; we become concerned with verification. If we come to doubt the legitimacy of conceptualizing language in elementarist, rule-bound, referential terms, then the process of checking the "fact" implied by a given proposition (that is, of seeing whether the location that the proposition specifies in state space is made true or made false by the corresponding situation in the object/attribute realm) may also be fallacious.

One implication of these kinds of critical analyses, then, is that the legitimacy of our usual preoccupation with individual linguistic elements and their corresponding referents is seriously called into question. There is a distinct possibility that the typical positivists' concerns about language, meaning, reference, verification, and so on may actually be concerns about pseudoquestions or pseudoproblems—artifactually generated issues that stem from basic misconceptions about what language is and does.

The psychological domain. Serious enough difficulties result from attempts to apply a referential theory of language to the domain of the natural sciences, to orange marigolds. According to the critics, problems escalate alarmingly when one also seeks to apply it to the domains of the behavioral disciplines. As I have said earlier, in mainstream psychology and other behavioral disciplines the usual, uncritically accepted way of representing and conceptualizing our inner domains is in terms of the standard object/attribute and subject/predicate referential framework of the natural sciences. From a formal point of view, the inner realm is treated in just the same way as natural science treats the external world. For instance, standard staples of psychology such as sense data, memories, perceptions, and affects are made to fit that kind of a framework. Formally, these and similar phenomena are treated as objects representable in terms of state process conceptions. But "the image of mental entities tallying with words in an exact one-to-one correspondence leads to obfuscation if taken seriously" (Black, 1970, p. 227; see also Louch, 1966, p. 134).

Extensive critical analyses about these matters have been available for some time. One of the more familiar is Austin's (1962) critique of the notion of "sense data." In general, the critics object to perception theories that typically invoke a sequence which begins with the notion of "physical event" and leads through a series of "magical transformations" to a conceptualization in terms of "inside-outside correspondences." This transformational sequential model adds up to a "scientific" picture of perception that is an "absurd belief" (Straus, 1969, p. 230). Barrett (1978) criticizes this framework in his examination of the "perceptual" statement "That picture is hanging askew" (pp. 142–143). Malcolm's (1971) analysis is in terms of the statement "My, that dog is shaggy!" (p. 390). Rorty (1979) presents yet another detailed analysis of "sensation," showing it to be an artifact of Cartesian thought (p. 47. See also Jaynes, 1966; Yankelovich and Barrett, 1970, pp. 259–261; Malcolm, 1977; other critics of mainstream psychology will be considered in Chapter 7.)

These and similar analyses seek to demonstrate how the usual ways of theorizing about sense data, perceptions, memory, and the like lead to models that, although usually accepted uncritically and taken as veridical, actually are fallacious, misleading impediments, or pseudoexplanations. Such analyses show, for instance, just how the usual perceptual model based on sense data leads one to problems of infinite regress; one escapes backward from one homunculus to another. To cope with this regressive situation, eventually one must decide to stop, arbitrarily, with some "explanation." Then, on closer examination, it becomes clear that this final "stopping place" of the supposedly explanatory framework leaves one with a situation that is at least as problematic as the original situation that the sense data theory purported to explain (e.g., Malcolm, 1971, p. 391).

Similar criticisms could be applied to another notoriously difficult subject area, namely, the realm of affects, emotions, and feelings (see Chapter 3, "State Spaces in the Behavioral Disciplines"). It is recognized in psychoanalytic theorizing to be an area full of difficulties and confusions (see, for example, Jacobson, 1971, especially pp. 4–29; Lichtenberg, 1983, pp. 21–26). These phenomena are also treated as referents of a state process system (e.g., "Emotion is a fact of human experience. Since it is a fact, it must be possible to describe it accurately and measure it adequately. . . ." [Arnold, 1960, p. 351]), with the usual undesirable consequences. I shall return to this subject in Chapter 7.

Reflexivity—the Remainder Problem, Again

A great deal could be, and has been, said about language and the self-reference problem. These kinds of problems were identified in Chapter 3. We recall some of the difficulties that are created when one initiates the knower/known dualism: problems of infinite regress, the elusive remainder, and fragmentation of wholeness.

Language adds another baffling dimension to these already baffling problem areas. To which side of the Cartesian equation does *it* belong? Knower, or object of study? We use it to study itself, and that inherently creates a paradox: "The very conception of a 'critique of language' confronts the difficulty that such a critique must itself be undertaken in and with words. It is born in contradiction and ends in silence, in what Mauthner has termed the 'suicide' of language" (Janik and Toulmin, 1973, p. 131). Any but comfortably positivistic models of language will necessarily embroil one immediately in an untidy, labyrinthine world:

> The appearance of the concept "language" [i.e., making it an "objective object"] presupposes consciousness of language. But that is only the result of the reflective movement in which the one thinking has reflected out of the unconscious operation of speaking and stands at a distance from himself. The real enigma of language, however, is that we can never really do this completely. Rather, all thinking about language is already once again drawn back into language. We can only think in a language, and just this residing of our thinking in a language is the profound enigma that language presents to thought [Gadamer, 1976, p. 62].

"The asking has always been part of the nature asked about" (Kovel, 1981, p. 64). How do we study the part that remains on the side of the knower—if there indeed is such a part? How do we study the part we study with? What about self-reference, "the special way in which our language works" (Bronowski, 1978, p. 98), the feature that is so central to discourse?

As the critics see it, these kinds of questions do not, cannot, receive satisfactory answers as long as one remains within a conventional Cartesian system of thought. Attempts to find answers in that framework must lead to the kinds of contortions exhibited in much of philosophy. For example, consider where the prevalent point of view that Rorty (1967) calls "methodological nominalism" leads. The premise of methodological nominalism is that questions which "(a) cannot be answered by empirical inquiry concerning the behavior or properties of particulars . . . and which (b) can be answered in *some* way, can be answered by answering questions about the use of linguistic expressions, and in no other way" (p. 11).

This approach ultimately leads to a host of contradictions and conundrums. For example, Danto (1968) has examined one prototype of the kinds of paradoxes that inevitably arise from these approaches: What about the sentence "Scientific sentences are made true by facts" (p. 8)? Is *it* itself a scientific sentence? Danto shows that it leads to the kind of self-reference paradox studied extensively by Russell (see also Bronowski, 1978, p. 98). If we maintain the sentence is scientific, we can show it is not; if we maintain that it is not scientific, we can show that it is. The issue cannot be resolved.

Moreover, when the knower's "tool" of language is added to the basic Cartesian bifurcation of knower and known, certain other "fissures" seem to appear as well. They arise as one begins to consider the various relationships that presumably hold between these three constituents (person, external world, language) of the state space model. It seems as though once compartmentalization gets started in this fashion, there is no stopping it—we encounter infinite reflections. Each constituent seems to generate further state spaces that are needed to "explain" that constituent, and so on; the state spaces needed to explain other state spaces proliferate, like the broom of the sorcerer's apprentice, and so do the interstices. For example, it has been suggested that philosophy occupies a special "crack": "The habitat of philosophy is the curious interspace between language and the world" (Danto, 1968, p. 9). Or that language occupies a crack between person and world: "Sentences serve as the interface between the knowing subject and what is known" (Hacking, 1975, p. 187). Again, in the views of the critics, these "cracks" are artifacts. The recommended way of dealing with these kinds of issues is to reconsider the Cartesian processes that had severed the prior unity so casually and cavalierly in the first place.

Explanation and Transparency

Yet another important area in which difficulties with state process referential conceptions of theoretical discourse arise concerns scientific explanation, a process that has been mentioned previously. Let us consider it further here.

The apparently straightforward notion of what it means to "explain" something has defied clarification. The issue is difficult enough in the natural sciences; it assumes new dimensions of difficulty in the behavioral disciplines. It seems that logical analyses just cannot adequately illuminate just what it is that an explanation accomplishes. (Reflexivity surfaces again: How does one explain explanation?) Thus, there has arisen a considerable body of literature about problems such as the distinctions between "scientific" and, say, psychoanalytic explanation, or between causes and reasons, or between description (sometimes referred to as "mere" description) and explanation proper. Authors who have written extensively about these matters include Kuhn, Braithwaite, Fodor, Louch, Nozick, Dray, Austin, Malcolm, Sherwood, von Wright, Hempel, Oppenheim, Scriven, and Grunbaum.

As part of the preliminaries of his examination of the relationships between logical reasoning and explanation in psychoanalysis, Sherwood (1969) summarizes the relevant literature. He sees explanations based on formal logical procedures (e.g., syllogisms or the application of covering law models) as inadequate. He observes that "there is no characteristic of logic or of grammar through which explanatory power is assured. . ."(p. 219). That is, the formal properties of any given explanation cannot satisfactorily account for its explanatory power. For example, the formal structure of good explanations is typically no different from that of poor explanations. Other illustrative issues that he discusses are (1) the inadequacy of inferential processes; the syllogism is an inappropriate model because in psychoanalytic explanations we are dealing with "construction" rather than "deduction"; (2) difficulties with generalization; if we attempt to make psychological laws more general, we end up by including implications that are psychologically clearly false; generality is bought at the price of correctness; (3) difficulties with specificity; if we attempt to make the laws narrower, more restrictive, then they become trivial and impoverished; they tend to lose explanatory power, become mundane, unable to add insight, novelty, creative contributions; their explanatory power is "removed" (Chapter 4). In short, attempts to impose logical models on theoretical discourse yield "grossly artificial, distorted, and inadequate" results (pp. 235, 238–239, 241).

These views and findings about the limitations of logical models have been expressed by Ryle (1964) in a more general context. His critical remarks pertain to the "formalizer's dream"—roughly, that everyday discourse can adequately be replaced by formalization, such as that attempted in Russell and Whitehead's *Principia Mathematica*. Critics of this dream

> maintain that the logic of everyday statements and even the logic of the statements of scientists, lawyers, historians and bridge players cannot in principle be adequately represented by the formulas of for-

mal logic. The so-called logical constants do indeed have, partly by deliberate prescription, their scheduled logical powers; but the nonformal expressions both of everyday discourse and of technical discourse have their own unscheduled logical powers, and these are not reducible without remainder to those of the carefully wired marionettes of formal logic [pp. 38–39].

Logical analysis, however, is not the only way to deal with the issue of explanation. The critics of the traditional formalistic view of language repeatedly make one important point about their conception of discourse as "embedded in the life world": Most of the time we know perfectly well what our discourse means!" We know how to use it. We understand it. We do not really profit from further explanations, and don't need them (except perhaps to satisfy obsessional kinds of motives for perfection or control).

This is the aspect of discourse extensively discussed in the literature under the label "transparency" of language. This label refers to the kinds of linguistic characteristics described in the various views quoted earlier: that most of the time language is "unfathomably unconscious of itself"; is understandable as part of an integrated situation—person, world, discourse; is "a region of being" inhabited by the person; is constitutive; is an irreducible integrated ontological given; is not a tool, and so on.

In his criticisms of computer models of skilled performance, Dreyfus (1979), drawing on the work of Heidegger, Merleau-Ponty, and Polanyi, invokes the metaphor of a blind man's use of his cane to illustrate the notion of transparency. When the blind man uses his cane, "he is not aware of its position in physical space, its features, nor of the varying pressure in the palm of his hand. Rather, the stick has become, like his body, a transparent access to the objects he touches with it" (p. 252). To analyze this situation in terms of the cane as a tool will lead, as usual, to gross errors, pseudoproblems, trivialization, and misconceptions, as Dreyfus goes on to show.

So it is with language. We usually know what we are saying when we say it, and we usually are understood. Rubinstein (1976) alludes to this matter in his discussion of psychoanalytic theorizing. When one considers the event of someone thinking, the meaning of "who *does* the thinking . . . is perfectly acceptable to commonsense. To our common-sense way of thinking about ourselves, a question like, 'What precisely does the word "does" mean in this context?' simply does not arise. . . . If we start to reflect about it . . . it seems quite nebulous" (p. 243).

I have earlier mentioned Rommetveit's (1974) criticisms and analyses of the standard linguistic approaches exemplified by the "Harvard-MIT school." In the course of his analysis, he questions the practice of explaining discourse by means of logical tools:

> Perfectly legitimate and comprehensible segments of everyday discourse may be shown to be contradictory when evaluated in terms of propositional attributes and gauged against the criteria of formal logic. . . . What, precisely, is achieved by mapping segments of discourse on to expressions of a semi-propositional form? [pp. 6–7].

In this regard, consider Freud's views about consciousness:

> Freud holds consciousness to be a fact of individual experience lying open to immediate intuition, and he makes no attempt to define it beyond this. It is "a fact without parallel, which defies all explanation or description. . . . Nevertheless, if anyone speaks of consciousness we know immediately and from our most personal experience what is meant by it" [Laplanche and Pontalis, 1973, p. 84].

In other words, most of the time language, including theoretical language, is "transparent," or at least transparent enough. (Which raises the question: For what? Pragmatic issues begin to insinuate themselves into our discussion of formal issues.) If we do understand discourse—even technical discourse—then why insist on analyzing it further? Obvious answers come to mind: clarification of ambiguities, specification of metrics for quantification, etc. But are these really necessary? The critical analyses cited earlier in this and the preceding chapter demonstrate that these "scientific" practices generate pseudo-answers that only lead to paradoxes and conundrums, buy us nothing, and maintain the illusion that one has gained in knowledge and understanding, that one has been appropriately "scientific." I am referring to the criticisms leveled against "explaining" perception or memory by theories invoking sense data, computer storage or hologram models, and so on, by workers such as Austin, Malcolm, Winch, Louch, Dreyfus, Barrett, or Rorty. Their criticisms will apply with equal force to the matter of "explaining" the meaning of discourse. If I know enough (for some *purpose!*) about what "I am angry" "means," why then gratuitously "explain" it further, say, in terms of formal state process models that remove meaning and leave us ultimately with at least as difficult a situation to "explain?" Why develop an *explanans* that on closer analysis is found to be at least as problematic as the *explanandum*?

Some comments concerning hermeneutics, the science and methodology of explanation, seem to be in order at this point. Originally, hermeneutic intervention—translation, clarification—was a special procedure to be invoked only in special circumstances. The generally accepted view was that the typical feature of discourse was transparency; texts were considered to be generally understandable as they stood; they were part of the life world and, as such, usually posed no special difficulties. One would need to implement hermeneutic interventions only in special circumstances, when "breaches of intersubjectivity" (Linge, 1976, p. xiv) arose, when the usually smooth-running, automatic, "unreflective" process of understanding failed for the moment, when the usually transparent discourse became opaque.

This is not at all the prevalent conception in current versions of hermeneutics. Hermeneutic intervention has come to be seen as a process that is constantly needed: "Initially one does not usually arrive at an 'understanding,' but rather at a misunderstanding, so the problem of 'understanding' becomes a theme of epistemology (the theory of knowledge)" (Thoma and Kachele, 1975, p. 52).

This conception of hermeneutics is decisively rejected by the writers I have been considering. Gadamer (1976), for instance, sees it as a trivialized version that arose in the 18th century, mainly with the work of Schleiermacher. Gadamer makes a plea for a return to the original hermeneutic practices. So does Hexter (1971), without using that terminology. Rorty (1979) argues for a rejection of epistemologies in any form and for a pragmatically based hermeneutics, not as a "replacement" for epistemology, but rather as a tolerance of its absence—a very large difference indeed, as Rorty goes on to demonstrate (especially Chapters VII and VIII).

As we have examined the notion of explanation, questions concerning its purpose have become more and more visible. It looks as though when we argue about whether some portion of discourse requires explanation, we not only need to consider what "explanation" means in some abstract, academic sense, but also need to examine the pragmatic issue—why explanations might be needed in a given instance. Hence, in the next chapter I shall look at the matter of pragmatism in clinical theorizing; further discussions about explanation will be postponed until pragmatic issues have been introduced.

IMPLICATIONS: REPRESENTATIONAL CAPACITY AND THEORETICAL DISCOURSE

The material in this chapter has been presented to support my contention that discourse conceptualized and used in the standard formalistic, logic-based, normal-science fashion is inadequate as a theoretical vehicle in certain behavioral domains. The Harvard-MIT approach, or any of its relatives, conceptualizes and uses language in ways that may be acceptable as long as one is speaking about inanimate objects situated in an external world. When, however, the same formalisms, methodologies, frameworks, and conceptions are used to speak about nontrivial aspects of *persons*, the approach does not work well.

In order to make my case, I linked up the general discussions of Chapter 3 with specific discussions about language. In Chapter 3 I sought to demonstrate the limitations of state process frameworks and formalisms in general, especially those limitations that are relevant to the behavioral disciplines. I mentioned a number of undesirable consequences of using these schema, such as the creation of conundrums and pseudoquestions, the construction of peculiar ontologies, the myth of veridical observations ("direct," "at the basement level"), and the remainder problem and its corollaries. The principal and most debilitating limitation, however, was the impoverished, trivializing representational capacities that any such formalisms must display. I sought to show that there are stringent limits on what such systems can portray.

In the present chapter, I repeated the general arguments of Chapter 3, but this time with the focus on language. In order to accomplish my goals, I needed first to show how our standard conceptions of formal discourse are state process conceptions. Demonstrating that claim allowed me then to apply to discourse, across the board, all the objections voiced earlier about state process representations in general. In other words, I sought to show that when one views and uses discourse as a state process logical system, it thereby becomes unfit to serve as an adequate vehicle for psychoanalytic theorizing; because of its internal characteristics and interpretive assumptions, language used as a state process formalism is unable adequately to represent, unable adequately to deal with, the domains of interest to, say, psychotherapy. That premise is at the heart of my criticisms of formal approaches. I shall return to formal issues in Chapter 6, in the context of my discussion of clinical pragmatism.

FIVE

The Focus of Theorizing

> The line between a belief's being justified and its being true is very thin.
> —Richard Rorty, *Philosophy and the Mirror of Nature*

> One might expect that of all the subjects with which psychoanalytic literature deals, questions involving what actually takes place in a psychoanalytic treatment and how the analyst's part therein may be made most effective would predominate. But this expectation does not prove to be correct. Questions of technique are approached in only a small proportion of psychoanalytic writings.
> —Otto Fenichel, *Problems of Psychoanalytic Technique*

In psychoanalysis, the traditional foci of theorizing—the targets, motives, themes, and goals of theorizing—have arisen from three interwoven strands. The first pertains to assumptions about the place of pure knowledge in theorizing; the second to the ambition that psychoanalysis be a general psychology; and the third to practices and beliefs adopted from medical theorizing and research. Together these strands combine to constitute a perspective, a belief system, a body of practice that I propose to call the "pure knowledge medical paradigm."

THE PURE KNOWLEDGE MEDICAL PARADIGM

Pure versus Applied Knowledge

In mathematics and the natural sciences, it is taken as a matter of course that theorizing requires no particular justification or motive. One is free to pursue any direction that seems interesting, important, or novel, and the presumption is that anything that will contribute to general knowledge is a legitimate target of theorizing. In the early stages of relativity theory, Einstein is said to have answered a question challenging the utility of that theory with another question to the effect, Of what use is a baby? The eventual payoff of unrestricted, far-ranging, "pure" theorizing is taken for granted—a position justified by history. As Graves (1971) has said, the standard leading principle in "normal science" is to try "to construct a coherent and intellectually satisfying picture of the world" (p. 3), "to *explain* observed phenomena" (p. 13). The quest for pure knowledge is primary and dominant; useful applications should eventually follow as a matter of course.

Not only is it taken for granted that pure theorizing must eventually pay off, but the view abounds that it is as lofty as applied work is crass—technology, engineering, commerce, industry, and the like. Consider what Davis and Hersh (1981) say about theorizing in mathematics, that discipline which seems to have become the ideal for other sciences:

> There is a widely held principle that mind stands higher than matter, the spirit higher than the flesh, that the mental universe stands higher than the physical universe. . . . The reputed superiority of mind over matter finds mathematical expression in the claim that mathematics is at once the noblest and purest form of thought, that it derives from pure mind with little or no assistance from the outer world, and that it need not give anything back to the outer world. Current terminology distinguishes between "pure" and "applied" mathematics and there is a pervasive unspoken sentiment that there is something ugly about applications. One of the strongest avowals of purity comes from the pen of [the mathematician] G. H. Hardy. . . [p. 85].

> Hardyism is the doctrine that one ought only to pursue useless mathematics. This doctrine is given as a purely personal credo in Hardy's *A Mathematician's Apology*. . . [p. 87].

> Hardy's statement is extreme, yet it expresses an attitude that is central to the dominant ethos of twentieth-century mathematics—that the highest aspiration in mathematics is the aspiration to achieve a lasting work of art. If, on occasion, a beautiful piece of pure mathematics turns out to be useful, so much the better. But utility as a goal is inferior to elegance and profundity [p. 86].

These authors go on to contrast Hardyism with "Mathematical Maoism . . . the doctrine that one ought to pursue only those aspects of mathematics which are socially useful" (p. 87). As we shall see, however, these are not the only available alternatives.

In Chapter 2 I presented a number of quotations from various workers in psychoanalysis that demonstrated their belief that sooner or later successful pure theorizing will necessarily lead to practical yields—that is, to clinically useful applications. I now submit that one also finds echoes of Hardy's position in the literature, although usually these are muted or implicit.

In one "theoretical" work after the other, authors take pains to point out that *this* particular work *is* theoretical, and that its implications for therapy and clinical technique remain to be worked out. Thus, Sherwood (1969) says of his book, "It is in pursuit of the former [theoretical soundness rather than clinical potency] that this study is directed" (p. 2). "The issue of the therapeutic function of psychoanalytic narratives lies outside the limits of this study and should not be allowed to distract us" (p. 251). "We have considered the logic of psychoanalytic explanation, but an entirely separate problem is its role in the therapeutic process" (p. 251). Similar sentiments abound—see, for example, Gitelson (1962, p. 194), Glover (1968, p. 114), Levenson (1972, p. 19), Loewald (1960, p. 16), Schafer (1976, p. 25), and Strachey (1934, p. 128). Kohut's (1977) statement summarizes the position to which I am referring: "Freud's values were not primarily health values. He believed in the intrinsic desirability of knowing as much as possible" (p. 64). "Freud's commitment to truth is admirable and . . . it has become, via our identification with him, the leading value of analysts" (pp. 65–66).

Theorizing for the sake of increasing the store of "pure knowledge," then, is one of the agreed-upon rationales for theoretical work in psychoanalysis. Hardyism finds expression in the tacit position that theorizing is lofty, concern with technique second-rate, a position difficult to illustrate directly but implicit in the literature's relative lack of focus on technique.

A General Psychology

A second, related strand in psychoanalytic theorizing pertains to the belief that psychoanalysis ought to become a general psychology. Consequently, the argument runs, any theoretical effort that advances the scientific status of psychoanalysis as a general science of behavior is justified. For instance, Fenichel (1941) writes, "The young science of psychoanalysis has as its object of study the totality of human mental phenomena. . . . The problem of therapeutic technique becomes just one subject among many others" (p. 1). The work of one of the early proponents of the general psychology theme is described by Sutherland (1963):

It is abundantly clear that in Rapaport's writings, as he himself states, he focuses on those aspects of the theory which are not obviously dependent on the clinical method and tries to avoid concepts which obviously are tied to them, like transference, interpretation, etc. A noteworthy instance of this divorce from the clinical findings occurs in Rapaport's earlier paper . . . on "The Conceptual Model of Psychoanalysis" [p. 110].

Loewald (1975) mentions general interests that go far beyond therapeutics:

I have no question that Freud was conscious of attempting to do more than heal neuroses of individuals. In fact, this latter purpose of psychoanalysis seemed more and more to take second place in his interests. That he and his friends spoke of psychoanalysis, not only as a science and as a form of psychotherapy, but as the psychoanalytic *movement*, that they were concerned with anthropology, mythology, and civilization and its discontents—all this shows that they had larger aims and vistas, namely to influence and change the outlook and behavior of a whole era in regard to the relationship and balance between rational and instinctual life and between fantasy and objective reality [p. 293; see also Schafer, 1983, p. 4].

Theorizing in Medicine

A third, consonant assumption that supports theorizing in psychoanalysis is adopted directly from medicine. In that discipline, it is usually taken as a matter of course that increased understanding of pathology—of its nature, origins, causal agents, and so on—will eventually lead to a corresponding increase in therapeutic effectiveness. History lends credence to this position: Much of the increase in medical therapeutic effectiveness has come about as a consequence of increases in understanding pathology.

It is widely assumed, furthermore, that this increased understanding will come about largely through pure research conducted along the lines described earlier. Thus, the typical theoretical or research effort in medicine is a combination of the search for pure knowledge and a focus on disease. I call this standard position the "pure knowledge medical paradigm."

This is also the paradigm that has guided most psychoanalytic theorizing (other than theorizing about wider subject areas—anthropology, general psychology, etc.) from the very beginning. The usual premise is that when we understand more about the "disease," about psychopathology, then we will thereby also have made corresponding progress in the technique of therapy:

> The theory of neurosis has the same relation to psychoanalytic therapeutic practice as pathology has to internal medicine: inductively arrived at through practical experience, it furnishes the foundation for further practical work. It represents an attempt to ascertain that which is regular in the etiology, the manifestations, and the clinical course of neuroses, in order to furnish us with a causally directed method of therapy and prophylaxis. Nothing could be demanded of such a theory that a medical man would not demand of pathology [Fenichel, 1945, p. 8].

Psychoanalytic theorizing has been and is virtually a synonym for pure theorizing about psychopathology—in other words, it is theorizing in the pure knowledge medical paradigm. Consider, for example, Freud's (1893) early paper "A Case of Successful Treatment by Hypnotism." After sketching some general features of the case and treatment (e.g., symptomatology, frequency of visits, method of treatment), Freud quickly turns to the task of explaining "the psychical mechanism of this disorder . . . which was thus removed by suggestion" (p. 121). He constructs a framework whose principal purpose and function will be to conceptualize, explain, and discuss "the mechanism of the disorder." The focus is on pathology, its description and conceptualization within some psychological "model of the mind," with considerations of development and etiology. At this early stage of theory-building, the proposed conceptual framework includes a formalized theory of ideas (two types: intentions and expectations), affects attached to those ideas (unspecified), and factors on which an attached affect depends (two kinds: degree of importance of the outcome and degree of uncertainty in expectation of the outcome, to which Freud gives the technical label "distressing antithetical ideas"). He then uses this pathology-focused theory to construct a rationally based nosology, to describe, organize, and explain symptoms, to conceptualize the status of the psychological apparatus before and after treatment, and so on. Furthermore, the need to generalize about psychological mechanisms is clearly evident: "The psychical mechanism which I have been describing offers an explanation not merely of isolated hysterical occurrences but of major portions of the symptomatology of hysteria" (p. 126).

The point I wish to make here is that in this example Freud's framework and theorizing are neither intended nor designed directly to illuminate the therapeutic action itself. His theoretical constructions are guided by a focus on pathology, not a focus on therapy. He is not looking specifically to construct a theoretical framework that would facilitate, for instance, inferences about technique. Indeed,

Freud says virtually nothing in his theoretical discussions that could have a direct bearing on the clinical procedure he "found." While he does report what he did as a clinician (how he induced the hypnotic state, etc.), he does not attempt to use his theoretical framework to derive inferences concerning, for instance, how one might make the clinical procedure more effective, to what alternative treatment approaches theory might lead one, and similar practical and clinically consequential issues (e.g., frequency or length of sessions, details of physical arrangements). Perhaps the closest he comes to making a theoretical statement about therapy itself is in one simple, general remark: "I made use of suggestion to contradict all her fears and the feelings on which those fears were based" (p. 119).

Thus, there is from the very beginning a marked contrast between Freud's theorizing about pathology and about technique. Theorizing about the former begins to take on the qualities of his later work, rich, complex, elaborate, with an intricate theoretical underpinning. By comparison, his theorizing about technique is brief, almost in passing; clinical phenomena—even central ones such as transference and resistance—tend to be viewed, once again, with a theoretical focus on pathology rather than technique. A number of the statements cited in Chapter 2 support this conclusion (see, for example, the section "Curative Factors and Technical Progress"). This focus on pathology rather than on "mere" technique would certainly be in line with the typical practices, values, and assumptions that Freud must have absorbed, at least to some extent, in his medical training. Surely it would have been difficult for him to emerge from that experience without partially accepting the usual medical assumptions: that progress in treating illness must come about largely as a result of progress in understanding the underpinnings of that illness, that theorizing is virtually equivalent to theorizing about pathology.

Although this example is drawn from Freud's early work, the era Yankelovich and Barrett (1970) call "Freud I" (pp. 17–25), it is, I submit, representative of almost all subsequent psychoanalytic theorizing in that the focus has remained overwhelmingly on pathology and, in that sense, on pure theory, pure knowledge, rather than "mere" practice. So far, the pure knowledge medical paradigm has dominated the theoreticians' approaches.

Perhaps we can now better understand the "overkill" phenomenon described in Chapter 2: A theoretical focus on pathology would largely account for the great disproportion, even in those works that advertise themselves as clinically or applications-oriented, between theorizing about pathology and theorizing about therapy. It would explain why it is that those portions that purport to theorize about therapy usually are disappointing. The remarks about treatment approaches tend to be brief, relatively simple, general, commonsensical, in comparison with the complex, dense, intricate theorizing about pathology.

Whether this approach really can contribute to therapeutic efficacy is rarely questioned. One of the few statements about this issue of which I am aware comes from Wilhelm Reich (1933–1934):

> It can be said that all questions of technique cluster around the one essential question, namely whether and how a clearly defined technique of analytic treatment can be deduced from the psychoanalytic theory of psychic illness [p. 3].

One might argue that the paradigm has carried psychoanalytic theory forward in the sense I referred to earlier, namely, that theory can now supply retroactively a "deductive" rationale for techniques that were at first found empirically. In Chapter 2 I sought to lay this argument to rest on the basis of several classes of indirect evidence. I also mentioned Graves's (1971) major reservations about the legitimacy of providing retroactive logical rationalizations for theories that actually evolved more or less informally. Graves discusses this issue in terms of "disinterpreting" and "reinterpreting" the ingredients of theory, tidying up the disorderly yield of empirical work by means of some neat logical system. One first "disinterprets" by removing the old rationale, thus returning to the unrationalized data and phenomena. Then one "reinterprets," providing a new, systematized logical basis, a new explanatory framework for the old data and phenomena. Advanced classical mechanics, honed to mathematical perfection by Hamilton, Jacobi, Lagrange, Hertz, and others, is an important example given by Graves of a system that has been obtained by these processes of disinterpretation and reinterpretation. It reinterprets Newtonian mechanics in terms of a mathematically more sophisticated analytical framework.

Graves presents an extended, closely reasoned criticism of the practice, noting that it "operates only after the real work of the theory has been done. Not only does it add nothing to our knowledge, but it prevents us from developing the theory further in useful directions" (p. 34; see also p. 41). He claims that this kind of "rational reconstruction" freezes and petrifies theory, causing one to "drop the pilot" (p. 35). Although for many applications the reconstructed version of classical mechanics is still very useful, as a theory it seems incapable of further significant evolution; according to

Graves, this is a typical consequence of the reformulation procedures we have been considering. His criticisms suggest that even if it were achievable, the disinterpretation and reinterpretation of analytic theory alluded to by Fenichel (1941) may not be a productive move.

PSYCHOTHERAPY AND MEDICINE

I submit that in psychoanalysis the practices, value systems, perspectives, and approaches of the pure knowledge medical paradigm have remained largely unexamined; they seem to have been taken over uncritically and unwittingly from science and medicine. Theorizing has focused on pure knowledge rather than on applications, on developing a general psychology rather than on clinical effectiveness, on pathology rather than on technique—the literature on therapy notwithstanding.

Let me emphasize that I am referring to a focus, a set of implicit assumptions and leading principles. I am *not* equating this paradigm with any particular scientific position, with positivism, for example, with its concern for operationalization, verification, accuracy, disconfirmation, and so on. Neither am I questioning any particular conceptual ingredient of traditional psychoanalytic theorizing at this time. I am only pointing out that a variety of tacit medical criteria, strategies, practices, and values have left psychotherapeutic technique largely in an orphan's position. I am suggesting that this position may, at least in part, be a consequence of a medical perspective.

The "medicalization" of psychoanalysis has been controversial for a long time of course (see, for example, Ingleby, 1980; Bettelheim, 1983; Jacoby, 1983, especially pp. 16–19, 138, 141–142, 145–149, 158). It is, indeed, an aspect of a much larger issue:

> Mental illness, we are told, is a major problem of our time. . . . But what exactly is this problem, and why do we seem so bad at solving it? According to most psychiatrists, it is a clinical problem like any other, which medical technology, in its relentless forward march, will eventually get rid of for us—provided the funds keep coming in. If we do not seem to have made much progress to date, that is because psychiatry is still an "infant science."
>
> To many thinking people, though, there seems to be something wrong with this answer. Mental illnesses, by and large, do not *feel* like other illnesses—the "symptoms" are not annoying externalities, like

the spots on the face of the chicken-pox victim; on the contrary, they seem to be features of the very life a person leads, and they reach down to the core of the personality [Ingleby, 1980, p. 1].

Seeman (1965) refers to the analogous situation for research in client-centered therapy; he might just as well have been speaking about psychoanalytic theorizing:

> Research has always followed theory and never led it. Innovations in practice have come from direct experience and not from research [more generally: theorizing]. This is in striking contrast to much medical research. A new drug or procedure is evolved and then tried out experimentally. If it works, it is used in general practice. Research in client-centered therapy has never served this discovery function. It has had, rather, the function of clarification and validation. Research has served to quantify the intuitive observations and findings and to check factually the validity of these observations. But research has not led to application; it has always trailed application [p. 1225].

If psychotherapy may not properly belong within medicine, then the pure knowledge medical paradigm may be a questionable leading principle for psychoanalytic theorizing. It has been recognized by some at least that knowing more and more about pathology may not necessarily benefit therapeutic technique:

> Much of the teaching of psychopathology and psychotherapy concentrates on the patient: Why he became the person he now is, why he developed his pathological defenses, what the pathogenic influences were in his life, what anxieties he defends himself against—as if this knowledge would automatically suggest how to approach him, and the best ways to help him [Bettelheim, 1974, p. 532; see also pp. 59, 415, 430, 433, 556].

Loewald (1981) makes a similar point: "Anna Freud . . . spoke of the difference between 'understanding a mental aberration' and the 'possibility to cure it,' suggesting that there is no obvious reason to assume 'that any mental affliction which is open to analytic understanding is open also to analytic cure'. . ." (p. 381).

Keat (1981), in an extended analysis of the relationships between theory and practice, demonstrates the tenuous logical connections between psychoanalytic theory (past and present) and therapeutic effectiveness:

> [There are logical] gaps between psychoanalytic theory and the success or failure of psychoanalytic therapy, so that the failure of therapeutic techniques is compatible with the truth of this theory, whilst the success of those techniques may provide little support for it. . . . Even in those cases where predicted therapeutic success is

achieved, it is possible that neither psychoanalytic theory nor its associated theory of technique are significantly supported, since it may be that this success is better explained by an alternative theory of technique [p. 159].

What I have been saying in this chapter, then, is that by following one particular leading principle, ideal, or cluster of ideas—the pure knowledge medical paradigm—psychoanalytic theorizing may have steered clinical thinking away from theoretical directions that would have led to greater clinical consequentiality. Perhaps Matte Blanco's (1975) lament, voiced in another context, applies here as well: "Psychoanalysis has wandered away from itself" (p. 10).

My discussion might well raise the question, Why isn't the usual theorizing about the clinical situation different from theorizing within the pure knowledge medical paradigm? Why, for instance, would not the kind of theorizing advocated and presented by such clinicians as Schafer (e.g., 1983), G. Klein (1973), Kohut (e.g., 1977), Kernberg (e.g., 1976), or Brenner (e.g., 1976) qualify as clinically relevant? Part of the answer has already been provided in Chapter 2; there is the issue of logical entailment. Additional considerations will be discussed in the next chapters, when I compare major proposals for presumably clinically relevant approaches with the suggestions and approaches that I am developing in this monograph.

In any case, I am proposing that this focus has characterized psychoanalytic theorizing from the very beginning. If that is the case, then the yield of theorizing within the pure knowledge paradigm may well bear, in some important ways, the stamp of that focus. It is to be expected in general that any framework will very likely be biased or skewed by the purposes for which it has been constructed. In the particular case of psychoanalytic theory, its framework will probably deeply reflect the fact that it has evolved under the tacit principal requirement that it be a pure knowledge framework, slanted toward investigating and explaining pathology. Its ingredients, models, and rationales all will show the influence of that focus. Its strengths will lie in its intended domain of application. It ought to excel in explaining or illuminating pathology, personality, development, etiology, and diagnostics, and in my view it does.

There is an obverse implication here as well, however: If, as the result of its focus, a framework shows strengths in certain areas, might it not concomitantly show weaknesses in areas that lie outside the domains of its principal intended applications? Could it not, then, be the case that a framework that evolved with a focus on pathology and on obtaining knowledge for its own sake might thereby also have become a framework that somehow, in some basic ways, would be ill-equipped to serve as a clinically consequential framework? Could it not be that a psychoanalytic framework whose development occurred under the pure knowledge medical paradigm would consequently lack the capacity to logically entail, and directly advance, therapeutic technique?

That is the main point of the present chapter. I suggested in Chapters 3 and 4 that there are *formal* characteristics inherent in any version of the state process framework that may make all versions of it unfit to serve as vehicles for clinically relevant theorizing. I am now suggesting, in addition, that theorizing that has evolved within the traditional leading principle may be deficient as a clinically consequential framework for *focal* reasons. Putting it simply: If you encourage the search for pure knowledge, if you seek to develop a general psychology, and if you maintain a medicalized focus in your theorizing, then the chances are that your theorizing will be unable to move therapeutic potency significantly forward.

A major implication of these considerations is of course that a framework with a different focus, a focus on therapy, would be somehow basically different from one that evolved under the usual pure knowledge medical paradigm. What would it mean to maintain a focus on therapy rather than on pathology in one's theorizing? What would a theory look like if it had been developed specifically with clinical relevance in mind? What would its ingredients be? What would a clinically relevant theory need to tell us, and how would it accomplish its functions? What would be the shape of a theory that would allow us to move technique forward, in a deductive fashion? I do not believe that we have clear answers to these questions. Furthermore, I claim that our lack of answers reflects not only, not even primarily, the difficulties that these issues raise; I have become persuaded that the lack of answers reflects first of all a lack of clearly formulated questions and tasks. Therefore, as I mentioned already in Chapter 1 and shall explore further in Chapter 7, the identification and formulation of generative questions is a necessary first step, one that should not quickly be shunted aside in favor of producing answers—premature answers to questions that we do not yet understand sufficiently well.

In the next chapters I shall attempt to bring the two major strands of my argument to bear on clinical and other issues. I shall further detail my proposed approaches, offer some formulations of questions, and make tentative, illustrative suggestions concerning the directions of future theorizing.

SIX

Clinical Pragmatism

> *Professions can survive the paradigms which gave them birth.*
> —Richard Rorty, Philosophy and the Mirror of Nature
>
> *What is urgently needed is a science that comprehends complex systems without, or with a minimum of, abstractions.*
> —Michael Polanyi, The Study of Man

A useful way of conceptualizing a clinical theory within psychoanalytic theorizing in general is in terms of Graves's (1971) epistemological framework, which I mentioned in Chapter 3. There I indicated that additional details concerning levels and the role of models remained to be presented; that will be done now. The presentation will provide the background for the discussions of formal and focal issues that follow.

What general features do theories display? I described several in Chapters 3 and 4. We should remember, however, that any broad generalizations about the characteristics and ingredients of theories have their limitations. Graves points out that such generalizations should be advanced only tentatively. There is a "risk of overestimating the importance of common features" (p. 6), especially when epistemologists indulge in abstract theorizing themselves. Graves recommends that philosophers of science use an empirical approach: When they themselves "practice in philosophy what they preach to science . . . [and] study actual scientific theories to see both how and why they have evolved and how they are presently understood by their users," it becomes evident that theories tend to be "related only by 'family resemblances,' in Wittgenstein's sense" (p. 6; see also p. 34). Generalizations tend to be made at the cost of accuracy. With that caveat, let us examine Graves's schemata.

LEVELS AND MODELS

Graves presents what he calls a "levels hypothesis," a rich framework within which one can usefully structure epistemological issues. He begins by drawing on the distinction, introduced by Bunge, between "cognitive" and "ontic" levels of theorizing. Cognitive levels play a major role in my presentation, and are described below. Ontic levels, which, according to Graves, pertain primarily to metaphysical matters (p. 19), are not discussed here, since they are tied only indirectly to cognitive levels (pp. 19, 22, 36), and since I shall not be considering metaphysics.

Ingredients of Cognitive Levels

Different theories have different domains, of course; they are useful primarily within some range of application. A theory located at a given cognitive level will have "a set of properties and laws peculiar to it" (p. 18), and will be "characterized by means of categories and concepts appropriate to it" (p. 21).

A theory at any one given cognitive level—say, the atomic level—has *formal* and *material* aspects—roughly, what in Chapters 3 and 4 I called the *internal* and *external* aspects of a theory. Specifically, a theory comprises (1) a language appropriate to the material constituents of that level; (2) laws or rules that connect the language constituents; (3) for some but not all theories, a quasihierarchical stratification of the theoretical language—a structuring of the formalism into various levels (say, of abstraction); (4) correspondence rules that provide the logical ties between any such levels of discourse (that is, when a given theory has such levels); (5) models, to be described below; and (6) interpretations—the logical mechanisms that connect the various constituents of a given theory (e.g., its language to its material aspects; see my discussions of interpretation in Chapters 3 and 4). Formalisms interpret material aspects and vice versa—"both support each other" (p. 42).

At a given cognitive level of theorizing, then, we have formalisms (language), material aspects (roughly, the real world referents of the formalisms), and models. At any one cognitive level, the entire complex constitutes a "theory."

Where, then, do models fit into theories? Usually, the term is used rather loosely in epistemological or scientific discussions, and there is no generally agreed-upon single meaning. Graves is specific in his

Psychoanalytic Theory and Clinical Relevance

usage. For him (Chapter 4), models occupy an intermediate position, conceptually somewhere between linguistic/formal and material aspects. Any model used within a given theory is usually some well-understood entity that "must have both material and formal aspects" (p. 46); frequently, an entity that now serves as a model for a theory at one cognitive level had at another time been the material constituent of a different theory. For example, while at one time theorizing in mechanics was "about" entities such as masses and gravitational or other force fields, once these became familiar and better understood, they in turn could become models within some other theory, at some other cognitive level. In Graves's usage, a model is a perfect embodiment or interpretation of a theory's formalisms. Also, models tend to have spatiotemporal features, to be visualizable, to come close to having "perceptible qualities."

Within a given theory, models can serve several functions. They can integrate and unify a cognitive level, stimulate and suggest productive ways of extending the theory (good models have "surplus value"), and mediate between language and material phenomena. One might say that for Graves models play a role close to that played by a useful, generative, suggestive metaphor.

I have sketched the properties and roles of models briefly here primarily in order to complete the epistemological description of theories that I began in Chapter 3. For detailed explanations, I refer the reader to Graves's extended discussions.

Hierarchies of Cognitive Levels

Thus far I have been describing the constituents and characteristics of a theory that pertains to a given cognitive level. Let us consider now how a group of such theories and associated cognitive levels might be related to one another.

The notion that theories can be stratified, that they pertain to different levels, is familiar and widely accepted. It is usually taken for granted that a set of theories can be arranged in a hierarchical order. One novel feature of Graves's scheme is that he rejects the notion of a simple, linear hierarchical order for cognitive levels or theories. In his view, usually there is no neat, universally applicable criterion according to which a set of cognitive theories can be arranged in a single sequence. He points out that a group of different theories can be ordered in various ways, according to various criteria, and that each way of ordering will yield its own hierarchy. For example, theories could be ordered according to the size of the "objects" of their respective domains (e.g., fundamental particles, atoms, everyday objects, astronomical bodies, etc.), or they could be ordered according to such criteria as evolutionary history, degree of abstraction, place on the inanimate-animate continuum, or range of velocities (e.g., relativistic, nonrelativistic). Thus, Graves tells us to give up the usual simple notions of hierarchy of theories, and to think in terms of a richer, more complex ordering. That approach has significant implications for the possibilities of reducing one level to another.

Relationships across Levels

We have seen that in Graves's framework the relationships between various cognitive levels are complex. Typically, it is not possible to make comprehensive reductions from one level to another, to reduce one theory completely to a second theory at a different cognitive level. (For Graves, the requirements for valid complete reduction from one level to another are quite stringent, and can but rarely be met in practice [p. 20].) Consequently, it is usually also not possible to make a transitive sequence of reductions, where level A would be reduced to B, B to C, and thus A to C (pp. 18–23). Neither, in the usual case, are levels fully coordinate or compatible, relatable to one another by complete and symmetrical translation.

What we often can do, however, is perform "partial reductions" between levels that are incompatible to some extent (neither fully compatible nor fully reducible). In those instances, it may very well be that different cognitive levels share terms ("cross-level" terms) and relations (laws). Although in these kinds of cases it would not be proper to speak of a theory at one cognitive level being "grounded" in, reducible to, another theory at a different level, it does seem to be legitimate to speak of "coordination" between such theories. In this view, then, "partial reduction," rather than being an asymmetrical reduction *from* a theory at level A to a theory at level B, refers to a symmetrical relationship, to the fact that one can discern a degree of coordination *between* levels. Coordination thus refers to a measure of translatability between theories of like rank at two (or more) cognitive levels; it does not imply a judgment concerning "higher" and "lower" theories and levels. I shall propose that this conception of cross-level relationships is appropriate for psychoanalytic theorizing. Let us, then, begin to consider the implications for psychoanalysis of this way of thinking about and organizing epistemological issues.

CLINICAL PRAGMATISM AS A SEPARATE COGNITIVE LEVEL

Levels in Psychoanalytic Theory

We have considered the issue of theory stratification in psychoanalysis in several contexts, beginning with the introductory discussions of Chapter 2 concerning the problematic status of a "clinical theory." There we saw that a consensus continues to hold for a version of hierarchical layering of psychoanalytic theory that is very close to Waelder's widely recognized notions. For example, Gedo (1979) defines "metapsychology as a set of psychoanalytic propositions further removed from observational data than are our clinical theories" (p. 244).

From time to time, questions have been raised about the legitimacy of these or similar established views that perpetuate the practice of hierarchical ordering within psychoanalytic theory. Basch (1973), addressing the issue from the perspective that "no hypothetical theory can be abstracted directly from observation," notes:

> The mistaken notion that clinical theory and the metapsychology used to explain it are opposite ends of a continuum and that the latter is an abstraction from the former is still current in psychoanalysis [p. 49].

Similarly, Keat (1981) speaks about the possibility that theories about therapy and general psychoanalytic theories may to some extent be logically independent from one another:

> Auxiliary statements [additional theoretical assumptions] would have to include *a theory about the therapeutic process itself*; and this may involve propositions that are to some extent independent of the general interpretations [general propositions on psychosexual development, structural characteristics of the apparatus, formation of neuroses, etc.] [p. 146].

> It is quite possible that additional theoretical knowledge would be required, which is not derivable from psychoanalytic theory, to enable effective therapeutic techniques to be developed. Thus successful results of psychoanalytically guided therapeutic processes cannot be regarded as a necessary condition for the truth of psychoanalytic theo-

ry: indeed its truth is compatible with a considerable degree of pessimism about the possibilities for therapeutic success [p. 150].

(This last issue seems to be an unpopular one: "Psychoanalysts do not like to dwell on the distinction between truth and their form of therapy" [Yankelovich and Barrett, 1970, p. 336].)

The framework I am about to propose is consonant with these and similar criticisms of the usual hierarchical notions. Later in this chapter I shall compare my suggestions with some important earlier proposals about a separate clinical theory.

As noted above, mainstream thought in psychoanalysis continues to retain the familiar hierarchical picture (see Thoma and Kachele, 1975, pp. 74–77). Let us now view this mainstream conception in terms of Graves's epistemological framework. In those terms, it becomes evident that the body of psychoanalytic theory has been traditionally treated as though it constituted *one* cognitive level. In the traditional view, it has (1) a material component: data of observation (the "'ground floor,' accessible to all" [Thoma and Kachele, 1975, p. 77]); (2) a general body of discourse "about" these data, divided into quasi-hierarchical levels according to the presumed "distance" from data (a typical "hierarchical" stratification of the language involves three levels of abstraction: generalizations of data, clinical theoretical concepts, and metapsychological concepts); and (3) models and metaphors (although standard psychoanalytic theorizing does not seem to have a clear conception of just where these third ingredients belong epistemologically). This psychoanalytic "level" of theorizing may then be contrasted with, say, the biological or the neurological (see, for example, Rubinstein, 1965; Peterfreund, 1971).

I would suggest, by comparison, that it would be more productive, lucid, and veridical to think of psychoanalytic theorizing in terms of *different* cognitive (and perhaps, ultimately, different ontic) levels. The clinical level would be one such separate cognitive level. Other psychoanalytic theories, at different cognitive levels, might then be, for instance, a theory of pathology, a theory of general psychology, a theory of group processes, and a theory of psychological development. Let me emphasize that I am not proposing here to develop any one particular comprehensive scheme of cognitive levels in psychoanalysis. I am primarily concerned in the present work with clarifying the notion of a clinical theory at its own separate cognitive level.

Advantages of a Clinical Cognitive Level

What would it gain for us to treat clinical theorizing at a single cognitive level? Graves points out that an important general function of a cognitive level is to furnish one or more regulative principles—leading ideas, ideals, paradigms, models. These will

> provide constraints on scientific theorizing. Once accepted, they then determine . . . the "ideals of natural order" for the scientific community, which in turn give criteria for deciding what sorts of phenomena need to be explained, and what counts as an adequate explanation of them [p. 8].

With this in mind, I would suggest that the construction or identification of a new cognitive level may free our thinking. In extreme cases, conceptualizations in terms of new cognitive levels may have a revolutionary scientific impact, according to Graves (pp. 41–42). On a more modest scale, a fresh cognitive perspective may have a liberating effect in several ways.

First, even though it may look like just a formal move, thinking of clinical theory as having its own distinct cognitive level could facilitate a shift in focus; it is easier to disidentify with old principles in a new framework. In our case, it might make it easier to consider exchanging the leading principles of the pure knowledge medical paradigm for other leading principles or foci. I shall illustrate this point later.

Second, it should clarify the matter of reductionism and the associated problems about levels of abstraction that have continually haunted (and, I believe, muddied) psychoanalytic theorizing. One could lay to rest the quest for a single, asymmetrical, transitive hierarchical ordering. The levels conception proposed here would promote epistemological clarity. Since coordination or partial reduction between different cognitive levels is a clear and legitimate relationship in Graves's epistemology, there now would no longer be any reasons why the theory at the cognitive level of clinical pragmatism should not comfortably share some ingredients (concepts, laws, models) with theories from various other cognitive levels (psychoanalytic and other); questions about which theory was higher, which was lower, or which terms belonged to which "layer" of theory, and the like would no longer be legitimate when theories are seen as partially correlated, as symmetrically and partially reducible. Furthermore, at its own cognitive level, clinical theorizing could introduce its own hierarchical structure of language, should that become necessary or advisable.

A third potential benefit that creating the new cognitive level might bring concerns the specification of formal requirements. A theory that has its own separate cognitive level could provide a convenient independent framework within which specialized needs for a new kind of formalism might be identified and met. We recall that a new cognitive level can redefine "what sorts of phenomena need to be explained, and what counts as an adequate explanation." A conceptualization that explicitly places different branches of psychoanalytic theory at different cognitive levels could encourage a corresponding differentiation between classes of formalisms; each theory would have the freedom to develop the formalism best matched to the needs of its cognitive level. Within that cognitive level, moreover, the possible need for a new formalism could be examined with a minimum of contamination from (and to) other, established formalisms and levels. Yet the premise of partial reduction would make discourse from other levels available as needed. Let us now consider the kind of formalism that might be appropriate for a theory at the cognitive level of clinical pragmatism.

FORMALISM: THE PROCESS NARRATIVE

The Requirements

What shall we select as the vehicle for theorizing at the cognitive level of clinical pragmatism? The premise that I have been developing, beginning with Chapter 3, is, of course, that *any* state process representation is inadequate to our needs. I have held that regardless of its specific form, any such representation is too impoverished to capture, and thus to allow us to deal with, the phenomena that are salient to a clinical enterprise.

It is a mistake, as I see it, to assume that any enterprise that seeks to be scientific must therefore use some variant of state process formalisms. As Hexter (1971) points out, "there is an irreducible divergence between the rhetoric of history and the rhetoric of the natural sciences" (p. 247); I submit that also applies to psychoanalysis and other disciplines that purport to deal with the subjective domain.

The general premise is not new, although, as far as I know, it has not previously been formally cast within a critique of state process representation. The search for an alternative to the standard logical conceptions of language seems to have a long, though not a prominent, history. According to von Wright (1971), one early attempt in this tradition was Aristotle's to develop an informal method of verbal meaning called the "practical syllogism." More recently, others who have searched, apparently unsuccessfully, in this direction include Dray, Anscombe, Taylor, and Winch (von Wright, 1971, pp. 25–29, 96–118, 180).

We recall that Wittgenstein's interest in formalizing language was motivated, to an important extent, by the goal of showing "that about which one must remain silent." This was to be accomplished indirectly, by comprehensively and meticulously specifying that about which a formalized language *does* allow us to speak; presumably, the remainder was the domain of the unspeakable, although, as Janik and Toulmin (1973) take great pains to point out, this remainder was for Wittgenstein by no means meaningless. On the contrary: The domain about which Wittgenstein thought one must remain silent was for him *the* important realm (see Chapter 3).

Similarly, as Wilber (1984) reports, several prominent physicists (e.g., Schroedinger, Eddington) have seen physics as dealing with a world of "shadow-symbols," and have turned to the metaphysical or mystical in their attempts to go beyond these representational limitations of formal systems. Langer calls on art, because of its nondiscursive nature, and on "feeling"—as "an 'image' rather than a scientific definition or a model" (Royce, 1983, pp. 494, 498)—to serve as representational systems.

Contemporary approaches in physics invite this open stance toward choosing one's theoretical vehicle. I think that Bohm (1980) has something like this in mind when he describes a way of theorizing in physics that integrates "fact and theory":

> To work in this way is evidently to give primary emphasis to something similar to *artistic perception*. Such perception begins by observing the whole fact in its full individuality, and then by degree articulates the order that is proper to the assimilation of this fact. It does not begin with abstract preconceptions as to what the order has to be, which are then adapted to the order that is observed [p. 141; see also Chapter 6].

Translating that into the clinical situation, one might say that preconceptions about the formal "order" or structure of theoretical discourse in psychoanalysis should be avoided. One should not try to decide ahead of time what would constitute acceptable theoretical discourse. The specification and understanding of one's vehicle for theorizing should be guided by a pragmatic focus; it should reflect the needs of one's practice and, indeed, grow out of them; it should not simply fall in line with some preconceptions about what supposedly constitutes scientific language.

At any rate, I trust I have demonstrated convincingly that while state process representational systems may be adequate vehicles for theorizing about the external world, about the world of matter, extension, mass, fields, or motion (Graves, Chapters 5–17), they will not do as vehicles for meaningful clinical theorizing. If that is the case, unless we decide that we must remain silent, we must find an alternative approach and vehicle. One such alternative is the kind of discourse Hexter (1971) calls a "process narrative" or "processive discourse." I shall describe that kind of discourse shortly, and later consider its relationship to apparently similar forms of discourse proposed for psychoanalysis in the past.

In Chapter 4, I suggested an alternative way of looking at language. I claimed that when one gave up conceptualizing language as a sort of imperfect state process formalism, when one rejected an elementaristic, referential, logician's conception, when one did not view language as a tool but treated it instead as an integral part of the life world, then one had made a start toward developing a language capable of dealing meaningfully and adequately with those phenomena that matter to clinicians, those phenomena that should matter to psychology in general. But how might one go about defining the specific kind of discourse that could serve as a vehicle for theorizing on the one hand and avoid the characteristics of a state process descriptive system on the other? An immediate and obvious problem is that if we wish to eschew a state process formalistic version of discourse, then we cannot use formal logic to specify its alternative:

> I doubt that the "adequate" or "satisfactory" [formal-logical] form of processive explanation is abstractable from the rhetoric of historical discourse which is its vehicle. If it were abstractable, I doubt that it would be much more relevant to an account of viable historical explanation than the covering-law and narrative [other formal-logical] forms have turned out to be [Hexter, 1971, p. 205].

In other words, here we run into the paradoxical situation that as soon as one tries to frame an alternative kind of discourse within logic, as soon as one attempts to define it in terms of logical specifications, the discourse thereby once again necessarily acquires the characteristics of a state process formalism. Then, by the arguments presented in the preceding chapters, it would once more lose its relevance and effectiveness, and again become "fruitless and vacuous" (Hexter, 1971, p. 198).

There are at least two other ways, however, to approach the task of specification: by proscription, and by example. Let us look at each in turn, and then see whether we can draw some useful inferences from the examination.

Specification by Proscription

Jaynes (1976), in addressing the issue of consciousness, opens his second chapter with this question:

> Thus having chiseled away some of the major misconceptions about consciousness, what then have we left? If consciousness is not all these things [here follows his list], what is it? [p. 48].

His comment reminds us that one way of specifying an elusive entity is by defining what that entity is *not*. In a general and obvious sense, then, non-state-formalistic discourse is what is left over after one removes the ill-advised conceptualizations and practices generated by state-formalistic, Cartesian approaches. That said, I should indicate that the important work of identifying those specific conceptualizations and practices in psychoanalysis remains to be done.

A model for such an approach to specification by way of proscription might come from linguistics. In his widely cited paper "A Plea for Excuses," Austin (1964) presents a collection of thirteen normative principles (pp. 52–63) in the form of proscriptions. He "proscribes," for example, the inappropriate use of negations and opposites in formal discourse, showing how pairs that apparently are logical opposites—e.g., voluntary/involuntary—in reality are not. As he states elsewhere, these are spurious dichotomies, dyads "that live by taking in each other's washing—what is spurious is not one term of the pair, but the antithesis itself" (1962, p. 4). Ingleby (1980) gives a similar example of two terms—individualism and collectivism—that superficially seem like opposites, but in reality are not (p. 44). In another vein, Austin points out the consequences of the failure of words to "shake off their etymologies and formations" and to shed pictures or simple (and misleading) associated models.

The same approach, I submit, can be brought to psychoanalysis. That is to say, if we wished to follow Austin's model in developing a theoretical discourse for the cognitive level of clinical theory, we might begin to assemble a suitable list of proscriptions. The first items of such a list might be culled from the remarks on processive discourse that follow. In addition, Austin's own proscriptions might be evaluated carefully for their relevance, possibly in a modified form, for psychoanalytic discourse.

Specification by Example

Examples provide a second way of specifying non-state-formalistic discourse. Consider, for instance, one bit of actual processive discourse. Melanie Klein (1948/1977), in a paper on the theory of anxiety and guilt, writes: "Regarding the manifestations of anxiety in young children, Freud said that anxiety is caused by the child 'missing someone who is loved and longed for. . . . If a mother is absent or has withdrawn her love from her child, it is no longer sure of the satisfaction of its needs and is perhaps exposed to the most distressing feelings of tension'" (p. 25). Do we understand that, or not? I claim we do. Yet Klein goes on to trace a history of "explanations" ranging from those couched in economic terms (e.g., transformations of unsatisfied libido) to those given in terms of object relations theory (e.g., good versus persecuting objects, processes of internalization and projection). From the perspectives of Chapters 3 and 4, we can say that the aim of these theorizings is to translate an understandable statement in narrative discourse into a state process formulation. Apparently, the judgment is that a narrative that is "transparent" requires explanation, formalization, translation, perhaps for the sake of satisfying the pure knowledge medical paradigm.

Another example of transparent processive discourse comes from one of Bettelheim's (1974) discussions of the therapeutic needs of patients. According to his findings, the most important factors in the treatment and recovery of the psychotic patient pertain to the patient's "conviction that he or she is an autonomous human being, one who has an important place in the particular segment of the world and society in which his life is unfolding at the moment. . . . [In a psychiatric hospital, it should be the case that] the patient's self-respect is of prime concern to everybody" (p. 226). How could that discourse be translated into state process form without major loss of meaning, without utter trivialization?

Let us next look at an extended example from Hexter's (1971) *The History Primer*, a work that I believe to be of major importance to our discussion for its comprehensive, lucid examination of processive discourse and related issues. Its major concern is with what constitutes an appropriate way of theorizing for the historian. The following cursory remarks fail to do justice to Hexter's presentation; the work repays careful study.

Hexter begins by contrasting the methodologies of physics and history. He discusses what he sees as the inappropriate yet ubiquitous aping of physics in the historian's quest to "assimilate" the "physical science norm." He comments, "Once formulated in this rigorous way the difficulty of assimilationists with history grew preposterously" (p. 17). He then compares the discourse of physics or engineering with a historian's narrative, the "processive discourse or explanation." He examines this theme from numerous perspectives, contrasting explanation by "boundary conditions/covering law" logical processes (roughly, state process formalisms) with the processive narrative. That narrative uses our common language, "a marvelously supple, superbly balanced, beautifully manageable means of communication" (pp. 51–52), "a versatile and well-tuned instrument" (p. 267).

Hexter is of course aware of the contradictions inherent in any attempt to define processive discourse logically. In his terminology, it is a form of discourse that is neither logical nor illogical but "translogical"; I take that to mean that it has validity, yet remains outside logical/formal, propositional systems. At any rate, it is because of this inherent difficulty with definition that Hexter specifies the characteristics of the process narrative primarily through a series of carefully worked out, highly detailed and analyzed examples. I shall summarize one here, but urge the interested reader to study the entire work with care.

The example is the following. Hexter presents three versions of an answer that Willie, a twelve-year-old, might give his father when asked why he has come home with his pants muddied (pp. 25–34). Willie's first answer, "Muddy Pants I" [MP I], is couched in impeccable scientific terminology. It addresses the question, and provides an answer, in terms of classical physics (surface adhesion, semirigid bodies, laws of dynamics, the instability of bodies whose height is great in comparison to their base, etc.). At the other end of the spectrum is "Muddy Pants III" [MP III], the kind of narrative a typical well-intentioned youngster might give in response to the parental request for explanation. MP III is given in terms of staying after school, taking shortcuts on the way home, and the like. For the father, MP I seems inappropriate, a sassy caricature, compared with MP III. The latter fulfills its purpose. The former does not. When Willie concludes MP I with "O.K.?" his father responds that it is "not O.K., and you know it."

Now, as Hexter knows very well, MP III may seem "antiscientific." He takes pains to point out that on any sensible "scientific adequacy scale" MP I would rank first, MP III last. For the actual recipient of the discourse, however, any reasonable "adequacy scale" constructed for *his* purposes would yield the reverse order: MP III would be "adequate and satisfactory because complete," while MP I would be "incomplete and a waste of time" (p. 32).

Furthermore, in terms of the father's needs the narrative is "confirmable" in straightforward ways. In this application, it would be ridiculous and inappropriate to verify the "data" by formal methodological tools, such as a statistically controlled experiment. We could check on Willie's story, and we would know quite well what it meant to confirm or disconfirm it. It is a matter of what kind of confirmation is appropriate to a given situation, purpose, or, more generally, discipline.

In Hexter's view, then, the *utility* of the discourse is the critical issue. Time and again, in different contexts, explicitly and implicitly, Hexter makes the point that when one considers what constitutes an adequate explanation, adequate discourse, adequate understanding, criteria for what constitutes adequacy should be posited in terms of adequacy *for* something (typically, practice), and not according to some arbitrary (even though scientifically sacred) canons of the pure knowledge paradigms of, say, physics or mathematics. The question is, When you have explained something by a professionally constructed processive narrative, then what more could one want? What more would one need? Typically, the narrative is transparent. Thus, Hexter arrives at the same position from a historian's perspective as do many of the critics from other disciplines whose ideas I presented earlier. Thought seems to converge on a "pragmatically based hermeneutics" as the appropriate framework for productive, nontrivial theorizing in those disciplines that lie outside the natural sciences.

In other detailed examples (a collapsing bridge, a lost pennant race, a man's death, etc.) Hexter shows in many ways and from several perspectives that scientific discourse is precise, logically structured, accurate (though highly incomplete), verifiable, unambiguous, and, for the historian's purposes, a waste of effort, inadequate, irrelevant. By contrast, processive explanations fail miserably according to the usual standards of normal science, yet they are rich, credible, coherent, not illogical but rather "translogical," patterned, the result of properly conducted investigations—and adequate for their purposes. Furthermore, processive explanations contain elements of creativity; they can surprise. In a processive explanation, "Each point about it has just that air of obviousness which everyone can agree to, but which no previous writer seems to have attained. . ." (p. 50).

Salient Features

Let us see whether we can extract some significant features and properties of processive discourse from the proscriptions and examples that have been presented.

Easy complexity versus difficult simplicity. One is struck by clear differences when one compares the theoretical discourse of historians with that of, say, physicists. Historians' discourse is easy and commonplace, in a way, obvious (especially after something has been said once), yet dense, rich, complex. The narrative integrates divergent factors in an orderly, rational way. (As I have said, however, and as we shall see again in my discussion of Sherwood's work, that does not mean that the rationale of an adequate process narrative can be satisfactorily specified or explained by means of formal logic.) By contrast, the formal language of the natural sciences looks frightfully difficult, especially to the uninitiated. When one has mastered the formalism, however, one sees that in a sense the discourse is simple. It is based on the relatively uncomplicated foundations provided by formal logic; the difficulties come largely from the continuous pyramiding and condensing of constituents at one level into higher-level abstractions at another level. (The move from arithmetic to algebra is an example.)

Terminology. The matter of correlation between cognitive levels becomes relevant here. Even if we adopt commonplace processive discourse, we should not hesitate to draw on specialized, even esoteric, terms, concepts, and the like *when necessary* (Hexter, 1971, pp. 55–56). That easy statement becomes difficult in practice: When are specialist's concepts "necessary?" The implication, of course, is necessary for *something*, and here again pragmatic issues intrude into formal considerations.

What one wishes to avoid is a scientistic, grossly inappropriate use of specialized discourse:

> Given the perverse appetite of men of learning to exalt their particular form of activity above those of other learned men, this danger exists throughout the learned world. It leads to self-satisfaction, pomposity, and mystagogy. This danger is especially acute in history [and in the psychological disciplines!], because of all learned disciplines it is the least mysterious, the least removed from common human experience [Hexter, 1971, p. 77].

The issues that I am addressing now have been explored, in a different context, by so-called ordinary language philosophers (Chappell, 1964; Rorty, 1967). Although this approach has so far been used primarily to cope with ontological issues (by philosophers such as Austin, Ryle, and Malcolm), it may profit us to take a brief look at some of their thoughts.

One major premise is that "ordinary language is all right" (Chappell, 1964, p. 2); it is effective, supple, adequate, useful, and does not need fixing up by formalization, by turning it into an "ideal language" through axiomatization, translation into formal notation, and so on.

Furthermore, ordinary language philosophers make an important distinction between "ordinary use of language" and "use of ordinary language." Use of ordinary language refers to the absence of esoteric, highly technical terminology, or even jargon. Ordinary use refers to what I have called "life world" use of language—integrated with person, world, tasks, transparent, "profoundly unconscious of itself" when it is functioning adequately. Apparently, there is no simple relationship between efficacy of language and complexity of one's terminology. That is, the power of one's language is not necessarily related to one's use of "plain and blunt" language, jargon, esoteric terms, or technical language. Thinkers who write plainly and bluntly may or may not be superior in thought to those whose writings are obscure (see Ryle's illuminating discussion, 1964, p. 36).

I would advocate that one should strive to use language in whatever ways are "necessary," no more and no less. I shall explore the implications of that pragmatic position in the next section. Ryle (1964) puts it in a nutshell:

> "Back to ordinary language" can be (but often is not) the slogan of those who have awakened from the formalizer's dream. This slogan, so used, should be repudiated only by those who hope to replace philosophizing by reckoning [p. 39].

Although it is not always clear whether he advocated use of ordinary language or ordinary use of language, Wittgenstein's general approach seems to have been consonant with what is being advocated here. According to Barrett (1978), it seems that Wittgenstein, after first pursuing Russell and Whitehead's vision of rigorously (mathematically) formalizing philosophical thought and argument, came to renounce "the domination of formal logic for the language of everyday use as a more adequate vehicle for philosophical clarification. The pretensions of exactness are given up for the more real satisfactions of adequacy to experience..." (p. 13). Wittgenstein proposed "the radical opening move that our colloqial speech is to be the medium within which we philosophize..." (p. 68). As Rommetveit (1974) has pointed out, "Wittgenstein's claim that an utterance has meaning only in the stream of life seems to hold true even for scientific and professional discourse" (p. 20).

This position is also consonant with much of what is being said about the way Freud used language in his theorizing (Bettelheim, 1983; Ornston, in press a,b). Not only did Freud tend to use ordinary language—that is, discourse that was homely, free of jargon, free of unnecessary esoteric terminology (yet potent)—he also used language in an ordinary way; he tended to let his discourse be expressive and meaningful in a holistic, coherent, integrated fashion, without undue worry about elements (formal or operational definition of terms), propositional or logical form, and so on.

In ordinary use of language, one can clarify one's ideas by restating them in other ways. Often, in attempting to express his thought, Freud relied on a constellation of mutually illuminating statements rather than on some formalistic, elementaristic approach. He allowed language to function normally, effectively, freely: "I think that Freud resolutely and steadily described a rich variety of ways of conceiving and unconscious, and that his fluid method of investigation [and, I would say, of using theoretical language] eluded Strachey's grasp" (Ornston, in press b, p. 5). "Freud thought that it was essential to describe a concept in as many different and detailed ways as possible. Therefore, he varied his descriptions of the most useful psychoanalytic ideas" (p. 20). "Freud almost always shifts and enriches his way of using any word as soon as one moves a bit further down the page. He uses the same term in many different ways and a wealth of descriptive language to sketch the same concept. Formal categories usually come unstrung as Freud compels one to think" (in press a, p. 4).

Freud's preference for avoiding state process theorizing is further illustrated by his attitude toward formal models. Again according to Ornston, when Freud did use diagrams, he apparently used them "wryly," with such ironic, irreverent labels as "ein Schema eines Apparatus," which Ornston translates as "a diagram of an apparatus/artificial contraption" (in press a, p. 15). These "vivid little diagrams" were not meant to be taken seriously, not meant to be enshrined as theoretical accomplishments: "Freud explicitly regarded any spatial portrayal as inherently primitive and misleading unless it was used to introduce a psychological conception; that is, a way of thinking about unconscious activity" (p. 22).

In the original German, then, before Freud's scientific systematizers and translators decided to make his discourse more respectable and formal, that discourse exhibited the spirit of the approaches I have been developing here. Much of the time, even though Freud was not explicitly concerned with state process considerations, his use of discourse eschewed the state process features and practices that I have identified and against which I have been arguing. Furthermore—and this is may be the crux of the matter—he demonstrated conclusively that with this kind of non-formalistic, holistic, narrative discourse one *can* speak effectively about highly complex matters, even matters that go against the established rules of common sense; an absence of formalism, of a state space framework, does not at all necessarily imply a concomitant superficiality of discourse or thought.

It is encouraging to find a similar attitude toward discourse expressed, albeit briefly and in passing, by Kohut (1984). He pauses to consider the differences between "harmless and excusable" and "noxious" use of imprecise, even internally inconsistent, theoretical discourse (pp. 50–52). Although he does not introduce state space issues, and even though he seems to adhere to some traditional notions about logical structure (e.g., the orthodox distinctions between experience-near and experience-distant "data," the hierarchical structure of psychoanalytic theory), clinical considerations and needs apparently brought Kohut to a life world, non-state-formalistic view of theoretical discourse that is quite compatible with the approach I am advocating here.

Adequacy. Throughout my discussion, the thesis that processive discourse is adequate has continued to raise the vexing question, Adequate for what purpose? I am proposing to use this form of discourse to theorize about therapy, so it will need to be adequate for that—whatever that may turn out to be. More generally, one can say that, at a minimum, the narrative will have to explain and, up to a point, predict. Let us look briefly at these two functions.

Can one predict by means of discourse that isn't formally structured? Hexter (1971) makes the interesting point that, at least for the historian, the trouble with prediction is not that it can't be done, but that often it is so easy that anyone can do it! It is not impressive enough; the esoteric, arcane quality is missing. When a physicist predicts the results of an experiment in quantum mechanics, *that* is prediction. The layman cannot do it. In history, however, and frequently in psychology, prediction may be so easy and commonplace that it is insufficiently appreciated (p. 45; see also p. 151 below).

There is another, more difficult aspect. Whether or not one likes it, and whether or not one articulates it, prediction about persons inevitably raises the specter of the free will/determinism issue. If, for instance, state space notions are not appropriate models of human psychological processes (a position carefully put forward by Bergson [1946]), then the requirement for prediction loses much of its potency. I will not complicate my general proposals by entering that quagmire here; I shall return to it briefly in Chapter 7.

What about explanations? I earlier considered that subject in terms of the transparency of language (Chapter 4). Here I shall consider it briefly in terms of adequacy.

One might try to maintain that explanation is a logical function. One might try to define it in terms of formal logic. Attempts to do so never seem to get very far, however (see, for example, Sherwood, 1969). I believe that Graves's (1971) view of explanation is more to the point. He sees it primarily as "a *pragmatic*, rather than [a] semantic or syntactic notion. To make a phenomenon intelligible is to make it accord, or fit in, with the standards of human rationality which prevail at a given time" (p. 14); it is a matter of making phenomena "intelligible in terms of the ideals of natural order of the scientific community" (p. 47).

If this view is correct, then it calls into question any arbitrarily selected, a priori impositions of formal requirements on one's discursive vehicle. Requirements stemming from the presumption that in order for a formalism to have explanatory power, it must necessarily be formalized, need no longer be accepted as gospel. For instance, I submit that it is arbitrary to insist on an elementarist view of language in which individual terms must be definable or operationalizable. If the discourse is intelligible and satisfactory for one's purpose (again, the complicating and crucial factor), then why insist on a logician's view of language? The relevance of such considerations to the comments presented earlier about Freud's use of theoretical discourse is obvious.

PRAGMATISM: BACKGROUND

Let us now consider more specifically questions about the *purpose* of theorizing. What do we mean by "pragmatism" when we speak of "clinical pragmatism?" How do formal and focal issues ultimately link up?

In the classical period of the natural sciences, it was held that the differences between the theoretical and the empirical realms, between thinking and doing, were quite straightforward and legitimate. Increasingly, however, that reassuringly simple belief has come under fire (see, for example, Powers, 1982). As usual, difficulties and complexities in the natural sciences are greatly compounded in the behavioral domains. In any case, there are several traditions and disciplines in which a great deal of thought has already been devoted to these issues, from which psychoanalytic theorizing might well profit.

Issues concerning the relationships between theory and practice are usually labeled "pragmatic." In philosophy the term has a variety of meanings. Although pragmatism as a movement (or set of movements) started formally about 1880 with Charles Peirce and William James, precursors go back to Socrates and Aristotle and continue through Hume and Berkeley. (For a historical overview and analysis, see McGill, 1962, or Thayer, 1967.)

The principal meanings and uses of the term are the following. First, pragmatism is often used interchangeably with "operationalism" or "instrumentalism" (e.g., concepts are synonymous with the corresponding set of operations). Second, it implies a particular scientific method, a technique for clarification (see Thayer, 1967, p. 432). Third, it has been used as a tool for evaluating equivalence among statements; if the empirical import of two statements is identical, then the statements are deemed logically equivalent. Fourth, pragmatism has been the basis for theories of truth (Ezorsky, 1967), of belief, and of value (Thayer, 1967, pp. 433-434). Finally, and this is how I shall be using the term, pragmatism implies a general approach to theorizing: Theory should be consequential "either in some action to be taken, or in an alteration in the way in which we now see or describe a problem. . ." (Kahn and Wright, 1980, p. 10).

Pragmatic approaches have sometimes been misperceived as necessarily antitheoretical, simplistically utilitarian, opportunistic, and generally "unscientific." Some proponents of one or another variant of the pure knowledge paradigm have even seen pragmatism as a threat to science. Rorty (1979) has discussed the "horror" with which certain writings of Quine, Kuhn, and Feyerabend were greeted; these and other "relativists" were seen as leading us toward "irrationalism," away from the path to certain, presuppositionless, objective truth (especially pp. 269, 376). Pure knowledge paradigms apparently hold a good deal of emotional appeal and fascination for their adherents. The pursuit of certain knowledge can be fascinating for extralogical reasons: "Reason is never satisfied with what experience has to offer. . . . the pressure in each human to not be satisfied leads [us], according to Kant, to indulge in reasoning which while in fact it does not extend our real knowledge, it seems to do so. . ." (Janik and Toulmin, 1973, p. 147; see also Barrett, 1978, pp. 82, 87, 94, 159).

I want to emphasize that pragmatism, as I shall use the term, does not say anything one way or another about sophistication, about the level of abstraction, about the mathematization or formalization of a theory. A pragmatic approach can be simple or complex, superficial or deep, concrete or highly abstract, clumsy or elegant. That point should become even clearer as I discuss specifics in later sections.

There are potential problems that abuses of pragmatic approaches can bring about, of course. As Bohm (1980) notes, "We have to be careful here not to identify truth [for Bohm, a pragmatic notion—as he calls it elsewhere, "truth in function"] as nothing more than 'that which works'. . . ." (1980, p. 43). A "vulgar," materialistic, trivialized version of pragmatism can be destructive. If one blindly insists on crass utility, commercial payoff, and the like as sole criteria for one's theorizing, then pragmatism may indeed have undesirable results. Such ill-advised versions may prematurely eliminate "important doctrines of science" in an early stage of theory building; there is the possibility that one might too quickly reject a theory on a pragmatic basis, rejecting it at some early stage where consequences of that theory are not yet visible (McGill, 1962, p. 247). All the same I doubt that is a realistic danger for psychoanalytic theorizing. There has been ample time to demonstrate the clinical relevance of the pure knowledge medical paradigm. I submit that the considerations I have presented in the earlier chapters support the presumption that it is time to consider an alternative.

A pragmatically illuminated position can provide guidelines concerning the kinds of questions one should, or should not, ask. It reminds us of the importance of the questions we ask—what kinds, and how formulated. At the same time as we become alert to issues of consequentiality we also become alert to the need to avoid asking "wrong" questions. The danger is that "we will not ask the right questions. . . . We will be like very clever men who have entered the maze at the wrong place. We will perform a series of extraordinarily clever maneuvers to get at the center, but we will never get there. And the more clever we are, the more fruitful our minds will be at dreaming up clever maneuvers. . ." (Hexter, 1971, p. 50).

A major guiding principle of pragmatism is the unity of doing and theorizing. In a pragmatic framework, it is unacceptable to separate (pure) knowledge from (mere) practice. Pragmatism seeks to eliminate "the Greek contrast between contemplation and action, between representing the world and coping with it. . ." (Rorty, 1979, p. 11). This is not a simple or superficial issue. It goes to the conceptual core of at least some disciplines.

With regard to contemporary physics, for example, Bohm is quite explicit: "It is useful to emphasize that experience and knowledge are one process, rather than to think that our knowledge is *about* some sort of separate experience. . ." (1980, p. 6). "Fact and theory are thus seen to be different aspects of one whole in which analysis into separate but interacting parts is not relevant" (p. 143; see also pp. 42–46, 56; Weber, 1982, pp. 44–104). Wittgenstein holds to an analogous view about mathematics. For him, "it is a mistaken conception of 'theoretical' to think of it as having meaning apart from human practice, operations, and usage..." (Barrett, 1978, p. 84).

Practice thus plays a major role in guiding the direction of theorizing: "Our choice of elements [constituents of theory] will be dictated by our understanding of the practice, rather than the practice's being 'legitimated' by a 'rational reconstruction' out of elements..." (Rorty, 1979, p. 319); "... theorizing over experience is, as a whole and in detail, fundamentally motivated and justified by conditions of efficacy and utility in serving our various aims and needs..." (Thayer, p. 435).

A highly complex and sophisticated application of a pragmatic perspective is Rorty's (1979) examination of the severe epistemological difficulties that perennially have plagued attempts to distinguish between viewing human beings as "subjects" and "objects." He uses the pragmatic perspective as a touchstone, and in so doing, demonstrates its potency and generality. Although it may very well be possible to adapt Rorty's general principles and approaches to psychoanalytic theorizing, his work amply demonstrates the conceptual complexities and difficulties inherent in a nontrivial version of pragmatism. To develop and implement a parallel approach in psychoanalysis would be no simple matter.

When one begins to view the tensions and relationships between theory and practice in these deeper ways, it becomes evident that a meaningful pragmatism is much more than merely a matter of "what works," or even of what makes a practical difference; it can become a way of enfolding praxis within a consequential theory. Thus, I have come to see that a proposal to shift the focus of theorizing from a focus on pathology to a focus on therapy is more than a minor issue. In fact, I believe that we don't even know much about what such a shift would mean or imply. I shall explore that subject further in the next chapter. I recognize, however, that the proposed shift may sound very much like the familiar, rather tired recommendations for a clinical theory. Later in this chapter I shall therefore say something about the differences between such other proposals and the present suggested perspective.

PRAGMATISM AND THE PROCESS NARRATIVE

Legitimate Questions

One important consequence of implementing a pragmatic focus in conjunction with a non-state-formalistic conception of theoretical discourse is that questions raised about theoretical discourse that previously would have been seen as legitimate now would have to be examined more carefully. An example is the matter of specifying the meaning of terms. Under the pure knowledge medical paradigm, a question such as "What do you mean by X?" (e.g., splitting, libido) would be taken seriously and would be a legitimate target for research, operationalization, and the like. The pure knowledge paradigm sanctions, without further question, the need to define and legitimize one's terms operationally, ostensively, or in terms of other atomic elements of language. Now, with the vision of discourse developed in Chapter 4, and of pragmatism developed in Chapter 5, that sort of injunction and procedure would no longer be accepted without question. Under the old paradigm, the need to be "clear and unambiguous," or the prospect of increasing one's store of pure knowledge, or the need to allow others to replicate one's findings would be sufficient reason to justify one's request to specify the constituent elements of discourse. Under a combined pragmatic and non-state-formalistic focus, in contrast, the first questions would be ones such as, How is your question clinically relevant? What pragmatic shortcomings does the discourse display as it stands? How is the narrative opaque? Why isn't it adequate for our clinical purposes? What else needs to be "explained" about the discourse that would move clinical consequentiality forward? On the basis of the many discussions and arguments about discourse and pragmatism presented earlier, it would seem reasonable, and profitable, to assume that in the usual case the discourse is transparent, at least transparent enough for one's purposes. When it is not, when in some particular instance discourse is judged opaque, that judgment should be made on the basis of pragmatic criteria. The issue should be, Opaque *for what purpose?* Theoretical effort would then be guided by the needs and inner directions of the subject matter. We would not simply continue automatically to apply standard state process formalisms and frameworks, nor adhere blindly to the foci and practices of the pure knowledge medical paradigm.

In that way formal and focal issues could begin to be integrated in one's work. In the past, although "positivists did distinguish among the pragmatics, semantics, and syntax of any language . . . they tended to concentrate on the syntax. . . . I would hold that all three are so intimately conjoined that they cannot be separated out in the case of any living and growing theory" (Graves, 1971, p. 33).

As a practical matter, my suggestions are meant to address the common complaint that mainstream psychoanalytic theorizing is clinically irrelevant, even obstructive to progress. They are meant to provide guidelines designed to keep theorizing from repeating the usual practice of wandering off on clinically irrelevant tangents. They are envisioned to be an antidote to standard pure knowledge medical paradigm practices.

Thought Experiments

We might get a bit more formal and develop tools that could help us decide whether a given posed question was clinically relevant or not. One such tool could be a variant of the so-called thought experiment. One conjures up some particular empirical situation, and thinks through the implications of one's theory in that context. That device was used productively by Einstein more than once to illuminate the empirical implications of relativity theory (see, for example, de Bono's discussion, 1981, pp. 150–151).

What I am suggesting as one possibility, then, is that when a clinician poses a theoretical question, or asks for the exact specification of a concept, or proposes a research task, these questions or proposals should be accompanied by a serious effort to demonstrate the clinical relevance of the request. The clinician would have the task of projecting from proposal to possible outcomes, from question to answer, and of demonstrating how a given solution would affect practice. If clinical relevance could not be demonstrated thus in advance, it might be better to set aside that particular question and cast about for an issue that was more demonstrably relevant. In this way, the thought experiment could provide a useful formal decision tool.

Furthermore, by introducing the issue of clinical relevance right at the start of a theoretical enterprise, one would encourage theoreticians to begin thinking about how to develop a clinically relevant theory—to begin to identify its characteristics, shape, features, needed ingredients, and so on. In other words, forcing ourselves to go through the exercise of constructing thought experiments could help to clarify what the properties and rationales are that make a theory consequential for clinical practice. For example, invoking a thought experiment when one felt the urge to dissect and analyze some piece of theoretical discourse could help to clarify the nature of processive discourse, and show us how to use it (see Chapter 7).

I should like to digress for a moment from the main argument to suggest that a similar strategy can also benefit diagnostics, in several ways. One way is by guiding clinicians toward more realistic criteria for deciding whether a formal psychological or psychiatric assessment is really justified in a given case. All too often, clinicians request such testing routinely, without adequately thinking through the request. Therapeutic issues such as the impact (current and longer term) of testing on a patient, or its meaning, are ignored. Questionable motives often spur requests for assessment: a clinician's magical expectations of testing; inappropriate reliance on the medical model (putting assessment in the class of "other laboratory tests"); protection against possible charges of not being thorough enough. Another common motive stems from the dogmatic conviction, fostered by the pure knowledge medical paradigm, that "knowing more about the case" will always be beneficial. In fact, premature information can be a handicap to therapy; as Winnicott and others have pointed out, it is not always necessarily a good thing to know more about a case at some particular stage of therapy (e.g., Winnicott, 1965, pp. 50–51).

In this kind of situation, the thought experiment would take the form of a charge to the requester that he specify in some reasonable fashion the clinical implications that various conceivable alternative outcomes of an evaluation might have. In other words, the clinician should be able to demonstrate the clinical consequentiality of the request. How will the information be used? What will be the effects on the patient? Will test results be relevant to therapy, to patient management, and so on? The response, "I don't quite know why I am requesting the evaluation—please do it anyway," at least is honest and clear. The standard ploy, "I need to know more about the case," should not be acceptable. The position I am advocating will often be unpopular; I strongly recommend the practice nevertheless. It is not unusual that a clinician, when confronted by this requirement, eventually comes to see that testing may be unnecessary, even counterproductive. Unfortunately, some requesters may eventually conclude that the extra effort demanded of them is just too much, that a request for testing engenders more trouble than it is worth. All the same I believe that, used judiciously, thought experiments lead to more discriminating, relevant, and thoughtful ways of using psychological assessment.

Thought experiments may also be helpful in teaching psychological evaluation. Before a student actually administers a battery of tests in a given case, all manner of thought experiments could be performed (about possible outcomes, possible applications of results, alternative test batteries, and so on), on the basis of preliminary information about the patient. The Barnum effect is more easily revealed; an active, thoughtful approach is fostered.

To return to the main argument: A few other matters should be noted about the proposal to use thought experiments. First, the procedure itself could well be temporary, a stopgap measure. Should the concept of a clinically relevant theory develop, clarify, and mature in a satisfactory way, theorizing might reach a point where a return to something akin to the pure knowledge paradigm (this time with greater clinical relevance) would be appropriate and achievable.

Second, the suggestion to explore thought experiments has little if anything to do with whether or not the technical means for actually doing a particular experiment are now available. Thought experiments, as Einstein demonstrated, may involve conceptualizations that lie entirely beyond the existing state of the art.

Third, the proposal also has little if anything to do with levels of abstraction, complexity or subtlety of thought, or intricacy of the concepts used in theorizing. As I have indicated previously, these kinds of matters are not the issue. The proposal to use thought experiments is not a proposal to confine theorizing to concrete or superficial thinking; it is silent on that matter. There is nothing intrinsic to thought experiments that would exclude abstract, or subtle, or complex thought. The point is to ensure relevance; theorizing should proceed at the particular complexity or depth needed for a given situation. The main purpose of the thought experiment is to keep the clinically pragmatic focus prominently in view, while using a vehicle that is properly matched to the needs at hand.

A CRITICAL REVIEW OF PAST PROPOSALS IN PSYCHOANALYSIS

On the basis of Graves's conceptual framework I have proposed that clinical theorizing be viewed as located at a separate cognitive level. That basic *focal* move invited a corresponding move with respect to *formalisms:* For the reasons advanced in the critical analyses of Chapters 2 through 4, the use of a non-state-process formalism seems to be indicated.

It may appear that what I am proposing is merely a warmed over version of past suggestions in psychoanalysis pertaining both to clinical focus and narrative discourse. For that reason, I should now like critically to review some of the more prominent and representative of these proposals, thereby to distinguish them from my own.

Linguistic Proposals

The suggestion to use non-state-formalistic language as a vehicle for psychoanalytic theorizing might very well strike the reader as anticlimactic and old hat. After all, have not psychoanalysts been exploring the "tool" of language for a very long time? And proposing to "reformulate" psychoanalytic theoretical discourse? Let us see now how some of these past proposals bear on the present discussion. The reformulation attempts will be considered in terms of four broad categories.

Antireductionism. One category contains those proposals whose aim is to get away from mechanistic, reductionist conceptions of language (and of its subject matter). In preceding chapters, I alluded to these and to an earlier paper (1978) in which I examined three representative examples. It was, and remains, my contention that these proposals in fact unwittingly return us to those very state process formalisms from which they sought to escape. In my view, they were prone to this kind of error because their proponents did not seem to recognize the presence and the consequences of state space conceptions.

I am not saying that it is absolutely necessary to recognize state process issues explicitly in order to avoid using, or returning to, a state process approach. Hexter, for instance, is an example (but a rare one) of a theorist who has managed consistently to stay away from state process methodologies even though he seems unaware of the formal frameworks discussed in Chapters 3 and 4. So is Schumacher, and, as we saw earlier, so was Freud. Apparently, well-functioning professional intuition can steer one away from unwitting returns to state process representations (but see the last sections in Chapter 7).

Hermeneutics. The second group are hermeneutic proposals. Thoma and Kachele (1975) define hermeneutics as "the science of interpretation according to which interpretation is based on a previous comprehension of the complete meaning of what is to be interpreted and proceeds to the exploration of presumed situational contexts" (p. 51). Past efforts have been discussed by Rosen (1974, pp. 201–202), Friedman (1976, pp. 260–263), and Thoma and Kachele (1975, pp. 51–75), among others. Hermeneutic approaches are usually applied to clinical material—dreams, free associations, and so on.

The usual hermeneutic assumption is that the material is opaque, in need of translation. In past proposals, the principal, if not the exclusive, function of hermeneutics has been to serve as a psychoanalytic "technology of interpretation" (Thoma and Kachele, 1975, p. 51). Hermeneutics has been conceptualized as a rather formal methodology that enables one to decode a coded message, a method of translation from one string of symbols to another.

As I indicated earlier, this current mainstream view has been criticized by those writers (Gadamer, in particular) whose approaches I have been recommending. It runs directly counter to the view that language is usually transparent, is an integral part of the life world, is not a formal-logical system of "strings" to be translated from one language to another, is something very different from a tool that is separate from the user and life world.

I have also mentioned that the hermeneutic approach typically is applied to *clinical* material; the concerns about language do not pertain to theoretical discourse (see, for example, the discussion of Habermas's work below). Thus, not only are there formal differences between this version of hermeneutics and the approaches I have been advancing, there are focal differences as well.

The psychoanalytic narrative. In the third group of past proposals are those concerning what is sometimes referred to as the "psychoanalytic narrative" (see Thoma and Kachele's review, 1975, pp. 90–101), or as "natural discourse at the commonsense level" (McIntosh, 1979, p. 410).

Sherwood (1969), whose work has already been mentioned with reference to the issue of explanation, has devoted a considerable portion of his book to matters pertaining to narrative discourse (see especially pp. 188–191, 220–257). I shall comment on past discussions concerning the psychoanalytic narrative in terms of his prototypical views and proposals.

As far as formal-logical issues are concerned, Sherwood, and others who discuss these matters, do not seem able to make clear cognitive distinctions between Cartesian and non-Cartesian conceptions of discourse. Although Sherwood's discussions center on the problematic relationship between narrative and logical, hypothetico-deductive frameworks, he makes little progress in distinguishing them. On the one hand, he clearly recognizes the limitations of logical methodology; he all but rejects formal logic as the tool for psychoanalytic explanation, as we have seen in the quotations presented earlier. On the other hand, he also rejects unorthodox alternatives that do not conform to standard scientific norms: "Let us immediately clear up a possible confusion concerning a criticism which would argue that what we are suggesting by the concept of narrative is somehow very different from what should be a truly scientific approach to behavior" (p. 191). His conception of narrative seems to be predicated on those same ingredients that characterize the usual scientific conception of language. There is, for example, the concern with the "meaning" and referents of excised propositions or terms, their "conceptual clarity" (pp. 204, 247, 253). There is also a continued focus on logical analysis, in spite of his remarks about the shortcomings of logic in terms of explanatory power. The truth values of propositions, their validity and self-consistency, and similar signs of orthodox formal analysis are very much in view.

If Sherwood is not at all clear about how to differentiate between his proposed alternative, the "psychoanalytic narrative," and standard forms of scientific explanatory discourse, I suggest that is so because he does not recognize and therefore does not use adequate conceptual tools in his analyses. That is where the formal notions about state processes—their use as decision tools, and so on—come into the picture. Analyses conducted in terms of state process issues should add considerable conceptual clarity to the subject matter of the psychoanalytic narrative. Although we have seen with Hexter's work that these kinds of analyses are not indispensable, it seems to me that one dispenses with them only at the risk of encountering the very sorts of problems I have identified in Sherwood's study.

Parenthetically, one source of Sherwood's difficulties might be called metalogical problems with his argument. In general, he rejects what he calls the "thesis of the separate domain" (Chapter 5; see also 1973, p. 359), the view that some features other than normal science practices and methodologies are needed in behavioral disciplines; specifically, he rejects any but formal discourse. The problem arises, as I see it, when he bases his arguments on formal logic (e.g., pp. 37–68, 125–184). Does that not raise an obvious difficulty? If logic is derivative, parasitic on the life world, then it would seem that to dismiss the thesis of separate domain by arguments predicated on logical formal analysis is an inherently and fatally circular procedure. One rejects life world approaches and perspectives by tools that depend on that ontologically prior domain. The argument invokes the Cheshire cat phenomenon.

I believe that these paradoxical difficulties reflect Sherwood's lack of appreciation of the formal nature of the problems with which he is struggling. He does not seem to be sufficiently aware of the difficulties and characteristics that *any* state process formalism will automatically and necessarily introduce. If he did, he would recognize the questionable nature of applying logical analyses to prelogical (life world) issues.

I have already discussed elsewhere (1978) the relationship of Schafer's (1976) action language to state process formalisms. Here, I shall only restate my conclusion that Schafer's approaches continue to operate within a formalized framework (although the formalization is masked). He is quite clear about his position toward ordinary language. While he advocates a use of language that to him seems "a return to Freud with fresh eyes" (1983, p. 273), he also makes it quite clear that he is against either "ordinary or common-sense locutions . . . [or] impressionistic, idiosyncratic, quasi-poetic rhetoric" (1978, p. 5). That would "not serve for systematic discourse. The reason . . . [these kinds of ordinary usage] will not serve is that . . . [they] follow tacit, elusive, and incompatible rules of every kind" (p. 5). He speaks approvingly of the "high degree of coherence" made possible by a mechanistic system such as metapsychology, noting that "a new language for psychoanalysis must do the same" (p. 6). I submit that the differences, in spirit as well as in specific practices, between his conception of theoretical discourse and the conception presented here are major.

Overzealous translators of Freud. The fourth and last category encompasses Freud's use of language, a matter on which I have already touched earlier. As we saw, recent studies show that in the original German Freud very frequently used discourse to theorize in a life world way that avoided implication of state process notions. It is beginning to look very much as though the formalistic aspects of the discourse were principally, and erroneously, introduced by overzealous translators, Strachey in particular.

The majority of theoreticians still continue to rely on the translated, formalized version:

> Freud used two primary narrative structures. . . . One . . . begins with the infant and the young child as a beast, otherwise known as the id, and ends with the beast domesticated. . . . Freud's other primary narrative structure is based on Newtonian physics as transmitted through the physiological and neuroanatomical laboratories in the nineteenth century. This account presents psychoanalysis as the study of the mind viewed as a machine. . . [Schafer, 1983, p. 213].

Thus, even though Freud's original use of narrative apparently avoided the practices that characterize state process formalisms, and even though it seems to have exhibited the salient characteristics of

Psychoanalytic Theory and Clinical Relevance   141

processive discourse, that is not how his theorizing is viewed by the majority of contemporary theorizers. In the mainstream view, Freud's narrative remains closely tied to metapsychological perspectives that include various mechanisms, psychological structures, or other spatio-temporal models; his process narrative has been turned into state process discourse; theoreticians generally lament, as unscientific, those instances when the absence of Freud's formalistic stance is still visible in the English versions.

Proposals for "Clinically Useful" Theories

The preceding discussions were intended to reveal the similarities and differences between past proposals pertaining to the use of theoretical discourse in psychoanalysis and those presented here. The emphasis was on formal issues. Next I shall present a view of proposals whose thrust is pragmatic, that is, proposals that stress issues pertaining to use of theory.

In earlier chapters, especially in Chapters 2 and 5, I sought to demonstrate that in a particular sense the great bulk of psychoanalytic theorizing has always followed the pure knowledge medical paradigm; that in itself implied a certain lack of clinical relevance. Still, so much theorizing in the literature is usually seen as clinically relevant that further clarification is in order.

The position I have been advocating is that it is no easy matter to specify what clinical relevance means. I have suggested that just because one may be theorizing *about* therapy (e.g., about transference, resistance, interpretation) does not automatically guarantee that the theorizing is clinically relevant. That may seem like a paradoxical claim, and I shall seek to remove the paradox by discussing examples provided by prominent theorizers whose work is usually considered to be clinically relevant.

It is difficult to summarize the differences to which I am referring in terms of simple labels, but perhaps the following all too crude ones will point the way. I shall try to show that one can be theorizing *about* therapy, and yet fail to theorize *for* therapy. By theorizing "for" therapy, I mean theorizing that has the capacity, the potential, to produce inferences that can move technique forward in significant ways. I trust the following discussion will show how that differs from theorizing "about" therapy.

Jurgen Habermas. Habermas is considered to be a theorist who pays a great deal of attention to the connections between theory and practice. Why, then, would I claim that his work fails to qualify fully as theorizing "for" therapy?

One set of shortcomings pertains to formal matters. Habermas does not address the issues concerning representational deficiencies displayed by state process formalisms. When he does address linguistic issues, his interest centers primarily on the verbal material produced by the patient in the clinical situation. For example, some of his principal linguistic concerns are with the opacity of the clinical verbal material, "self-misunderstandings," unwitting distortions, or hermeneutic translation. Thus, he does not attend to the principal linguistic concerns addressed in this monograph: the limitations of state process theoretical discourse, and the usefulness of transparent life world language for theoretical discourse.

Some other formal issues also receive a treatment that differs from the approaches developed here. For example, Habermas emphasizes conventional formal/methodological concerns—e.g., the place of "truth," validation, confirmation, or testing of interpretations; the role of logic and structure in hermeneutic translation; the conventional hierarchical layering of psychoanalytic theory (Thoma and Kachele, 1975, pp. 76–88; Keat, 1981, Chapter 5).

I might add that some of Habermas's criticisms of the formal aspects of positivism do seem close to, and congenial with, the criticisms I presented in Chapters 3 and 4. His objections to scientism, his critique of presumably presuppositionless scientific objectivity, his call for a special methodology to deal with the internal, subjective domain, his concern with meaning, and his ideas about the undesirable constitutive consequences that follow from one's adhering to traditional scientific norms and procedures (see Keat, 1981, Chapter 1) all seem quite compatible with criticisms of state process practices that I have presented.

Let us now consider the pragmatic foci of his theorizing. His pragmatism posits norms that define what the practical consequences of successful therapy ought to be, but he does not emphasize technical issues, does not theorize with an eye to advancing therapeutic effectiveness. It seems that his work is pragmatic in the particular sense that he is concerned with the *kinds* of results that therapy achieves; his pragmatism pertains primarily to desired goals (e.g., emancipation, autonomy) and to social, moral, and political normative values such as class distinction, economic oppression and exploitation, and freedom versus repression.

As far as clinical technique itself goes, Habermas apparently assumes that adequate technique is already available. "Therapeutic" is seen as equivalent to "overcoming the power of the unconscious" by

Psychoanalytic Theory and Clinical Relevance 143

self-reflection and by hermeneutics (Keat, 1981, p. 107; see Chapters 4 and 5). In terms of my shorthand labels, I would say that his is a theory of therapy; he already "knows how to do it." It is not a theory for therapy. It is not focused on moving technique forward, on, for example, developing clinical methodologies that would be significantly different from the standard mainstream practices. Thus, even though he is concerned with pragmatic issues, with relationships between theory and practice, Habermas's is not a clinically pragmatic focus, in the sense in which I use the term.

Helmuth Kaiser. Even though Kaiser's work does not seem to be the subject of much current attention in the literature, I mention him here because he is one analyst who seems to have made a serious attempt to maintain a clinical orientation in his theorizing. He meticulously chronicles the evolution of his thought, and in doing so demonstrates an approach that is entirely in the service of developing an "effective psychotherapy." He emphasizes that his theorizing is guided by constantly asking himself, "How will all this thinking and theorizing affect my principles of psychotherapy?" (1965, p. 137).

Although Kaiser's writings have had some impact (see Paul, 1973, 1978), it seems to have been a rather minor one. Perhaps one reason is the relative simplicity of his "theoretical armamentarium"; the theoretical tools and conceptual ingredients that Kaiser developed may not be sufficiently formal, "scientific," and abstract to attract many theoreticians. He did not construct intricate models or apparatuses. Another possible reason for his lack of impact is a certain ad hoc quality in his thinking. He seems to have proceeded largely on the basis of unstructured exploration, by intuitive trial and error, in haphazard fashion; there do not seem to have been unifying guiding principles that served his search for clinical effectiveness and relevance. At any rate, except for Paul's work, there does not appear to be an evolving, cumulative body of theorizing based on the recommendations Kaiser developed.

I shall now return to some of the major clinical theorizers whose work I considered earlier, particularly in Chapter 2: George Klein, Schafer, Gedo, Kernberg, and Kohut.

George Klein. One proposal for reformulation that has received a good deal of attention is George Klein's. His paper "Two Theories or One?" (1973) has been viewed as a reconstruction proposal with a radically clinical focus (Yankelovich and Barrett, 1970, pp. 169–177; Gill, 1973). I have already referred to it in the context of formal issues; there I indicated that it unwittingly retains a state process underpinning and therefore remains vulnerable to all the problems that such an underpinning entails. What about pragmatic issues, its focus?

There are, it seems to me, two major characteristics of Klein's pragmatic focus. First, there is his emphasis on the ingredients of psychoanalytic theory. Klein (1973) proposes to replace a theory of mechanisms—apparatuses, forces, structures, drives, energies—with a theory of meanings, purposes, directions, and aims of behavior, focusing not "on the 'how', but on the 'why'. . ." (p. 114). Thus, for Klein, "clinical theory" means a "theory framed in terms of meaning," which is contrasted with that part of psychoanalytic theory which presumably lacks clinical relevance: the "second theory," metapsychology, the "theory supposedly explaining" the clinical theory (1976, p. xiii).

The second characteristic is his reliance on the pure knowledge medical paradigm. Within the "first theory" (the "clinical" portion of psychoanalytic theory), any theorizing about clinical phenomena is deemed legitimate: "The analytic situation produces coherent, perceivable regularities, which need not have any immediate or distant relevance to therapeutic intent, yet which are legitimate for study and may even have basic importance for psychoanalytic theory. . ." (1973, p. 125). He shares the paradigm's characteristic concerns with general understanding of pathological phenomena, empirical truth, systematic rigor, definition of terms, lawfulness of data, valid experimental procedures, and operationalization of experience-remote concepts (e.g., 1973, pp. 113, 120, 123–126, 128). He shows the usual interest in the matter of a general psychology (1976, Chapter 1). Nowhere are focal distinctions such as those I pointed out in Chapter 5 (e.g., between theorizing about pathology and theorizing consequentially about therapy) even mentioned.

Thus, even though he theorizes *about* therapy, about some of its phenomena, regularities, and so on, Klein's approach remains very much within the pure knowledge medical paradigm. His focus is not specifically and explicitly on theorizing designed to advance clinical technique and effectiveness. I doubt that he would have supported the pragmatic proposals I have introduced here; I believe he would have rejected, for example, the application of the thought-experiment criterion to theoretical questions, on the ground that it might impede advances in pure knowledge.

Roy Schafer. Another major proposal for psychoanalytic reconstruction is represented by Schafer's (1976) action language theory. I have already discussed formal aspects of his proposal in different contexts.

Two points can be made about the focal aspects of Schafer's approach. First, it seeks to be a general methodology. Action is "human activity of every sort" (1983, p. 83), and action language therefore is a language about psychological actions in general (1978, pp. 187–199). His theoretical vehicle is developed within a broad context rather than, as I have been advocating, within a single clinical cognitive level. As Graves suggests in his approach to partial coordination between levels, this difference between Schafer's and my notion does not in itself mean that his general vehicle could not serve within that one specific cognitive level, nor that the vehicle I propose could not serve outside its original level. The point here is that in Schafer's theorizing there does not seem to be the kind of principal clinical focus I have advocated, and sought to formalize by means of a separate cognitive level.

My second point is that Schafer is not seeking to develop a new theory, let alone a new clinical theory: "Action language is not a set of empirical psychoanalytic propositions; it is a strategy for stating these propositions clearly and parsimoniously" (1978, p. 185). In terms of Graves's analyses, his theorizing qualifies more as an instance of "disinterpretation" followed by "reinterpretation" than as theorizing that could generate fundamental technical or methodological improvements in clinical practice. It is designed to purge theorizing of fallacies and other epistemological sins—reification, misplaced location, substitution of a mechanism for a responsible actor, inappropriate separation of the "person" into various parts (but see Kovel's [1978] criticisms). Schafer proposes to formalize and generalize "the extensive and varied content of writings with which psychoanalysts are well acquainted" (1978, p. 185), but he is not calling that content into question. He apparently believes that the essentials of psychoanalysis can now be specified. For example, its "principal business" is to interpret and reinterpret in a certain way (1978, p. 6); to clarify and make sense of what the patient is doing "in terms of unconsciously defined danger situations" (1983, p. 112); to follow a "set of rules for interpreting human action along certain lines in a certain context" (1978, p. 199). Thus, while in a limited sense his theorizing does remain open ("Many of these rules [for interpretation] are still to be worked out" [1978, p. 199]), his approach suggests that the essentials of therapy are already established, that there is no need to search for any fundamentally new approaches.

For these reasons, I do not view Schafer's action language as geared to relevant theorizing, that is, theorizing that would enable one to draw major new inferences about technique. His notable contributions to clinical practices (e.g., 1983) fail to demonstrate a potential for moving therapeutic practice forward in significantly new ways. His writings are essentially clarifications of the standard mainstream position, as well as attempts to remedy various questionable scientific practices in psychoanalysis. (For other analyses and criticisms of Schafer's proposals, see Wallerstein, 1976, pp. 139-140; Kovel, 1978; Spiro, 1979).

John Gedo. Gedo's explicit goal is "to articulate a new clinical theory for psychoanalysis" (1979, p. xi). Earlier we saw that he offers a correlational scheme that links five developmental modes with five corresponding therapeutic modalities.

Gedo presents his various principles as axioms (e.g., pp. 18-25), basic hypotheses justified on the basis of commonsense reasonableness and an appeal to empirical findings. Examples are that the actual curative step in modes I-III is the reduction or elimination of parameters (p. 22); that one cannot afford to neglect any modes—all antecedent difficulties must be dealt with (p. 21); that therapy must raise unrecognized psychobiological needs into awareness (p. 23); or that interpretation is "the modality devised for the handling of unconscious conflicts [mode IV]" (p. 25). Once again, we have a theory *of* therapy, in the sense that as presented it is a near-finished product that seems to have little room for further evolution, other than in relatively minor ways. The hypotheses specify pathology, therapeutic action, and technique. Thus, within Gedo's proposed scheme, all that seems possible is to fill in a gap here, amplify a point there.

I might also note in passing that he retains, more or less, the standard views concerning the hierarchical structure and characteristics of psychoanalytic theory (see my earlier remarks in Chapter 2).

Otto Kernberg. Kernberg's theorizing falls well within the pure knowledge medical paradigm. As suggested in Chapter 2, a major focus of Kernberg's work is the delineation of a particular class of pathology, a delineation set within a comprehensive nosological-diagnostic scheme. The tacit assumption seems to be the usual one, that understanding pathology will profit therapy. The "overkill" phenomenon predominates. For example, a paper whose title refers to "implications for technique" (1979) has a good deal more to say about the relevance of object relations theory to pathology and nosology (pp. 207-211, 218-222) than about technique (although Kernberg does refer the reader to earlier works).

In Chapter 2, I also illustrated Kernberg's correlational approach to clinical theorizing. Therapy rules, apparently derived from clinical experience, intuition, and trial and error, are correlated with various clinical events or phenomena: With *this* manifestation (e.g., splitting, aggressive envy, transference manifestation) do *that* (e.g., be technically neutral, confront, attend to the negative transference phenomena). It is hard to see how this approach could lead to improved clinical techniques. Indeed, Kernberg does not claim that his theorizing has either the capacity or the aim to generate a basically different technique:

> It must be stressed that, with this reformulation of aspects of the theory of psychoanalytic technique, basic psychoanalytic technique itself does not change, but, in addition to expanding its boundaries, is enriched in daily practice [1979, p. 218].

Heinz Kohut. Kohut's is essentially a correlational theory of therapy. As outlined in Chapter 2, this kind of theory correlates two pairs (child development and early environment; adult pathology and therapeutic needs), relying on informal translations (from child to adult pathology; from early environment to the therapeutic environment). I have already discussed the relationships between these kinds of correlational theories and the pure knowledge medical paradigm. The dominant focus is on pathology, on particular kinds of transference phenomena and correlated recommendations to the therapist (see Chapter 2).

In the next chapter, when I attempt further to specify the differences between theories "of" therapy and theories "for" therapy, I shall return briefly to Kohut's work in the context of that discussion. For the moment, I wish to point out that although Kohut's work is seen (and criticized) in some quarters as a major modification of traditional theorizing, he himself maintains that, especially as far as technique is concerned, he hews to the traditional approaches, although the self-psychology-oriented therapist does tend to be more relaxed, and to have an expanded scope available for his observations (1984, pp. 104–108, 172): "Self psychology does not differ from traditional psychoanalysis in its characterization of what is going on between analyst and patient that eventuates in a cure" (p. 104).

Summary of Findings

Some general conclusions about formal and focal matters can be drawn from the preceding representative examples of psychoanalytic theorizing. First, the formal issues that I discussed in Chapter 3 and 4 usually are addressed inadequately, if at all. State process underpinnings are retained, at least tacitly. Formalization and rigor remain ideals. Even Schafer, the theoretician who seems most explicitly to be searching for linguistic vehicles that will avoid inappropriate mechanistic practices, rejects a life world approach to psychoanalytic discourse in favor of a formalized action language. Other traditional formal characteristics are very much in view. For example, the usual hierarchical assumptions tend to be perpetuated; by and large, theorizers do not treat the "levels" issues in any but the orthodox ways.

Second, the focal characteristics inherent in the pure knowledge medical paradigm are retained. There is the familiar focus and dominant emphasis on psychopathology, and the tacit assumption that increases in pure knowledge will eventually move therapeutic technique forward.

The third and perhaps most important general feature is that, on the whole, alternative approaches and theories are presented as near-finished constructions. This seems to be true whether a given proposal is a significant extension of standard theory or a disinterpretation/reinterpretation. These almost completed conceptions (e.g., Schafer's, Kernberg's, Gedo's, and, with some qualifications to be discussed in Chapter 7, Kohut's) comprise a theory of pathology, a theory of therapeutic action, and specific technical recommendations. Each of these three ingredients is presented in a nearly closed version; that is, each is so specifically and highly developed that further significant developments seem to be unattainable.

Together, all these features contribute to what I have called the lack of clinical relevance of the usual psychoanalytic theorizing. When a given theory is a theory *of*, rather than a theory *for* therapy, all that followers of that school can do, it seems, is dot the i's and cross the t's. The principal constituents—hypotheses about therapeutic action, pathology, and technique—are presented in final form. I submit that that is why Freud's and subsequent theorizing about therapy has failed to move technique significantly forward, once the theory had been promulgated. Each new set of hypotheses attracts attention and followers, and then stagnates while controversies about details occupy center stage.

What, then, would distinguish a theory "for" therapy from a theory "of" therapy? Let me tentatively offer several general observations. The language of a clinically pragmatic theory must have the required representational capacity. To safeguard against the inadvertent use of state process formalisms, a policy concerning formalisms should be spelled out. I have attempted to do that in the early part of this chapter, in my discussions of the process narrative.

Focal characteristics ought to follow the general recommendations developed in the preceding sections about the role of pragmatic considerations. The pure knowledge medical paradigm should be set aside, replaced by the clinically pragmatic approaches outlined earlier. Focal policies should work together with an adequate formalism to eschew pointless scientism, reject vacous, misguided "pure" theorizing, and identify consequential issues.

A final, and in my view, a most important consideration concerns the matter of generative principles. The nearly complete clinical theories I have discussed are closed theories primarily because they lack those kinds of principles. From the standpoint of a psychoanalytic theory that seeks to advance technique in significant ways, the principles of the prototypical examples that I have presented are static: Do this, don't do that. In my view, it is absolutely vital, if a discipline is to move forward significantly, that such generative principles be developed. Examples from physics will illustrate what I mean.

Hoffmann (1983) shows conclusively that three apparently simple principles played a key generative role in Einstein's theorizing about relativity. For special relativity, there were two: the equivalence of all inertial systems, and the constancy of the velocity of light in these systems. For general relativity, the major generative principle was the equivalence of gravitation and accelerated motion. Working together, these principles had an explosive impact on theorizing. They not only led to the mathematical formulations of relativity theory, but also to drastically new empirical implications and findings (e.g., the bending of light in gravitational fields, time dilation).

I am proposing here that a theory "for" therapy be similarly grounded in some set of generative principles. These principles, rather than the prescriptions contained in a fully formed theory "of" therapy, could provide the dynamics that would move practice forward in nontrivial ways. The focus of such principles would be on how to advance therapeutic technique, on how to theorize *about* therapy in ways that would lead to an evolution of technique, in contrast to the usual proposals for a clinical theory. To develop a clinically pragmatic theory, one needs to do more than offer yet another closed way of conceptualizing and doing therapy. I shall attempt to sketch such an approach in the next chapter.

Some Possible Objections

My suggestions to reject—or at least for the time being set aside—state process frameworks and the practices subsumed under the pure knowledge medical paradigm invite certain obvious objections. I shall consider three of these now.

But is it psychoanalysis? Unorthodox approaches tend to be open to the charge that they fall outside psychoanalysis (see, for example, Kovel's [1974, 1978] remarks concerning Erikson's and Schafer's work). That charge naturally implies that there are some consensually validated criteria that would allow one to evaluate a given proposal to see whether it did or did not fall within the domain of psychoanalysis.

Unfortunately, that is not the case. There seem to be no clear, uncontroversial decision rules that can be applied. To some extent, the criteria that define what analysis "is" differ among analysts. Schafer (1983) speaking of "the modern Freudian analyst," cautions "that there is considerable dispute among those who do their work under this banner as to what is modern, what is Freudian, and what is analysis" (p. 240).

For Matte Blanco (1975), the "most distinctive characteristics" of psychoanalytic theory are those of "the system unconscious" (p. 9). According to him, to the extent that the focus on that system has been diffused—say, by structural or other approaches that theorize "in terms of material space and energy" (state process formalisms?)—psychoanalysis "has wandered away from itself" (p. 10). For Guntrip (1961), the essential ideas are "repression, resistance, transference, dreams as a revelation of the unconscious, the centrality of the Oedipus problem in neurosis, and the 'super-ego' " (pp. 57–58). Lacan (1968) lists four elements: the unconscious, repetition, transference, and drive. Glover's (1955) essentials include transference, analytic or transference neurosis, and resistance (p. 367; see also Fenichel's consonant views, 1941, p. 24).

Kovel (1978) emphasizes the repressed unconscious, the "foundation-stone of psychoanalytic theory" (p. 46), which in his view is intimately tied to the "problemacity of the idea of a person" (pp. 34–41). Ultimately, the repressed unconscious finds its "nuclear formulation" in terms of "a proposition built of heteronomous elements: *words* and *things*" (p. 46). As far as therapy itself is concerned,

> the essential feature of the analytic situation is its moment of emptiness. It is a caesura in the ordinary flow of existence, a kind of space or rather, an occurrence in which the customary becomes momentarily transparent. At that moment, something deeper is manifested, as when we can see the bottom of the sea while the surface waves are stilled. Freud called the process regression. . . . Whatever is grossly called analytic technique consists of the fostering of such moments of regression [1981, p. 69].

In Kohut's (1977) view, "psychoanalysis is a psychology of complex mental states which, with the aid of the persevering empathic-introspective immersion of the observer into the inner life of man, gathers its data in order to explain them" (p. 302; see also 1984, pp. 162–169).

Others (e.g., Loevinger, 1966; Yankelovich and Barrett, 1970, pp. 277–448; Levenson, 1972) identify yet other defining elements. Plainly, the question of what psychoanalysis "is" does not have an agreed-upon answer. For that reason, and also because I do not see anything in my proposals that would obviously place them outside psychoanalysis, I suggest that the question ought not be taken as a serious basis for objection to my argument.

But is it science? The suggestion to give up, or at least set aside for now, both state process frameworks and the pure knowledge medical paradigm might be interpreted as a suggestion to give up science and clinical research. I have already presented numerous examples of Bohm's thought with regard to physics that seem quite consonant with much of what I have been proposing, yet clearly fall within the general domain of science. Let us briefly consider how others have dealt with this issue.

Hexter (1971) reports that a professor of engineering challenged him during a lecture to show that historians could make predictions. He responded by making several predictions about the professor's own activities. The professor's response

> was peculiar but instructive. He might have faulted my predictions on two grounds. He might have said they were wrong. The only thing that barred that course to him was his evident belief that they were right. His second line might have been that one did not have to be a historian to make that sort of prediction. He did not take that line either. What he did was say, "Do you call *that* predicting the future?" and smiled at me contemptuously and triumphantly [pp. 143–144; see also pp. 272–273].

Weizenbaum (1976) looks at these issues in terms of the distinction between rationality and scientific methodological orthodoxy. He notes that being rational can mean

> something other than the mere application of science and technology . . . [that] it need not automatically and by implication [be] equated to computability and to logicality. The alternative to this kind of rationality . . . is not mindlessness. It is reason restored to human dignity, to authenticity. . . . Instrumental reason has made out of words a fetish surrounded by black magic. And only the magicians have the rights of the initiated. Only they can say what words mean. . . . In fact, I *am* arguing for rationality. But I argue that rationality may not be separated from intuition and feeling. I argue for the rational use

of science and technology, not for its mystification, let alone for its abandonment [pp. 255–256].

It has been said that doing science is simply thinking clearly and hard about one's subject. That seems as good a definition as any to me. As long as one does not resort to flagrant mysticism, *ad hominem* argument, or other obviously antirational practices, one remains within a realm that can reasonably be called scientific, in the broad sense. There seems to be decreasing support for the once highly popular "unity of science" position. Graves (1971) rejects this notion, preferring, as he puts it, to think of "science" ("the totality of the various special sciences") as "knowledge in general" or "Science with a capital S":

> Unlike physics, biology, etc. this "Science" cannot be characterized in terms of its subject matter or degree of abstraction. Therefore it would have to be defined in terms of method or logical structure, independent of content. What I am claiming, on the other hand, is that there is no such thing as "science," except as a collective name for "the sciences" [p. 32].

Similarly, Jaynes (1966), writing about the behavioral disciplines, "scorns"

> the unity of science. My impulse is a disturbed feeling that, as science folds back on itself and comes to be scientifically studied, it is being caricatured into a conformity which is nonsense, into a neglect of its variety which is psychotic, into a nagging and insistent attention to its cross-discipline similarities which are of trivial importance [p. 94].

I submit that any approach that is matched to the needs of its domain, that is public, and that explains that which needs to be explained in an intelligible manner should qualify as scientific (see Graves, 1971, pp. 6, 7, 13, 32). I am not aware that anything I have put forward runs counter to the spirit of that view of science.

But is it practical? Strangely enough, while pragmatic approaches in general have been criticized for being antiscientific, for being merely opportunistic and simplistically oriented toward "what works," the proposals I have been developing have been criticized by some as "too abstract, too theoretical."

Judging from this and other similar experiences, it seems to me that all too frequently we discuss the issues of theory and practice in terms of erroneously posed polarities. One is given the choice between the Scylla of impulsive, action-oriented, "let's do something" antitheoretical attitudes and the Charybdis of sterile, meaningless, irrelevant, overintellectualized obsessing that often passes for "theorizing." It should be clear by now that I am advocating neither; rather, I am for the kind of integration of praxis and theorizing proposed by those workers (e.g., Bohm and Rorty) whose approaches I have referred to so frequently in this monograph.

The basic outline of my argument has now been presented. I have put forward general principles, formal as well as focal, that should guide the search for a clinically relevant theory. I believe that these general suggestions (e.g., the various uses of state process analysis, the conception of non-Cartesian theoretical discourse, the idea of a separate cognitive clinical level, the substitution of a clinically pragmatic for a pure knowledge medical paradigm) are useful in themselves. There may be some merit, however, in cautiously exploring some specific possible implications of the views I have presented. That is the goal of the final chapter.

SEVEN

Speculations and Generalizations

> But first might it not be better to abide with the questionable character of our modern situation a little longer, a little more persistently and a little more submissively, before we rush off into one or another of all the proposed ideologies of salvation? Let us at least grasp the question before we invent our answers.
> —William Barrett, Time of Need

> What is the point of a psychology that is confused about the fundamental fact of human personality, which is consciousness itself? It will only end by assimilating itself clumsily to an imitation of what goes on in the physical sciences. Its researches go off in all directions but lack a unifying center.
> —William Barrett, The Illusion of Technique

> The arrangement does not force itself upon us irresistibly; it comes from ourselves; what we have done we can undo.
> —Henri Bergson, The Creative Mind

ABOUT CONSTRUCTING SOLUTIONS

Systematizing versus Edifying Traditions

In his far-ranging and fundamental critique of epistemology, Rorty (1979) contrasts two classes of theoretical efforts: "therapeutic rather than constructive, edifying rather than systematic," revolutionary rather than within "normal" practices (p. 5). He is distinguishing between those mainstream works on the one hand which primarily continue along, and systematically add to, an established tradition, and those radical critical analyses on the other hand which look at the status quo in new ways, but do not necessarily offer alternative "systems" or prescriptions. His own book is an analysis and radical extension of the "anti-Cartesian and anti-Kantian revolution" (p. 7), and falls largely within the edifying rather than the systematizing tradition. (Rorty carefully notes, though, that a therapeutic, edifying, revolutionary work always needs some tradition against which its critical analyses can be applied [p. 365].) Although I have made some suggestions and recommendations in the preceding chapter, and will make further ones in this final chapter, I view the monograph as a whole as falling largely within the edifying tradition. I have mainly presented considerable nontraditional criticism, both formal and focal, that by its very nature requires assimilation and critical examination.

At the same time, of course, the common response to an extended critique seems to be a challenge to produce alternatives to the criticized approaches. And yet, even if I could produce a full-blown theory at this point, I would have great reservations about doing so; it is so easy to present yet another closed system, or, at least, a system that is closed enough to preclude significant further development within that system. Therefore, before "rushing off into one or another of all the proposed ideologies of salvation," as Barrett puts it, let us briefly review, as a possible antidote, the virtues of deliberation and questioning.

The Value of Generative Questions

A major contribution of these kinds of "therapeutic" enterprises is the formulation of generative questions:

> Now, in scientific inquiries, a crucial step is to ask the right question. Indeed, each question contains presuppositions, largely implicit. If these presuppositions are wrong or confused, then the question itself is wrong, in the sense that to try to answer it has no meaning. One has thus *to inquire into the appropriateness of the question.* In fact, truly original discoveries in science and in other fields have generally involved such inquiry into old questions, leading to a perception of their inappropriateness, and in this way allowing for the putting forth of new questions. To do this is often very difficult, as these presuppositions tend to be hidden deep in the structure of our thought [Bohm, 1976, p. 63].

In my view, the value of that questioning function is widely underestimated. Axelrod (1979) shows by case studies of major creative accomplishments the essential role that questioning of commonly held assumptions plays in enabling a worker to move beyond "what everybody knows to be true." He demonstrates that it is this selective questioning of the obvious that is the most difficult aspect of the creative process. One difficulty is that it will not do to question just any currently accepted views; creativity, well-functioning intuition, and perhaps luck enter into the process of choosing. The same point is made by Hoffmann (1983) in his book about Einstein's development of relativity theory; according to Einstein, by far the most difficult part was the formulation of the right questions—for example, to question the notion of simultaneity during a scientific age when everybody "knew," with utter certainty, what it meant to say that events occurred simultaneously. Well-chosen questions are likely to entail productive avenues of investigation and, eventually, useful answers as well.

Thus, the superficial assumption that answers matter more than questions is probably quite wrong. Yet that assumption prevails, bringing with it the usual rush to produce answers, and the usual impatience with questions that are posed without accompanying solutions.

Incidentally, the arena in which these misguided views probably do the most damage is in politics. One can see the widespread demand for answers to national and international problems, when most of the time, in my opinion, we do not even know what the actual central questions and issues are.

Looking before Leaping

When one begins to acknowledge the intrinsic value of generative questions, one automatically tends to look before one leaps. That procedure is recommended by some of the thinkers whose work we have been considering, by Barrett, for example, in one of the epigraphs to this chapter.

Hexter (1971) advises historians to this effect: "Before rushing in to seek explanation, carefully examine the question that the explanation is supposed to answer" (p. 33). David Bakan introduces the notion of idolatry into the discussion: "Idolatry is the *loss of the sense of search*, of the sense of freshness of experience. It is the overquick *fixing upon any method or device or concept*" (Braginsky and Braginsky, 1974, pp. 28–29).

In physics, Bohm's "emphasis is on the methodology of the self-deconditioning process, not on the promised land which might lie at

Psychoanalytic Theory and Clinical Relevance

the end of it" (Weber, 1982, p. 39). That is, at this stage of theorizing in physics, Bohm is more interested in achieving progress by shedding old frameworks than by prematurely constructing new ones: When we ask for a solution to some particular problem,

> it is presupposed that while we begin not knowing the answer, our minds are nevertheless clear enough to discover an answer. . . . But if our whole way of thinking is penetrated by fragmentation, this implies that we are not capable of this. . . .
>
> It does mean that we have to give pause, so that we do not go with our habitual fragmentary ways of thinking as we seek solutions that are ready to hand. The question of fragmentation and wholeness is a subtle and difficult one, more subtle and difficult than those which lead to fundamentally new discoveries in science. To ask how to end fragmentation and to expect an answer in a few minutes makes even less sense than to ask how to develop a theory as new as Einstein's was when he was working on it, and to expect to be told what to do in terms of some programme, expressed in terms of formulae or recipes [Bohm, 1976, p. 16].

In an imaginary dialogue, Bateson (1979) responds to a request to define the implications of his "few strong presuppositions and a great stochastic system" in this way: "I think I would like to call my next book *'Where Angels Fear to Tread.'* Everybody keeps wanting me to rush in. It is monstrous—vulgar, reductionist, sacrilegious—call it what you will—to rush in with an oversimplified question. It's a sin against all three of our new principles. Against aesthetics and against consciousness and against the sacred" (p. 236).

"Of Course"—the Obvious

Typically, a major consequence of rushing in prematurely with solutions is that the edifying criticism is bypassed or misunderstood. There is the premature, impatient "yes, of course, it is obvious, we knew all that, let's get on with solutions" reaction. Let me give two examples.

One concerns the work of Karen Horney. Her ideas "seem like simple common sense, something that could have occurred to anyone. They did not occur to anyone, however, before Horney. Too often people do read her thinking, 'Yes, of course,' and then forget that they had not known it all before. The fact that her theory is deceptively simple and unfashionably clear tends to obscure both its originality and its explanatory power" (Paris, 1981).

The second example is from an introductory physics text by the Nobel Prize winner Richard Feynman (Feynman, Leighton, and Sands, 1963). In the course of discussing the issue of relativistic mass, he demonstrates that in a relativistic framework, when two inelastic masses collide,

> The mass of the object which is formed when two equal objects collide must be twice the mass of the objects which come together. You might say, "Yes, of course, that is the conservation of mass." But not "Yes, of course," so easily, because *these masses have been enhanced* over the masses that they would be if they were standing still, yet they still contribute to the total M, not the mass they have when standing still, but *more*. Astonishing as that may seem, in order for the conservation of momentum to work when two objects come together, the mass that they form must be greater than the rest masses of the objects, even though the objects are at rest after the collision! [p. 16–8].

It seems to me that it would be equally easy and tempting to react to the formal and focal criticisms I have developed in Chapters 2 through 5 in these several ways. Obviously, what I am suggesting, and what the various quotations I have cited suggest, is that the critical analyses themselves need to be considered with some care, without hurry, without immediate pressure to produce answers. In a sense, as Bohm has said so clearly, answers and progressive solutions are contained in the way one formulates one's questions.

In short, I believe that what one needs to do first is become immersed in the critiques, digest and critically evaluate the proposed positions, work them through. Afterward one could expect that some promising paths would begin to emerge from a better grasp of the issues and questions. In this way, relevant solutions would have a chance to evolve naturally; new and appropriate directions could grow organically out of the critical analyses; the construction of forced, artificial, hurried, shallow, inadequate, prematurely closed solutions might be averted.

Having said all that, I shall nevertheless attempt at least to indicate some possible implications of the critical analyses I have presented so far. In doing this, my purpose is not so much to propose new answers as it is to clarify and illuminate further the perspectives I have been advocating. In the next few sections I shall attempt to sketch very roughly an outline of an approach to theorizing. In many respects, it will incorporate familiar material and approaches. That is as it should be, it seems to me. One needs to build on previous work as much as one can.

After this attempt to outline a "theory for therapy" come five brief sections of comments pertaining to various other subjects. The main purpose of these discussions will be to indicate the potential that my general approach could have for wider applications.

SPECULATIONS: THE CLINICALLY RELEVANT FRAMEWORK

Although I have proposed to locate a clinically pragmatic theory at a separate cognitive level, and have suggested certain formal and focal principles and strategies, it will obviously not do to reinvent the wheel. It would be ludicrous to fail to take advantage of the enormous amount of accumulated experience, wisdom, and knowledge about clinical matters (see, for example, overviews in L. Friedman, 1978; Lichtenberg, 1983, Chapter 13, Schafer, 1983). For that reason, I shall begin with a review of areas of consensus.

Consensus: The State of the Art

Is there a consensus about key issues? It bears repeating that there are many "schools" of psychoanalysis, each

> having a substantial body of literature and eminent members who make persuasive claims as to their special vision of the psychoanalytic truth and the results to be obtained by those who share this vision [Schafer, 1983, p. 282].

Nevertheless, one would think that it should be possible to tease out significant areas of basic agreement.

The comparative analysis of various schools of psychoanalysis has scarcely been addressed, according to Schafer (1983). Such comparative study "is a virtually undeveloped intellectual pursuit" (p. 282). It is undeveloped probably because even within any one school the problems of untangling its structure, contents, assumptions, evidence, or methods are formidable; the task of analyzing the relationships across various schools therefore adds an extra order of difficulty (p. 282).

Obviously, a comparative study falls outside the scope of this work. I shall, however, identify some major landmarks. Since the clinical issues are so complex and massive, I shall have to settle for some very simple obvious commonalities exhibited by the various schools.

Two classes of pathology. There are within psychoanalytic thought various ways of conceptualizing pathology, but two large categories can be discerned. It seems to be almost universally accepted on the basis of accumulated clinical experience that pathology can be divided into oedipal and preoedipal classes. This basic distinction seems to emerge independently of the nosological criteria one has employed—whether one discriminates on the basis of developmental accomplishments, classes of defenses, types of transference manifestations, quality of object relationships, existing structures and/or defects within a psychological apparatus, energic considerations, or analyzability.

Two modes of therapy. Similarly, there seems to be very general agreement that psychoanalytic therapy displays two principal facets: "attachment," pertaining primarily to affective ties, and "understanding," pertaining to cognition (Loewald, 1960; L. Friedman, 1978; Schafer, 1983, Chapters 2, 4, 16). (A third factor, "integration," is sometimes separated out.)

Two classes of therapy. Finally, although there is less agreement on this matter, there appears to be a majority view for two major classes of analytic therapy. One is the cluster of therapeutic approaches that can be subsumed under the label "classical," the other includes various expanded analytic approaches (e.g., Kohut's, Gedo's, Winnicott's) involving the use of "parameters" and the like. For the sake of convenience, I shall refer to this latter group of approaches as "expanded analytic therapy."

I shall draw on these crude distinctions and labels in the illustrative sketch of a clinical theory that follows. That theory adopts two assumptions: The first is that, in one way or another, both modes enter into each class of therapy. There seems to be a convergence "to an acceptance of the interconnection between understanding and attachment at all stages of therapy" (L. Friedman, 1978, p. 560). The second assumption is that, generally speaking, oedipal pathology is to be coupled with classical therapy, preoedipal pathology with expanded analytic therapy. This correlation is exhibited, for example, in the ways in which one identifies the therapy of choice (or, perhaps, a specific therapist) for a given patient. The same coupling is also found within any given case (e.g., Gedo and Goldberg, 1973); that is, the therapist tracks the shifting manifestations of pathology, drawing on classical therapy when manifestations of oedipal pathology appear, and on expanded analytic therapy when manifestations of preoedipal pathology predominate.

The above notions are not only quite familiar, but also highly oversimplified. In spite of their obvious defects, they provide a useful skeleton for the sketch that follows.

Oedipal Pathology and Classical Therapy

It seems to me that from a pragmatic perspective one major issue pertaining to therapy of oedipal pathology—whether conceptualized as part of the therapy in a given case, or as therapy in "pure classical" cases—is whether or not classical therapy is essentially a finished product. I have the impression that there is wide agreement that it is, even though that agreement generally is implied rather than explicitly stated. Many of the opinions previously cited support that conclusion. Further support would not be difficult to come by. Winnicott (1965), for example, in the context of his many discussions of preoedipal issues, frequently refers to the finished state of therapy for classical cases as a foregone conclusion; more recently, Schafer's remarks (cited earlier) have the same implication (e.g., 1978, pp. 6, 185, 199; 1983, p. 112); so do many of Kohut's statements (e.g., 1984, pp. 4, 6, 65–66, 94, 104–106, 172).

One task of a clinically pragmatic theory, then, would be to find some way of addressing and resolving this question. If classical therapy indeed were complete in all essentials, then a pragmatic perspective would indicate that questions pertaining to it ought to be set aside for higher-priority questions. My impression is that within the prevalent pure knowledge medical paradigm this issue is neither explicitly identified nor significantly addressed. It may very well be, too, that if we did attempt to answer this question, we should find that it is quite difficult to discover ways of investigating it, or even of thinking about it. Such a finding could be salutary, as I see it. That kind of difficulty would not only point to a pragmatic shortcoming in theorizing (that we do not know how to search for an answer to this clinically relevant question), but could also serve as a nodal point for a pragmatic orientation. That is, in struggling with finding ways of addressing the question, we would at the same time be struggling with the meaning of pragmatic theorizing.

Let me raise a second question, one about verbal interventions in classical therapy: What alternatives to interpretation are available? Should we rely on "transference interpretations *only*?" (Leites, 1977, p. 279). That pragmatically important question seems to have received very little attention indeed.

The question is general: What about the role of construction, specifically, in classical therapy? (Laplanche and Pontalis, 1973, pp. 88–89). It is interesting that even Leites (1977) in his extensive investigation of the role of alternatives to transference interpretations ignores the matter of construction in analysis completely. Furthermore, the standard literature on technique (e.g., Glover, Paul, Greenson, Fenichel) fails to present any significant discussion. Yet, as Schafer (1983) points out, Freud's paper "Constructions in Analysis" raises a major question about therapeutic action and technique. That paper contains a very brief, cryptic allusion that amounts to a "significant reversal of Freud's usual emphasis on how much depends on making the unconscious conscious" (Schafer, 1983, p. 27). Surely the pragmatic importance (even the "theoretical" importance) of this issue for classical therapy should be beyond question. Once again, it may be difficult to find a way of entering the problem; and, once again, such a difficulty could have the beneficial results discussed in connection with the question I posed previously.

The preceding issue could be viewed as a special case of a yet wider question: How much does the patient need to understand, ultimately? There are occasional hints in the analytic literature that at least in some cases, or at some time, the answer is not all that much (see, for example, Winnicott, 1975, p. 115; see also Bettelheim, 1967, Part 2). This difficult issue is connected, for example, with the role of veridicality in interpretations (see, for example, Glover, 1955, pp. 353–366; Schimek, 1975; Gedo, 1979, pp. 256, 260; Spence, 1982; Schafer, 1983, p. 204 and Chapters 12, 13; Kohut, 1984, pp. 91–94; 153–154). Although, once again, from a pragmatic perspective the question seems to be central, it does not seem to have received nearly the attention it deserves. One factor that may have contributed to this neglect has already been mentioned, namely, that "psychoanalysts do not like to dwell on the distinction between truth [or understanding?] and their form of therapy." Of course, if one takes the position that the theory of classical therapy is a closed issue, then this question can be ignored. L. Friedman (1978), in analyzing the work of the Edinburgh Conference on "The Curative Factors in Psycho-Analysis," concludes that the panelists "did not want to hear about any curative factor except understanding as conveyed by interpretation" (p. 535). Perhaps this attitude still influences mainstream approaches to these important questions about classical therapy.

It seems to me that a good case can be made for the premise that some significant changes in classical therapy still might be possible (and advisable). I submit that there could be major variants of that therapy that still would be analytic, that is, not suggestion or indoctrination, provided one continued to pay attention to the principal factors of transference, resistance, and the dynamic repressed unconscious. Even that "paying attention" might be satisfactorily accomplished in cases of oedipal pathology by therapeutic means other than the traditional interventions that constitute classical therapy. For example, there might be more emphasis on construction, or on a mode such as Gedo's (1979) "witnessing," or even on a judicious integration of Rogerian views (e.g., Rogers, 1977, p. 250).

The notion that classical therapy could profit from extensions is not new, most certainly. One can occasionally find very radical inquiries in this direction—explorations of the relationships between classical analysis and meditation, Zen Buddhism, and the like. The question is perhaps more one of emphasis than content. The point I have been making is that the problem areas I mentioned above, while identified, have scarcely been investigated. I am suggesting that a pragmatic stance leads one to question the priorities for theorizing. Practical but nonsuperficial considerations suggest that the preceding questions deserve considerably more "theoretical" attention than they have received to date. In future work, I hope to present illustrative examples of how one might actually go about addressing them.

Preoedipal Pathology and Expanded Analytic Therapy

There seems little question that in more recent times the clinical subject area that has received the greatest attention in the analytic literature is preoedipal pathology and its therapy. There is much discussion about borderline, narcissistic, and psychotic patients and phenomena, and about therapeutic approaches to this broad and highly diverse class of patients.

A basic question is, Does classical technique require fundamental modifications in these cases? (Schafer, 1983, p. 14). Do we need an expanded analytic therapy for preoedipal pathologies? I have assumed that we do; there seems to be a great deal of past and current support in the literature for this position. What I shall attempt here is to identify one task that, it seems to me, pragmatic considerations point to as of the highest priority for a theory of expanded analytic therapy.

I shall assume that a central ingredient of that therapy comprises analogues to the mother-child setting and interactions. According to some, that is true of analysis in general: "The prototype of the analytic experience is not hard to identify. There can be no doubt that analysis is, in essence, an artful reconstruction of very early transactions with the mother" (Kovel, 1981, p. 69); "the analytic setting itself . . . [contains] some elements of the mother-child relation"

(Modell, 1976, p. 289; see also L. J. Friedman, 1975, pp. 142, 144; Lichtenberg, 1983, pp. 211–213). It seems to be generally agreed, however, that this aspect of psychoanalytic therapy tends to recede into the background in classical cases, and only becomes prominent in cases where preoedipal pathology dominates.

In Chapter 2 I outlined a general correlational structure that formally organizes this situation. Let us quickly review the essentials. We have two pairs: (1) the "internal" psychological development of the child and the correlated "external" responses of the early environment, and (2) the "internal" pathological state of the adult's psychological apparatus and the correlated "external" therapeutic interventions and arrangements. These correlations are linked by a double translation: The psychological status of the child is translated into the analogous adult pathology; childhood environmental phenomena, benign as well as malignant, are translated into analogous environmental phenomena in the therapeutic situation.

According to Winnicott (1965), "it will profit us to look at the needs of infants, and then to translate these needs into language that is appropriate at all ages. . ." (p. 69). I maintain, however, that from the point of view of formal theorizing these translations from the first to the second pair typically are accomplished quite casually. For the most part, the process has been implicit and highly informal. That is, clinicians and theoreticians have moved from pair one to pair two without a careful examination of the bases of their translations, without, for example, explicitly stating principles that provide the rationales for the translations. Obviously, the two pairs (child and environment, adult and therapeutic environment) describe entirely different situations. These differences have been described, for instance, by Heimann, Anna Freud, and Spitz (see L. Friedman, 1978, pp. 537, 543, 545), and more recently by Lichtenberg (1983, pp. 212–213), Winnicott (1965), and Bettelheim (1956, pp. 516–517), among many others. It is not, then, that theorists are unaware of the differences in the two situations. It is rather a problem of focus, of emphasis.

In Chapter 2 I referred to Gedo and Goldberg's (1973) correlational scheme. These authors use the model of the "flooded" reflex arc to represent the psychological trauma that occurs in a child's earliest development phase; they call the modality required of the adequate environment at that stage "pacification." They then translate these notions into a corresponding regressed mode of functioning in the adult and a correlated treatment modality. The flooded reflex arc becomes adult "disorganization" (e.g., Gedo, 1979, pp. 66, 159; but see Bettelheim's [1967, pp. 292–294] cautionary remarks on the use of the concept and term "regression"); the correlated therapeutic modality remains "pacification" or an aspect of "the holding environment" (e.g., pp. 18, 24).

I maintain that in proportion to their central importance these translations are given short shrift. Discussions of how one arrives at the modalities for treating manifestations of archaic phases are disproportionately brief (e.g., Gedo, 1979, pp. 18–19, 23–25, 159, 194). It is assumed—in my opinion, too quickly, too casually, without theoretical examination—that these modalities involve "no actual departures from the usual analytic *procedures*. . ." (p. 18). Does not this pragmatically central issue deserve more "theoretical" consideration? Should we not think about specifying generative principles that could provide a deeper base for accomplishing the necessary translations?

Another example of these characteristically informal ways of achieving translations comes from Kohut's writings (e.g., 1971, 1977). He translates the environmental needs of the child during the narcissistic developmental era into analogous therapeutic needs of the adult who exhibits disturbances of the self. As I noted in Chapter 6, Kohut's technical approach is but little affected by his theorizing: "In principle, the approach of self psychology toward patients with analyzable self disturbances is the same as the approach of traditional analysis toward patients regarded as analyzable" (1984, p. 81; see also pp. 104–108, 172). (Kohut does, however, immediately amplify his remarks.) The general premise is that, in therapy, defects in the self become reactivated and worked through "via a wholesome psychic activity that has been thwarted in childhood, [and which] lays down the structures needed to fill the defect in the self" (1984, p. 4; see also pp. 6, 65–66, 94; 1971, pp. 85–90, 148–151, 210–220, 257–258). The building of new structures is a central matter in Kohut's conception of child development and in his recommendations for therapy of narcissistic disturbances in the adult. He outlines three general conditions for benign process: readiness of structures, gradualness, and depersonification of the internalized situation (1971, pp. 40–41). Yet I cannot find the translation from the first correlated pair to the second explicitly identified and methodically discussed as a theoretical issue. Parallels are drawn directly and literally.

Kohut's, or Gedo and Goldberg's, or similar recommendations may find empirical support, may be quite effective therapeutically, may seem reasonable, and may have face validity. That is not the point. What I am calling attention to is a matter of emphasis and of formal theoretical treatment. I maintain that given the pragmatically central role that translation plays in the kinds of correlational frameworks I have just outlined, it follows that these translations merit much more focused attention, a much more explicit, methodical treatment than they have received to date. Where are the specific, orderly procedures that provide and spell out the rationale for a given clinician's translations? How does a given author get from pair one to pair two? I maintain that clear, explicit explications are nowhere to be found.

This situation provides a major example of the impact that the pure knowledge medical paradigm can have on theorizing, it seems to me. The usual focus on understanding and conceptualizing pathology takes its toll. The notion that as simple an idea as translation could qualify as a major theoretical issue does not seem to have been articulated, at least not with any prominence. Under the pure knowledge medical paradigm, translation comes to be seen as a minor theoretical issue. It is "merely" a practical issue; it may be addressed in passing, implicitly, casually; it usually becomes lost or buried among the theoretical discussions concerning the "important" "pure knowledge" issues—conceptualizations of borderline or narcissistic disorders and their transference manifestations, retrospective theoretical arguments that justify empirically derived technical rules and recommendations.

Let me make a seond point. My impression is that various theoreticians' proposals display varying degrees of "openness." That is, while I suggested in Chapter 6 that many of the systems proposed by major clinicians are nearly closed, it does seem as though some are inherently more closed than others. The closer a proposal is to being one that contains set technical recommendations, to being what I called earlier a theory "of" therapy, the less capable it seems to be of significant further development. (These closed theories of therapy include those that are "disinterpretations and reinterpretations" of already available findings.) What I should like to propose now is that the more open clinical theories (meaning those that support significant further development of technique) consist of correlational frameworks that focus on translation issues and at the same time avoid making set recommendations about technique. For instance, Kohut's approach, even though it does not theorize explicitly about the processes of translation, somehow seems to have encouraged clinicians to pay more attention to these kinds of translational issues. In my view, it is more open, more flexible, than some of the other correlational frameworks I considered earlier, or than some of the approaches and proposals that are seen to be primarily reformalizations (what I have been calling disinterpretations and reinterpretations). I believe that this flexibility, this degree of openness, this implied emphasis on translation, explains at least to some extent why Kohut's approach continues to foster some development of technique, and why, say, Schafer's proposals for an action language (which fall into the class of disinterpretations and reinterpretations) seem to have had relatively little impact on clinical practices.

Winnicott and translation. In general, it seems that the therapist's expanded view of developmental issues will have a beneficial impact on technique (Kohut, 1984, p. 82). It therefore seems reasonable to assume that the richer one's view of the first pair (child/environment), the greater the clinical potential of a correlational theory would be. In my judgment, a promising point of departure is Winnicott's theorizing. He provides a comprehensive, subtle developmental framework that seems comfortably to encompass both classical notions and clinical concepts about infancy culled from his own experience as a pediatrician. Thus, not only does it have significant content of its own, it is also open, flexible, and able to integrate material from other frameworks as needed. All in all, Winnicott's theorizing seems to have considerable potential for serving as a foundation for a more methodical, formalized, clinically pragmatic correlational framework.

Winnicott divides the period from birth to the beginning of latency into three major eras. In each of these three epochs, the child's complex needs are correlated with certain complex environmental requirements. In the first era, which lasts a few months (Winnicott eschews precise dating), the environment is expected to provide a "holding" function, and the infant is said to be in a state of "absolute dependence." In the second era, which seems to last until about the start of the oedipal period, the environment is needed to provide "handling" for the child in a state of "relative dependence." The third period requires "object presenting" as the child moves "towards independence."

Winnicott has much to say about benign and malignant interactions between the child and its environment in terms of the above framework. He spells out in great detail the aspects of the "good-enough" as well as the failing environment, with extensive discussions of the consequences for the child, and later for the adult, of various clusters of benign and malignant experiences at various stages of development. Basically, good-enough environmental provision amounts to an appropriate matching across the various strands indicated above. Development can then proceed in near-optimal fashion. Environmental failure can be conceptualized as one or more of a variety of the many possible mismatches—an impingement, abandonment, defect in tracking the child's needs, mismatched degree of identification, and the like. Corresponding to various kinds of failures there are the various pathological developments that then become necessary (e.g., premature self-care, defensive separation of psyche and soma, exaggerated development of a compliant, "false" self). Representative questions examined by Winnicott include: How does the environment deal with the child's initiative and activity on the one hand, and passivity on the other? Does the environment respect the child's quiescent state, and respond appropriately to his active, excited times? Does the environment track accurately, provide the correct, graduated degree of failure? Does it allow for experiences of omnipotence? Does it sustain the paradox of transitional phenomena? Does it foster clarity, or does it allow too much confusion, complexity, "muddle?"

What about the all-important shift from this dyad (child/environment) to the other (adult patient/therapeutic environment)? Winnicott does have a great deal to say about adult psychotherapy and pathology in the light of his developmental framework. Examples of themes in the therapy of adults that Winnicott has examined in this manner are: the environment's provision of ego coverage (1965, pp. 166–170; 1971, pp. 26–37; 1975, pp. 285–261); the presence of the false self (1965, pp. 151–152; 1971, pp. 56–64); dependency (1965, pp. 233–241, 249–259); dealing with unconscious destructive wishes (1965, pp. 79–82); and the pathological localization of "mind" (1975, pp. 248–252). In his discussions, Winnicott usually pays great attention to the implications that developmental issues have for interpretations—their timing, mode, and content. (For him, interpretation is central in the therapy of adults: ". . . there is no more than interpretation, correct and penetrating and welltimed. . ." [1975, p. 292].)

Still, there is a certain ad hoc quality, a high degree of informality, about Winnicott's approach. At times, the rationales for his moves from the child's needs to those of the adult patient seem obscure, even arbitrary. One then has the impression that the translation process may have been accomplished intuitively and without formal reflection, or at least without Winnicott's sharing his thought processes with the reader.

My suggestion, then, is the obvious one. Pragmatic considerations support the premise that a principal task of a theory of expanded analytic therapy is to clarify the translation process. While one does not wish to encumber the openness and flexibility of Winnicott's approach with rigid "translation rules" that would turn his thought into yet another prematurely closed system, it still might be profitable to search for and articulate generative principles of translation that could be applied to his framework. I shall therefore present an organized outline of some of Winnicott's developmental notions, as a challenge to would-be translators in general. I shall use the format of developmental lines introduced by Anna Freud (1965).

From the side of the child, a number of developmental lines can be identified along which the child moves through Winnicott's three major developmental eras. Here are examples of major themes:

(1) The movement from the perspective of ego development, ranging from near-total absence of ego functions, through occasional brief episodes of partial mastery, to more effective and mature relationships between ego and id, ego and superego, and ego and environment.

(2) The movement in terms of differentiation between psyche and soma, from an undifferentiated state, through a stage of fluid relationships between the psyche and its embodiment in the soma, to stable "personalization," facilitated by adequate maternal "handling."

(3) Development in terms of a shift in typical anxieties from unfathomable basic existential dreads (of falling, going to pieces, having no relationship to the body, having no orientation) to more mature anxieties over loss of love.

(4) Development in self-awareness, from the totally undifferentiated state (with neither self nor other having any meaning), through moments of being aware of "being," to "going-on-being," now differentiated from the environment and integrated over time (continuity of being).

(5) Development in terms of necessary defenses, for instance, of the compliant, reactive "false" self, and the manner in which the "true" self protects itself.

(6) The movement from occasional experience of omnipotence through paradoxical transitional experiences to full recognition of, and distinction between, that which is "found" and that which is magically created or projected.

(7) A closely related movement, namely, the gradual establishment, clarification, and growth of the "transitional" domain, from paradoxical illusion to play, and to cultural, religious, or moral matters.

(8) The development from aggressive motility through hate, ambivalence, guilt, finally to the capacity for concern.

For the mother, there are a number of corresponding, complementary developmental lines and tasks. Major examples are:

(1) The movement from "absolute maternal preoccupation" to a

return to other concerns—other family members, work, creativity, etc. It is the movement from intense identification to normal individuation.

(2) A movement from magically knowing and meeting the unstated needs of the infant, through a period of waiting for signals, to a period of normal empathy—a movement in terms of graduated failure.

(3) Changes stated in terms of ego functions, from virtually complete "ego coverage" for the infant to full differentiation between the two egos.

(4) The concurrent development of two differentiated aspects of the maternal environment: the object (or part object) mother, and the environmental mother.

(5) The graduated adaptive provision for realizing the creative impulse, from fostering illusion and brief experiences of omnipotence to provision of appropriate cultural or moral enrichment.

(6) The movement in terms of the ways mother meets aggression and hate.

It is all very well, then, to say that "it will profit us to look at the needs of infants, and then to translate these needs into language that is appropriate at all ages." *The question is, How is one to achieve this translation?* How is one to move methodically—by means grounded in a clinically pragmatic theory—from issues in child development to parallel issues in the therapy of adults? What do the differences between the child and adult imply for the kind of translation we are considering? How might one go about developing a mature theory of translation? (Lichtenberg, 1983, pp. 212–213).

Some basis for addressing these and analogous issues is clearly needed. How might one develop an adequate rationale? That kind of quest may be important in itself, as I suggested earlier; the pursuit of well-chosen questions may usefully illuminate the meaning and characteristics of clinically relevant theorizing. In any case, it is necessary to start by identifying and articulating the issues, questions, and needs, and I have attempted to do that. For the present, that is where my suggestions about clinical theorizing stop.

GENERALIZATION I: OTHER CLINICAL FRAMEWORKS

The implications for other clinical frameworks of the criticisms and suggestions put forward earlier should be fairly obvious. For example, it should hardly be necessary to demonstrate the presence

Psychoanalytic Theory and Clinical Relevance 171

of state process formalisms in either behaviorally or cognitively oriented clinical theories. To the degree that the premises of Chapters 3 and 4 are valid, then, these and similar clinical frameworks must be severely limited by the class of formalisms they employ. (As we know, however, clinicians of all persuasions tend to do much more than is defined or contained in their presumed frameworks. Therefore, a clinical discipline may transcend the limitations imposed by its official theory: "A good deal of clinical judgment and even research is possible in partial, not to say fantastic, theoretical frameworks" [Langer, 1967, p. 18]—and the same might be said about effective therapy.)

Nevertheless, it may be useful to point out how the patterns I criticized earlier repeat themselves in some unexpected quarters. Consider, for example, family therapy. Currently, it is quite fashionable in that field to develop a theory based on formalized, systems-oriented approaches (e.g., Minuchin, Whittaker, Malone, Scheflen, Watzlawick). Let us consider one particular example, the "paradoxical" methodology advocated by Palazzoli and her co-workers (Palazzoli et al., 1978). Theirs is obviously an approach that relies heavily on General System theory notions, and thus on frameworks that automatically bring with them state process underpinnings—feedback, homeostasis, logical rules and transformations, and states and changes of state (see, for example, pp. 6–7). Furthermore, key aspects of the pure knowledge medical paradigm are very much in evidence. There is the usual focus on pathology, on what is wrong with a given "family system," on how it got that way, on what mechanisms maintain it, and so on.

We have, then, the familiar general situation whose characteristics I considered earlier: from a formal point of view, a state process theory—in this instance, rooted in General System theory notions; from a focal perspective, an instance of the pure knowledge medical paradigm.

According to the arguments of Chapters 3, 4 and 5, such theorizing should be severely limited in direct clinical consequentiality; the formal and focal characteristics of the theorizing would lead us to expect to find, just as we did in psychoanalysis, that therapeutic technique has actually been based on empirical findings, and has not been derived from the elaborate theorizing itself. We would expect to find once more that state process formalisms and the pure knowledge paradigm had, in combination, been unable to provide a framework that could logically entail clinical practices.

That expectation seems to be confirmed in our present example. Although these therapists have developed a ponderous systems-theoretical framework, they say that their therapeutic techniques and approaches were found, not deduced: "Therapeutic interventions in the family, as we have gradually devised, applied, and critically examined them, appear to be . . . no more than a learning process acquired by the therapists through trial and error" (p. 47). Perhaps, then, these and similar approaches to family therapy could profit from the general formal and focal considerations developed earlier in the context of psychoanalytic therapy. (It should not be necessary to point out again that my remarks say nothing one way or another about the actual effectiveness of the approaches proposed by Palazzoli et al.)

GENERALIZATION II: CRITICS OF MAINSTREAM BEHAVIORAL DISCIPLINES, AND BACKSLIDING

Unorthodox Criticisms

We have seen repeatedly in the previous discussions that there is a common thread of radical criticisms of normal behavioral science scattered throughout various disciplines. In Chapter 4, for example, we saw a commonality among certain criticisms of the standard views and practices of linguistics. Other subject areas in psychology and related disciplines that have been similarly criticized include memory, perception, and artificial intelligence. Reference to such radical criticisms of mainstream approaches has been made throughout the earlier chapters; additional extended discussions may be found in Bergson (1946), Lecky (1961), Jordan (1968), Giorgi (1970), Braginsky and Braginsky (1974), Langer (1967, 1982), Winch (1958), Louch (1970), Harth (1983), Wilber (1983), Matson (1976), Bunge (1976), Settle (1976), and Merleau-Ponty (1962, 1963).

Let us briefly look at further examples of these kinds of criticisms. Langer (1967) examines and criticizes in considerable detail various practices and characteristics of mainstream behavioral disciplines. Her general targets are the "idols of the laboratory": physicalism, methodology, jargon, objectivity, mathematization (p. 47). She illustrates the widespread use of pretentious jargon, "language which is more technical than the ideas it serves to express" (p. 36), and corresponding mathematical pretensions—the mathematization by psychologists of their findings "as fast as they are found and even faster" (p. 39; see also Royce, 1983, especially pp. 494–497; London, 1944).

Psychoanalytic Theory and Clinical Relevance 173

The unrestrained use of stimulus-response models, the staples of experimental psychology, comes under her critical analysis as well. In the course of her discussion about "the deceptiveness of simple achievements [in animal psychology] as models for highly complex ventures" (p. 44), she refers to Tolman's reservations about such practices:

> "I still feel that 'response' is one of the most slippery and unanalyzed of our current concepts. We all gaily use the term to mean anything from a secretion of 10 drops of saliva to entering a given alley, to running an entire maze, to the slope of a Skinner box curve, to achieving a Ph.D. or to the symbolic act of hostility against one's father by attacking some authority figure. Now, I ask you!
> "As for perception, I have always been about as sleazy about it as I have been about responses. The 'stimulus' as we use it today seems to be just as slippery a term as that of response" [p. 287].

In general, this misappropriation and misuse of the standard tools and methods of the natural sciences have not produced worthwhile results:

> Here, I think, we have the central and fatal failing of all the projected sciences of mind and conduct: the actual machinery that their sponsors and pioneers have rented does not work when the "conceptualized phenomena" are fed into it. . . . The intellectual results are disappointing. Such a powerful machinery should make the behavioral sciences rocket to success. Instead of that, it has so far left psychology, sociology, anthropology, and ethical theories just where they were before [pp. 41–42].

One major theme in Langer's criticisms is the trivialization of phenomena by mainstream behavioral frameworks. These methodologies can deal with significant subject matter, such as art, music, or poetry, only by reducing such material in ways that remove significance. We have encountered this point before, particularly when we considered linguistic issues; it is a recurring theme among the criticisms to which I have been referring.

In a similar vein, Koch (1961) objects to the use of simple models of behavior (goal-directed, a "rough and ready 'instrumentalism'" [p. 631]) that cannot adequately deal with nontrivial aspects of the human experience. He, too, uses an example drawn from the realm of art—the examination of a painting—to illustrate the failings of mainstream methods and frameworks. In his discussion of such general methodological shortcomings, Koch makes an interesting reference to the problem of the representational capacity of systems, a problem to which I devoted a good deal of attention in the discussions of formal issues. He observes that psychology has constructed a language which renders virtually impossible a differentiated exploration of the content of man. Such a constraint upon the very possibility of a sensitive analysis of experience is precisely what has kept psychology away from questions that could be of concern to the humanist [p. 631].

We shall meet yet other examples of these kinds of critical perspectives below, in the context of the critics' vulnerabilities to error.

The Return of Disclaimed Practices—
Formal Issues

How might the concepts and approaches developed in Chapters 3, 4 and 5 be relevant to these kinds of criticisms? In general, I would say that these widespread critical views about the shortcomings of, say, psychology have failed to understand clearly the bases of the shortcomings that they are criticizing. That seems to have been especially true about formal issues. Since they have not fully understood the issues, critics (such as Langer, Koch, or George Klein) who on the one hand have objected to certain characteristics, shortcomings, or weaknesses in the behavioral disciplines have, on the other hand, tended to advocate alternatives that, according to the views I developed earlier, would still rely on the same ill-advised frameworks. I believe that the difficulty is this. While they recognize the limitations of the currently used formal frameworks, they do not seem to recognize that the common and limiting feature is the use of state process notions, in any of its many guises. As Langer (1967) herself has pointed out, "the concept of mechanism [state process formalisms, in my view] . . . has not received . . . critical treatment or careful definition from the philosophers who declare it inadequate to the task of describing vital phenomena" (p. 271).

Rorty's (1979) work illustrates Langer's point. In the course of presenting a radical and sophisticated criticism of conventional epistemology, he claims that "the notion of 'state' is sufficiently obscure that neither the term *spatial state* nor the term *nonspatial state* seems useful" (p. 21). (I would, of course, strongly disagree with this view, on the basis of the perspectives and thoughts developed in Chapters 3 and 4.) Consequently, although Rorty criticizes mainstream psychology (e.g., Chapter V), ultimately he still retains state process frameworks in what presumably are proposals for radical alternatives. For example, he makes extensive (although implicit) use of state process notions in his analysis of internal subjective experiences such as "pain" (p. 66).

One can find criticism after criticism that repeats the pattern I am describing. Practices, methodologies, characteristics, and the like that are decried and criticized are then unwittingly reintroduced in proposals that presumably would bring about remedies. I shall mention several more examples, but I maintain that the number could be multiplied at will.

Langer (1967), even after her extensive, detailed critique of methodological abuses in mainstream psychology, continues to invoke state process notions. For instance, she hopes that emotional expression in works of art can be explained in terms of logical structure (pp. 29–30). Similarly, a concept central to her discussion of art, the "act," implicitly invokes state process notions (pp. 261ff).

The same is true of her view of language. It remains a logician's view, concerned with formal rules, syntax, structure, definition, reference. For example, hers is an elementarist, and a typically referential, view; she thinks about language in terms of its constituents, its building blocks, and their external referents. Thus, she notes that the characteristic of language is "its atomic structure" and talks about "ways of bringing words with unduly many meanings back to a strict sense by agreement, if only in a given context" (p. 103). She very explicitly questions the idea that narrative discourse has the capacity to serve as an adequate vehicle for theorizing: "The abstraction of pure concepts may occur under stringent controls of technical terms, but the inveterate tendency of even such terms to become assimilated to common parlance and share the ways of 'ordinary language' leads me to wonder whether the great frame of science can possibly be made of word-borne thought" (1982, p. 209). We can discern the features that characterize the orthodox, state-process view of scientific discourse: a focus on elements (terms), their exact specification and their referents, the preference for formalized symbolic systems, the disdain of "ordinary language."

She holds these and related views in spite of her recognition that the difficulties in psychology arise "because we are trying to transfer methods of observation simply and directly from physics . . . without taking account of the fact that the intraorganic character of the material presents a special difficulty and does not lend itself to those methods" (1967, p. 65). Again, it seems to be a matter of not recognizing fully all that necessarily accompanies the use of state process forms.

Similarly, as radical a critic of formalistic views of language as Rommetveit on occasion invokes state process notions; when he does, it is without any recognition of inconsistency. One instance in which he proposes an explicit state process framework is in the course of his discussion of the "*here-and-now* of the dialogue. . . . [of the] interpersonal speaker-to-listener coordinate of the speech act" (p. 36). Indeed, his figure 1 is a sketch of just such a coordinate system.

The same could also be said of Louch's (1966) criticisms and proposals. While he criticizes psychologists' unproductive aping of physics, he proposes analyses in terms of actions and their verbal referents, "units of examination of human behavior . . . observed, identified or isolated through categories of assessment and appraisal" (p. 56).

Yet another example is furnished by Dreyfus (1979). As we have seen, he criticizes the use of Turing machines as models of persons. Yet when he suggests presumably alternative theoretical frameworks, what are they? He suggests, for example, that we replace computer models—"dry engineering"—with "wet" ones, or with certain kinds of analogue frameworks (p. 247); another proposed alternative is information processing models based on the properties of optical holograms (p. 20). These models would presumably allow one to deal successfully with, say, gestalt processes. As we know by now, however, such models retain state process formalisms. Such alternatives—wet, dry, optical, it does not matter which—all fall within the standard formal structures of scientific models, and thus must exhibit the usual characteristics and limitations described generally in Chapter 3.

The premise I am presenting, then, is this. Outside of physics, it seems that, workers typically fail fully to understand, recognize, or appreciate the central theoretical role of state process formalisms and the consequences that necessarily follow from their use. Critics of mainstream practices may clearly recognize the defects and limitations that a given discipline exhibits. But to the extent that these critics fail fully to understand and appreciate the formal issues, they remain prone to proposing "solutions" that will ultimately lead to the same defects and limitations from which the critics had sought to escape; the culprit is the unwitting retention of the very same state process frameworks that have brought about the difficulties in the first place. Therefore, a process of analysis that can illuminate and clarify the formal issues, a process that can identify the presence of undesirable formalisms, should be valuable in a wide variety of circumstances and applications.

To repeat, it is not absolutely necessary for criticisms to rely on analysis of state process formalisms in order for them to be effective. We have seen two important cases—Freud's use of ordinary lan-

Psychoanalytic Theory and Clinical Relevance

guage, and ordinary use of language, and Hexter's linguistic proposals—that show that a critic can intuitively avoid a return to state process representations. Another compelling example is Schumacher's work. He presents an effective criticism of Cartesian frameworks (e.g., 1977, pp. 50–60), demonstrating an excellent grasp of their limitations—their trivializing effects, their representational restrictions, and so on. And even though he seems unaware of the formal state process perspective that I developed in Chapters 3 and 4, his recommendations consistently stay away from making use of such frameworks. He is the exception rather than the rule, however.

As the preceding examples suggest, then, it seems that without the benefit of an explicit understanding or analysis of these formal issues, one remains vulnerable to the errors I have mentioned above. Ingleby (1980) refers to this general situation in psychiatry:

> Many who have sought to escape from the paradigm adhered to by traditional psychiatry have fallen short of their goal, and ended up merely by embracing a different (psychological or sociological) version of positivism. Indeed, the hegemony which natural-scientific ideas have enjoyed over the last hundred years has made it hard to do otherwise, since it has become virtually taken for granted that there *are* no other valid forms of knowledge [p. 46].

The identification of the state process formalism as the key formal ingredient in mainstream scientific conceptualizations suggests that one potential application of state process analyses would be as an evaluative tool. Given a particular model, theory, conceptualization, we can now ask, Is it some variety of state process framework? If necessary, we can analyze it explicitly and methodically to see whether it exhibits those standard ingredients that I have described in some detail. And should the theory under examination indeed turn out to be a varient of a state process formalism, then we may expect that all the limitations, implications, and features discussed above will follow automatically; these consequences should be expected regardless of the particular version of state process frameworks used in a given instance. In this way, then, an analysis performed in state process terms can provide a particular kind of criterial evaluation of any given conceptual framework.

That kind of analysis does not seem to exist in the literature. It is the kind of analysis I introduced in 1978—very briefly and sketchily—in my consideration of the "alternative" conceptualizations of Schafer, Rubinstein, and George Klein within psychoanalysis. It is nowhere in view in the many published works I have cited that concern themselves with developing an alternative to Cartesianism.

Focal Issues

Is there a corresponding contribution this monograph could make to understanding or clarifying focal, pragmatic issues? That is a more difficult question. In clinical areas, one obvious useful pragmatic focus—therapeutic relevance—lies readily at hand. In more general behavioral areas, say, learning, memory, perception, or cognition, the corresponding meaning of a pragmatic focus is much less clear—to me, at any rate, since my concerns have primarily been clinical.

It does seem to be the case, though, that focal or pragmatic issues, at least the kinds I introduced in Chapters 5 and 6, have not been widely recognized or discussed in disciplines such as psychology. The potential which a pragmatic yet unvulgarized pragmatic focus has for being a leading principle, integrated with formal practice, does not seem to have received attention. In the majority of instances, these disciplines tend to embrace one of the many versions of the pure knowledge paradigm, or a shallow form of pragmatism. The role of "praxis" does not seem to have been discussed in any significant depth. (It is true, though, that one can occasionally find facile, token references to presumed parallels between the indeterminacy principle of quantum physics and observer influence in behavioral experiments.) My intuition is that it would profit workers in the behavioral disciplines to consider those issues I have labeled "focal," but at this time I am not prepared to say much more than that.

Let me mention a few examples of what seem to me superficial views of pragmatic issues that fall short of the approaches I reported in Chapter 5. In Jordan's (1968) very general critical analysis of psychology, he briefly turns to pragmatic issues in a quite simple, routine way. He speaks about "pure" versus "applied" goals of the academic researcher, the oversimplification of research techniques, and limitations in the academic setting of research programs (pp. 216–229, 235). This is hardly a view that links up with the kinds of pragmatic issues I considered in Chapter 5.

Similar comments apply to Braginsky and Braginsky's (1974) study. Their brief mention of "pure" versus "applied" science issues (pp. 8–9) is primarily a straightforward standard commentary about research motives and rationales.

One area in behavioral disciplines that presumably does focus on the relationships between practice and theory is the area of experimenter effects and artifacts (e.g., Rosenthal, 1966; Rosenthal and Rosnow, 1969). One might expect that studies in this area would examine focal issues in greater depth. In fact, however, the analyses are again conventional as compared with the approaches I presented earlier. These studies concern themselves primarily with such issues as pretest contamination, subjects' set, demand characteristics of experiments, volunteer subject bias, and suspiciousness of the experimenter's intent. The assumptions and implications seem to be that these and similar characteristics of empirical practice contaminate "pure" results predicted by valid theory; if one only could avoid or correct for these kinds of experimental weaknesses or errors, then truth would be reached, or at least asymptotically approached. The pure knowledge paradigm features remain; there is no sense of a holistic, integrated approach to experimentation and theory. Perhaps explicit attention to this issue would be beneficial.

GENERALIZATION III: FIRST LANGUAGE ACQUISITION

Let me conclude with some observations about three specific subject areas that each cut across several disciplines: first language acquisition, determinism, and affects.

Bridging the Gulf

I have proposed that in certain clinical applications conceptions of language as a logical system composed of elements lead to inadequate views of discourse. Difficulties created by the standard view arise in still another context. The integrated wholeness of language, world, and being suggests that the process of acquiring one's first language may not be represented well in terms of standard models such as those drawn from cognitive psychology or learning theories. These kinds of orthodox theories, whether based on an empiricist or innate conception of language acquisition, rely on some kind of a formal-logical model of language (see Hacking, 1975, pp. 57–69). For instance, there is the reliance on "abstractionism": "the doctrine that a concept is acquired by a process of singling out in attention some one feature given in direct experience—*abstracting* it—and ignoring other features simultaneously given—*abstracting from* them" (Hacking, 1975, p. 59). Even some less orthodox notions of first language acquisition, such as Wittgenstein's (Hardwick, 1971), rely on some scheme similarly based on a logical formalism—for example, rules of a game.

Language acquisition is a move from having no language at all to having at least some. While it has importance in its own right as a linguistic issue, the acquisition of one's first language is also a prominent example of a much more general class of conceptually problematic developmental processes. In each case, the key (and problematic) issue is the move from a condition in which something is absent in an organism to one in which something is present. The transitions are reminiscent of those encountered in mathematics when one tries to move from discrete to continuous variables. Even in mathematics, those two realms cannot be bridged conceptually in some easy manner, by some smooth transition. One has to construct special notions such as the idea of a limit in order to accomplish the change. There is still no smooth transition; for example, the usual approach in mathematics—to use a procedure based on the idea of a limit to account for those changes—glosses over the problems of qualitative changes essentially by substituting "and so on, ad infinitum" for a finite argument.

The same objections apply to the class of developmental issues that I have mentioned. The paradoxes and conundrums that arise when one considers any of these transitions from one basic condition to another—say, from an undifferentiated to a differentiated state—are glossed over in mainstream theorizing. Typically, one is satisfied, in principle, with conceptualizations such as progressive integration (e.g., of ego nuclei) and differentiation. A careful analysis can show, however, that the schemes that are usually advanced cannot really adequately account for the fundamental qualitative change that they seek to explain. I mentioned in Chapter 3 that Feffer (1982) has demonstrated this inherently problematic aspect of developmental theories. He shows that any and all versions and variants of developmental explanations (e.g., instinct theory, behaviorism) must encounter the paradox of discontinuity—what Feffer calls the problem of "immutability and discontinuity." He identifies the fundamental Cartesian world view and its presumptions as the root cause for this paradoxical situation (especially Chapter 2), and shows how Cartesianism constructs an "unbridgeable gulf," a necessary discontinuity, between developmental stages that require continuity. Cartesianism seeks to connect events that it has rendered unconnectable. From this perspective, first language acquisition becomes yet another special case of a more general problem of discontinuity and immutability.

Laplanche and Pontalis also point to these general conceptual difficulties that usually are passed over so glibly: "Deriving an object from an objectless state seems so unpromising a theoretical task to certain analysts that they do not hesitate to affirm—in a reaction which is laudable in its intentions but which only leads to a different error—that *sexuality per se* has an object from the beginning" (Laplanche, 1976, p. 19); "just how are we supposed to picture the transition from a monad shut in upon itself to a progressive discovery of the object?" (Laplanche and Pontalis, 1973, p. 257).

Schumacher (1977) considers problematic aspects of theories of development from the broad context of biological evolution. He, too, identifies difficulties with traditional developmental views (pp. 111–119) that arise from the kinds of Cartesian presumptions Feffer has subjected to formal analysis.

I would suggest, on the basis of analogy and extrapolation, that the conceptual difficulties faced by the usual theories of language acquisition are, at bottom, just those faced by all attempts to explain theoretically *any* developmental change that involves drastic qualitative changes in status—that is, development that is a movement across a gap, from one condition in which some function or capability is lacking to another condition in which that competence is exhibited. The theoretical "explanations" may look like explanations, but closer examination always reveals some smoke-generating step that bridges an unbridgeable gulf. Let us remind ourselves of the cavalier treatment these kinds of issues usually receive.

Trivialization of the Problem

As I said, these kinds of inherent problems and limitations associated with orthodox attempts to represent and conceptualize various kinds of basic developmental steps remain insufficiently appreciated in much of the literature, analytic and other. For example, Stoller (1975) considers that explanations of the kinds of phenomena about which I am speaking just "have not been worked out" as yet (pp. 147, 151), with the implication that further standard work, further effort along the same lines, will eventually provide answers.

Another example of a standard treatment is provided by Kernberg (1976). In his discussion of the transition from a primary undifferentiated state to "the state of primary, undifferentiated self-object representations," he makes casual statements about, for example, "the gradual building up of the normal, primary, undifferentiated self-object representations" (p. 60). His "solutions" to such developmental discontinuities are traditional, relying, for example, on innatist notions such as Hartmann's "primary autonomous ego functions" which elaborate into internalizations.

Graves (1971) is equally casual when he refers to the phenomenon of language acquisition: "Thus an infant's senses may be stimulated, but he cannot be said to have any experiences until he has learned at least the rudiments of a language" (p. 12); "Popper has pointed out that even infants have certain expectations (which may be called 'low-level theories' for them), which are constantly being revised to the extent that they fail in helping adjust to present and future events" (p. 27).

Just as the developmental move in general receives insufficient treatment, so does the specific case of first language acquisition. The inherent gap between the stage of having no language and the stage of having some is glossed over, explained by some superficial developmental scheme such as stages of vocalization or cognition, or acquisition of syntactic competence. I maintain that these contribute little to understanding the process. The real problems, such as the question of how generalization really is possible in first language acquisition (the problem of the "universal word" [Goodstein, 1960, pp. 85–86]), are swept under the rug or "solved" by superficial and fallacious arguments and lists.

Application of State Process Analysis

If the view of language presented earlier has any validity, then learning language—and most especially one's first language—cannot be treated adequately by the usual explanations grounded in formal logic and Cartesian frameworks; these kinds of attempts *must* fail. Language acquisition cannot be treated as rule learning, for example. Neither can it be treated as learning to use a complex tool. Gadamer (1982) describes the situation by invoking Aristotle's image of a fleeing army regrouping. One by one, as the individuals stop, the army continues to flee, "and yet, in the end, the whole army regroups. Now the same is true of learning to speak. There is no first word and yet, while learning, we grow into language and into world—these inseparable unities" (p. 492; see also the epigraph to the beginning of Chapter 4). Formal logic cannot encompass the image that Gadamer uses for his analogy.

Dreyfus (1979) offers these remarks:

> What is involved in learning a language is much more complicated and more mysterious than the sort of conditioned reflex involved in learning to associate nonsense syllables. To teach someone the meaning of a new word, we can sometimes point at the object which the word names. . . . But Wittgenstein points out that if we simply point at

a table, for example, and say "brown," a child will not know if brown is the color, the size, or the shape of the table, the kind of object, or the proper name of the object. If the child already uses language, we can *say* that we are pointing out the color; but if he doesn't already use language, how do we ever get off the ground? [p. 110].

Winnicott (1965) alludes to language acquisition in his discussion of what it means when an individual is able to say "I am alone" (pp. 32–33). Acquiring a first language, then, is intimately a part of the fundamental but entirely obscure developmental processes by which internality and externality *both* become established from a prior undifferentiated state in which neither notion applies (see, for example, Loewald, 1962, p. 493).

Once again, we can identify those approaches that inherently must lead to dead ends. I have pointed out many times that these limitations seem to escape the notice of those who seek to solve the problems within orthodox frameworks (e.g., Goodstein, 1960; Popper and Eccles, 1977, pp. 69, 309–310, 333). The retention of methodologies that cannot succeed is also practiced by some critics of orthodox approaches, however. For example, I think it likely that Feffer, in spite of his unusual and productive critique, will remain stymied in his search for solutions. While he notes that he is still struggling for a way out of the Cartesian dilemma (pp. 5, 258–285), he apparently also continues to assume that *some* logical-formal schema will enable him to move forward (e.g., pp. 282–285). In my view, the very best that such attempts can accomplish would be to remove the problems one stage further, or to obscure them with some new brand of logically based handwaving. Somehow, one will need to address the basic set of paradoxes, the problems represented by the move from a world that is entirely undifferentiated and unintegrated to a world that displays differentiation and integration both. Perhaps we shall have to enter the prenatal domain to do so.

Winnicott (1965) seems to have a sense of that problem. To cope with the translogical movement across stages, he develops the conception of transitional realms and phenomena. These notions serve as undefined intermediaries between a situation in which there is no inside/outside, no self/other differentiation, and the situation of differentiation, where objects are "objective," found, differentiated from a rudimentary self. He recognizes the highly paradoxical nature of the transition from subjective "making" to objective "finding," and suggests that the paradoxes that arise should be tolerated, not glibly resolved. Furthermore, he suggests that these intermediate realms continue to play an important role in adult life, certainly an interesting and generative suggestion. Although to some his proposals may not provide a satisfactory solution, at the very least they highlight the paradoxes without offering facile (and fallacious) Cartesian answers.

The acquisition of one's first language, then, falls into the same class of mysterious, bootstrap, paradoxical transitional phenomena as differentiations from an undifferentiated state into self/other, psyche/soma, inside/outside—at least in the view of the critics. It is questionable whether one can get very far in understanding them if one separates these processes into various compartments, if, for example, one believes language acquisition can be treated separately from more general developmental phenomena. I am reminded of Robinson's (1975) remarks, quoted earlier in Chapter 4:

> I suspect that if there can be anything called "psycholinguistics" it will have to work by meditating on the psychology built into our language, the ways in which the psyche makes itself in speech [p. 160].
>
> One cannot study language without studying human nature [p. 185].

The implication for formalisms should by now be obvious. State process formalisms, the formal expressions of the Cartesian world view, simply cannot hope adequately to capture or represent these developments. Worse, they will necessarily engender paradox and dead ends. What is needed in order to address these kinds of issues is a theoretical vehicle that will not introduce Cartesian presumptions "at the front end."

I am suggesting, then, that to address these kinds of subjects by means of the processive, life world discourse presented in Chapters 4 and 6 may be useful. It may provide an approach that would avoid a return, once again, to the frameworks that cannot do otherwise than entrap us in insoluble paradoxes. My very tentative and general suggestion is that a non-state-process use of language, coupled with a pragmatic focus that can guide us to productive and relevant questions, may allow progress in this and related subject areas pertaining to developmental phenomena.

GENERALIZATION IV: FREE WILL, DETERMINISM, CAUSALITY

I venture into this philosophical minefield only in order to add some speculative comments. General discussions of perennial disputes in this area can be found, for example, in Danto and Morgenbesser (1960, pp. 315–470), Keat (1981, pp. 110–112), Rorty (1979), Margenau (1934), Schumacher (1973, pp. 210–216), and von Wright (1971, Chapter 2).

While controversies continue about the compatibility of freedom and determinism, it seems to me that, once again, key representational issues have been neglected. When "compatibilists," "hard determinists," and "libertarians" (Keat) argue about whether there is such a thing as free will, or determinism, or causality pertaining to human actions, whether free and unfree actions somehow refer to different levels, and the like, certain ambiguities and confusions are perpetuated. Perhaps an analysis in terms of state process notions can shed additional light on these perennial and unresolved questions.

What is determinism? We saw in Chapter 3 Laplace's familiar state space specification. Roughly, it amounted to saying, first, that knowing all about a system (say, the "world") is the same as knowing all the variables, laws, and initial conditions that are required to represent completely that system within a state space; second, that determinism then is simply equivalent to working out the evolution of the state within that all-encompassing mathematical/formal space, and then retranslating the formal results into their referent, the system. In this way, total prediction will be accomplished with certainty. On the other hand, there are perspectives, such as Bergson's (1946), that reject the very idea of human predictability, in certain creative situations at least. Bergson, for example, begins with the premise that an adequate view of persons and their creativity is simply incompatible with the Lapalacian picture. I shall limit myself here to two observations.

The first concerns the distinction that is usually made between deterministic and teleological conceptualizations. According to that distinction, determinism is at one end, the Laplacian end, of a spectrum with teleology at the other. The organism is either "blindly impelled from one act to another" or acts "from the outset in the light of its foreknowledge" (Feffer, 1982, p. 199; see also pp. 79–83). Teleology and causal/deterministic frameworks are seen as alternative, logically incompatible views.

What does the state process perspective have to add to this commonly held view? I would suggest that from the point of view of state space analysis this standard polarization is a misconception. In physics, "causal" frameworks such as the classical Newtonian framework of forces (causes) and accelerations (effects) can be, and have been, recast into logically equivalent teleological versions that remain entirely mechanistic. In classical mechanics, one can just as well specify the Newtonian world by means of teleological (variational) principles as by means of the better known "causal" principles that involve pushes and pulls and their effects. In the teleological versions, one assumes that systems behave in ways that minimize certain mathematical functions or variables. For example, one can say that in a mechanical system of fields and particles the paths of these particles will be "sought" by the system according to certain teleological principles. The paths followed over time by a set of mass points subjected to a force field will be selected in such a way that some particular quantitative value (say, the so-called action) will be minimized, will be less over the "chosen" paths than it would have been over any other available alternative path. One can think of these "choices" as being made locally, as it were, one short step at a time, with the macroscopic "selected" path being the final expression of the cumulative local decisions.

Similar variational, teleological principles can be found in classical optics (e.g., Fermat's principle) or in quantum theory. A well-known yet highly paradoxical example of a combined mechanistic and teleological situation comes from the kind of experiments in which single particles are allowed to pass through one of two slits, one particle at a time. The experiment can be performed in one of two ways; one can either cover the slits one at a time, or one can leave both slits open all the time. Common sense predicts that the accumulated outcomes would be the same in either case. (Remember that only one particle at a time is directed at the slits.) That is not borne out; although common sense has no explanation, the results of these kinds of experiments plainly show that particles act as though each single particle "knew ahead of time" whether it had one slit available (whether one of the two slits had been covered) or whether it had to "choose" between two available slits.

(An often cited but in my view erroneous example of systems that supposedly display teleological but not deterministic behavior are cybernetic, feedback-governed systems. I believe these to be vulgarized pseudo-examples, because, properly speaking, these kinds of systems basically are just standard mechanical deterministic systems operating under conditions of variable inputs. They can, of course, also be viewed from a teleological perspective, but they are teleological only in the most superficial sense. For a discussion of the irrelevance for epistemology of cybernetic, homeostatic, and similar engineering "teleological" systems, see von Wright, 1971, pp. 22–23.)

At any rate, as various examples from theoretical physics have shown, one has the option of "explaining" the behavior of some inanimate systems in ways that ascribe teleological features to them. From a formal point of view—that is, in a state process sense—

teleological and causal versions of events are, in many cases, logically equivalent conceptualizations. Thus, a state process analysis suggests that the usual presumption—that these two varieties of explanations are polar opposites—is wrong.

Second, on the basis of the preceding considerations, state process analysis suggests a legitimate alternative basic polarity. The analysis suggests that the true polarity is between state process and non-state-process frameworks. (It might be worth reminding ourselves, though, that these two do not have coordinate status; ontologically, the state process view is derivative, parasitic on the life world, non-state-process framework.)

Accordingly, it seems to me that discussions about these issues (e.g., Rorty, 1979) ought to keep these facts in mind. Once the discussions are placed and conducted within a state process format—tacitly or explicitly—then the issues must perforce be plagued by paradox, and must necessarily become unresolvable. One's options for solutions come to be restricted. Once one becomes trapped within the assumptions and constraints of a state process formalism, only mysticism can offer a way out; otherwise, all formal moves must come up against the innate limits of the conceptual framework. One cannot expect to deal adequately with non-state-process aspects of the world within a state process framework. Even such unorthodox thinkers as Lewontin, Rose, and Kamin (1984) flounder when they attempt to explicate free will within a framework that harbors standard state process notions (pp. 287–290). In my view, they are unable to find a compelling alternative. They do not recognize clearly the state process issues to which I am calling attention, and therefore remain stuck with the principal features of the standard Laplacian world view: equating knowledge and understanding with the availability of a complete state process representation of the world. They are forced to conclude their discussions of the issue with what is to my mind a rather lame argument:

> Our biology has made us into creatures who are constantly recreating our own psychic and material environments, and whose individual lives are the outcomes of an extraordinary multiplicity of intersecting pathways. Thus, it is our biology that makes us free [p. 290].

It would seem that in spite of rejecting much of the standard Cartesian framework (e.g., Chapter 10), they still must call on the enormous dimensionality of the (Cartesian) world to provide a means for explaining freedom. That is all they have available.

In the life world view, in the view in which a derivative state process net has not yet been cast over one's experience, the notion of determinism likewise is not yet rigidly specified, and thus there is still room for productive exploration of the concept. A generative approach to these issues, then, might be to see what it means to remain outside a state process perspective, to see what that implies, how it might be accomplished, and so on. An application of the formal and focal principles and methods that I have been advocating may help to illuminate the questions.

GENERALIZATION V: AFFECTS

I have already discussed on several occasions the scientific treatment of affects. I sought to demonstrate that in the behavioral disciplines they are conceptualized, whether explicitly or implicitly, as states or state processes.

It is quite clear that affects have been and continue to be a nagging problem for psychoanalytic theorizing: "We do not possess a systematic statement of the psychoanalytic theory of affects" (Rapaport, 1953/1967, p. 476). "Hartmann has said that Freud's inability to solve the problem of quality, that is, the nonquantitative aspects of a structure, was his greatest disappointment" (Gill and Klein, 1967, p. 28). "Psychoanalysis has always been aware of the focal significance of affect and, at the same time, of its inability to define and describe the nature of that concept satisfactorily" (Basch, 1976, p. 759).

Brenner (1974) puts it this way:

> The complexities and difficulties inherent in any attempt to arrive at valid and useful generalizations concerning mental phenomena have been very evident in the field of affect theory. Every psychoanalyst who has approached the subject has begun by emphasizing the meager and unsatisfactory state of our theoretical knowledge in spite of the importance of affects both in psychoanalytic theory and in clinical practice [p. 532].

Brenner goes on to review the standard psychoanalytic conceptualizations. His own model, while perhaps not quite standard, can nevertheless be considered as representative for the purposes of the present discussion. His model subsumes the standard views of affects as aspects of quantitative instinctual discharges:

> Psychologically an affect is a sensation of pleasure, unpleasure, or both, plus the ideas associated with it. Ideas and sensation together, both conscious and unconscious, constitute an affect [p. 535].

Brenner enlarges on this definition in other works (1975, 1976); it seems to be compatible with other mainstream conceptualizations (e.g., Kernberg, 1976, pp. 111–115).

From a formal point of view, what do we have here? First, we have a quantitative component, the "sensation." Formally, it has the same features as those implied by a view of affects as aspects of energic discharge: The sensation is conceptualized within a simple one-dimensional space that spans the range from unpleasure, through a mixture of unpleasure and pleasure, to pleasure. A given sensation is representable by a point in that space.

What about the "associated ideas" component? The idea of an "idea" has been around for a long time, and has gone through many phases. For example, in the 17th century's Port Royal *Logic,* there is the following opinion: "Some words are so clear that they cannot be explained by others, for none are more clear and simple. 'Idea' is such a word" (quoted by Hacking, 1975, p. 12). Descartes, drawing an analogy between vision and inner ("direct") perception, advocated that one needs to avoid becoming enmeshed in inner speech, which can confuse us. Instead, we must study our ideas, giving them "that degree of mental illumination that each of us possesses" (p. 31). More recently, Deese (1978) states unequivocally that "linguistic rules and psychological limitations in processing information determine how we put ideas into words" (p. 314). I doubt that anyone would care to support the position that "idea" is a simple, self-evident notion that can serve to illuminate explanations.

It seems, then, that we are at an impasse. If we stick to a quantitative conception of affects (e.g., an energy-based discharge notion), obviously we then remain within a state space conception and can expect to be limited in the usual ways. Adding the notion of "process" does not really help. If we widen the conception to include such an "action" representation, that turns out to be only an apparent change: "There is nothing specially explanatory about the term 'process'; it is simply a label for 'activity' of some kind, and activity can be activity of either an impersonal or a personal object" (Guntrip, 1961, p. 145; see also Berger, 1978). Whether implicitly or explicitly, "process" typically turns into "path in state space." Formally, all we have done is move from a point representation to a path representation, all still within the state process formalism.

This seems to be the trap into which theorizers about affect typically fall. Seemingly unaware of the implications of invoking a state process framework, they attempt to cope with the affective aspect of the life world within a formalism that, in my view, dooms such attempts in advance.

This is the limitation inherent in Basch's (1976) view of affects, for example. He sets his examination of the affective domain within an implicit state conception—in terms of communicational, symbolic-logical, patterned activity of the facial muscles (in infants and animals); referential, atomic conceptions of language; muscular and glandular responses of the body, and other formalisms that implicitly invoke state models. Basch neither identifies nor discusses this common underlying formalism. As one would expect from my earlier discussions, by remaining within this formal class of frameworks, he necessarily must remain stymied; he is, for example, forced to speak about "'feelings,' so-called" (p. 762). Life world phenomena cannot be adequately represented or treated.

The same kinds of critical comments also apply to Laplanche's (1976) extended analysis of Freudian approaches to affect. He, too, struggles with models—from Freud's 1893 *Project*—that are circumscribed from the very start by state process features: neuronal configurations on the one hand, and a quantifying economic component on the other (pp. 54–58). (Laplanche specifically identifies the formal identity between the Freudian system and Descartes' earlier version—"figure/movement" [p. 54].) Since the two apparently different models—neuronal configuration and quantified psychic energy—are both state process representations, they ultimately must reduce any and all affective experiences to state properties (e.g., p. 116) and thus, to impoverished, inadequate entities.

Obviously, I am maintaining once again that difficulties from which one cannot recover are introduced at the very start of one's scientific analysis when one proposes that there are phenomena, entities, events, or experiences that can be referentially labeled as affects, formally excised, and then treated as a state space "object" by the observer. We are back to the issue of the standard Cartesian practices. The earlier criticisms imply that there may be something very wrong with treating affects separately from the total situation within which they are experienced; there also may be something very wrong with representing the now excised affects as points in an impoverishing and impoverished state space. As far as consciously experienced feelings go, there is no consciousness without affects, and, conversely, no affect without consciousness. If that is the case, it would seem that one should be suspicious of conceptions of affects that sever them from the fact of consciousness: being, the integrated life world experience. That point has been explored generally in previous chapters. Perhaps one needs to be very careful before one compartmentalizes the experience of the person-in-the-world into affects, ideas, thoughts, inner speech, perception, and consciousness, let alone into person, external world, and language. Perhaps we need to give careful and explicit thought to the representational issues. Perhaps we need to screen more carefully the "theoretical" questions we formulate about affects; pragmatic perspectives, thought experiments, might provide productive alternatives to the pure knowledge paradigm. Perhaps a significant number of the aggravating difficulties that arise in theorizing about affects are artifacts that must inevitably arise in the course of Cartesian compartmentalization and state representation. We have taken the situation apart quite easily, but apparently we can neither deal effectively with the separate constituents that our framework has created, nor put them back together in a satisfactory fashion.

COMMENT

I shall leave matters in this incomplete state. I trust I have made a plausible case that certain important formal/focal issues arise in a great many different contexts in those disciplines that seek to deal with the domain of the person.

Schumacher has worked out very carefully the implications that Cartesian world views and techniques have for global well-being and, indeed, for survival (e.g., 1973, pp. 72–94; 1977, Chapter 10). His works can be read in many different ways (Kumar, 1981, p. vii), but for me, his dominant message is the urgent need, on a scale that greatly transcends clinical issues, to reconsider very generally the consequences of our wholesale and inappropriate application of Cartesian thought and methodology. It may be, then, that the issues I have gathered, integrated, and reported in this work have significance for clinician and nonclinician alike, and that they may merit and repay further consideration for that reason as well.

References

Abelson, R. (1984), Review of *Mathematical models in the social and behavioral sciences*. American Scientist, 72: 92.
Arnold, M. B. (1960), *Emotions and Personality*. New York: Columbia University Press.
Aronson, G. (1977), Defence and deficit models: Their influence on therapy of schizophrenia. *Internat. J. Psycho-Anal.*, 58: 11–16.
Austin, J. L. (1962), *Sense and Sensibilia*. New York: Oxford University Press.
———— (1964), A plea for excuses. In: *Ordinary Language*, ed. V. C. Chappell. Englewood Cliffs, NJ: Prentice-Hall, pp. 41–63. (Reprinted from *Proceedings of the Aristotelian Society*, 1956–1957, 57: 1–29.)
Axelrod, C. D. (1979), *Studies in Intellectual Breakthrough: Freud, Simmel, Buber*. Amherst, MA: University of Massachusetts Press.
Barker, S. F. (1969), Introduction. In: *Observation and Theory in Science*, eds. E. Nagel, S. Bromberger, & A. Grunbaum. Baltimore, MD: Johns Hopkins University Press, pp. 1–14.
Barrett, W. (1972), *Time of Need: Forms of Imagination in the Twentieth Century*. New York: Harper & Row.
———— (1978), *The Illusion of Technique: A Search for Meaning in a Technological Civilization*. Garden City, NY: Anchor/Doubleday.
Bartley, W. W. (1973), *Wittgenstein*. Philadelphia: Lippincott.
Basch, M. F. (1973), Psychoanalysis and theory formation. *The Annual of Psychoanalysis*, 1: 39–52.
———— (1976), The concept of affect: A re-examination. *J. Amer. Psychoanal. Assn.*, 24: 759–777.
Bateson, G. (1979), *Mind and Nature: A Necessary Unity*. New York: Dutton.
Bellman, R. (1967), Mathematical models of the mind. *Mathematical Biosciences*, 1: 287–330.
Berger, L. S. (1974), *The logic of observation in psychotherapy research*. Unpublished doctoral dissertation, University of Tennessee, Knoxville, TN.

References

―――― (1978), Innate constraints of formal theories. *Psychoanal. Contemp. Thought*, 1: 89–117.
Bergson, H. (1946), *The Creative Mind: An Introduction to Metaphysics*. (M. L. Andison, Trans.) New York: Philosophical Library. (Original work published in 1934.)
Bettelheim, B. (1956), Schizophrenia as a reaction to extreme situations. *Amer. J. Orthopsychiat.*, 26: 507–518.
―――― (1967), *The Empty Fortress: Infantile Autism and the Birth of the Self*. New York: Free Press.
―――― (1974), *A Home for the Heart*. New York: Knopf.
―――― (1983), *Freud and Man's Soul*. New York: Knopf.
Black, M. (1970), *Margins of Precision*. Ithaca: Cornell University Press.
Bohm, D. (1976), *Fragmentation and Wholeness*. Jerusalem: Van Leer.
―――― (1980), *Wholeness and the Implicate Order*. London: Routledge & Kegan Paul.
Boring, E. (1950), *A History of Experimental Psychology*. New York: Appleton-Century-Crofts.
Bowlby, J. (1979), Psychoanalysis as art and science. *Internat. Rev. Psycho-Anal.*, 6: 3–14.
Braginsky, B. M., & Braginsky, D. D. (1974), *Mainstream Psychology: A Critique*. New York: Holt, Rinehart & Winston.
Brenner, C. (1974), On the nature and development of affects: a unified theory. *Psychoanal. Quart.* 43: 532–556.
―――― (1975), Affects and psychic conflict. *Psychoanal. Quart.* 44: 5–28.
―――― (1976), *Psychoanalytic Technique and Psychic Conflict*. New York: International Universities Press.
Bronowski, J. (1966), The logic of the mind. *American Scientist* 54: 1–14.
―――― (1978), *The Origins of Knowledge and Imagination*. New Haven: Yale University Press.
Buber, M. (1970), *I and Thou*. (W. Kaufmann, Trans.) New York: Scribners.
Bunge, M. (1976), The relevance of philosophy to social science. In: *Basic Issues in the Philosophy of Science*, ed. W. R. Shea. New York: Science History, pp. 136–155.
Campbell, K. (1982), The psychotherapy relationship with borderline personality disorders. *Psychother.: Theory, Prac., Res.*, 19: 166–193.
Capra, F. (1982), Holonomy and bootstrap. In: *The Holographic Paradigm and Other Paradoxes: Exploring the Leading Edge of Science*, ed. K. Wilber. Boulder, CO: Shambala, pp. 113–116.
Chao, Y. R. (1968), *Language and Symbolic Systems*. London: Cambridge University Press.
Chappell, V. C. (Ed.) (1964), *Ordinary Language*. Englewood Cliffs, NJ: Prentice-Hall.
Chessick, R. D. (1977), *Intensive Psychotherapy of the Borderline Patient*. New York: Aronson.
Chomsky, N. (1972), *Language and Mind*. (2nd, enlarged ed.) New York: Harcourt Brace Jovanovich.

Church, A. (1981), Formal logic. In: *Dictionary of Philosophy*, ed. D. D. Runes. Totowa, NJ: Littlefield Adams, pp. 170–181.

Danto, A. C. (1968), *What Philosophy Is: A Guide to the Elements*. New York: Harper & Row.

———, & Morgenbesser, S. (Eds.) (1960), *Philosophy of Science*. Cleveland: World.

Davis, P. J., & Hersh, R. (1981), *The Mathematical Experience*. Boston: Houghton Mifflin.

de Bono, E. (1981), Lateral thinking. In: *The Schumacher Lectures*, ed. S. Kumar. New York: Harper Colophon, pp. 144–164.

Deese, J. (1978), Thought into speech. *American Scientist*, 66: 314–321.

Deikman, A. J. (1982), *The Observing Self: Mysticism and Psychotherapy*. Boston: Beacon.

d'Espagnat, B. (1979), The quantum theory and reality. *Scientific American*, 241: 158–181.

Dorpat, T. L. (1973), Research on the therapeutic process in psychoanalysis. *J. Amer. Psychoanal. Assn.*, 21: 168–181.

Dreyfus, H. L. (1979), *What Computers Can't Do: The Limits of Artificial Intelligence*. New York: Harper Colophon.

Edelson, M. (1975), *Language and Interpretation in Psychoanalysis*. New Haven: Yale University Press.

Eissler, K. R. (1953), The effect of the structure of the ego in psychoanalytic technique. *J. Amer. Psychoanal. Assn.*, 1: 104–131.

Engelmann, P. (1967), *Letters from Ludwig Wittgenstein*. (L. Furtmueller, Trans.). Oxford: Basil Blackwell.

Erickson, S. A. (1970), *Language and Meaning: An Analytic Phenomenology*. New Haven: Yale University Press.

Ezorsky, G. (1967), Pragmatic theory of truth. In: *The Encyclopedia of Philosophy*, ed. P. Edwards. New York: Macmillan & Free Press, pp. 427–430.

Fairbairn, W. R. D. (1958), On the nature and aims of psycho-analytical treatment. *Internat. J. Psycho-Anal.*, 39: 374–385.

Feffer, M. (1982), *The Structure of Freudian Thought: The Problem of Immutability and Discontinuity in Developmental Theory*. New York: International Universities Press.

Fenichel, O. (1941), *Problems of Psychoanalytic Technique*. (D. Brunswick, Trans.) New York: Psychoanalytic Quarterly.

——— (1945), *The Psychoanalytic Theory of Neurosis*. New York: Norton.

Feyerabend, P. (1975), *Against Method*. London: New Left.

Feynman, R. P., Leighton, R. B., & Sands, M. (1963), *The Feynman Lectures on Physics*. (Vol. 1). Reading, MA: Addison-Wesley.

Fliess, R. (1949), Silence and verbalization: A supplement to the theory of the "analytic rule." *Internat. J. Psycho-Anal.*, 30: 21–30.

Fodor, J. A. (1968), *Psychological Explanation*. New York: Random House.

Freud, A. (1965), *Normality and Pathology in Childhood: Assessments of Development*. New York: International Universities Press.

References

Freud, S. (1893), A case of successful treatment by hypnotism. S.E., 1: 115–128.
_____ (1904a), Freud's psychoanalytic procedure. S.E., 7: 247–254.
_____ (1904b), On psychotherapy. S.E., 7: 257–268.
_____ (1910), The future prospects of psychoanalytic therapy. S.E., 11: 139–151.
_____ (1912a), The dynamics of the transference. S.E., 12: 97–108.
_____ (1912b), Recommendations to physicians practicing psycho-analysis. S.E., 12: 109–120.
_____ (1913), On beginning treatment. S.E., 12: 121–144.
_____ (1920), A note on the prehistory of the technique of analysis. S.E., 18: 263–265.
Friedman, L. (1976), Problems of an action theory of the mind. *Internat. Rev. Psycho-Anal.*, 3: 259–275.
_____ (1978), Trends in the psychoanalytic theory of treatment. *Psychoanal. Quart.*, 47: 524–567.
Friedman, L. J. (1975), Current psychoanalytic object relations theory and its clinical implications. *Internat. J. Psycho-Anal.*, 56: 137–146.
Furlong, F. W. (1981), Determinism and free will: Review of the literature. *Amer. J. Psychiat.*, 138: 425–439.
Gadamer, H-G. (1976), *Philosophical Hermeneutics*. (D. E. Linge, Trans. & Ed.) Berkeley: University of California Press.
_____ (1982), *Truth and Method*. New York: Crossroad.
Gedo, J. E. (1979), *Beyond Interpretation*. New York: International Universities Press.
Gedo, J. E., & Goldberg, A. (1973), *Models of the Mind: A Psychoanalytic Theory*. Chicago: University of Chicago Press.
Gedo, J. E., & Pollock, G. H. (Eds.) (1976), Freud: The fusion of science and humanism. *Psychological Issues*, 34/35. New York: International Universities Press.
Gill, M. M. (1973), Introduction to G. Klein's "Two theories or one?" *Bull. Menn. Clinic*, 37: 99–101.
_____ (1976), Metapsychology is not psychology. In: *Psychology Versus Metapsychology: Psychoanalytic Essays in Memory of George S. Klein*, eds. M. M. Gill & P. S. Holzman. *Psychological Issues*, 9, 36. New York: International Universities Press, pp. 71–105.
_____, & Klein, G. S. (1967), The structuring of drive and reality—David Rapaport's contributions to psychoanalysis and psychology. In: *Collected papers of David Rapaport*, ed. M. M. Gill. New York: Basic Books, pp. 8–34.
Giorgi, A. (1970), *Psychology as a Human Science*. New York: Harper & Row.
Gitelson, M. (1962), The curative factors in psycho-analysis—the first phase of psycho-analysis. *Internat. J. Psycho-Anal.*, 43: 194–203.
Glover, E. (1955), *The Technique of Psychoanalysis*. New York: International Universities Press.

——— (1968), *The Birth of the Ego*. New York: International Universities Press.

——— (1972), Remarks on success and failure in psychoanalysis and psychotherapy. In: *Success and failure in psychoanalysis and psychotherapy*, ed. B. B. Wolman. New York: Macmillan, pp. 131–152.

Goldstein, H. (1980), *Classical Mechanics* (2nd ed.). Reading, MA: Addison-Wesley.

Goodman, N. (1972), *Problems and Projects*. New York: Bobbs-Merrill.

Goodstein, R. L. (1960), Language and experience. In: *Philosophy of Science*, eds. A. C. Danto & S. Morgenbesser. Cleveland: World, pp. 83–100.

Graves, J. C. (1971), *The Conceptual Foundations of Contemporary Relativity Theory*. Cambridge: MIT Press.

Greenson, R. R. (1967), *The Technique and Practice of Psychoanalysis* (Vol. 1). New York: International Universities Press.

Grene, M. (1948), *Introduction to Existentialism*. Chicago: University of Chicago Press.

——— (Ed.) (1969), Toward a unity of knowledge. *Psychological Issues*, 6, monograph 22. New York: International Universities Press.

Guntrip, H. (1961), *Personality Structure and Human Interaction*. New York: International Universities Press.

——— (1969), *Schizoid Phenomena, Object Relations and the Self*. New York: International Universities Press.

Hacking, I. (1975), *Why Does Language Matter to Philosophy?* New York: Cambridge University Press.

Hanson, N. (1971), *Observation and Explanation: A Guide to Philosophy of Science*. New York: Harper & Row.

Hardwick, C. S. (1971), *Language Learning in Wittgenstein's Later Philosophy*. The Hague: Mouton.

Harman, G. (1973), *Thought*. Princeton: Princeton University Press.

Harth, E. (1983), *Windows on the Mind*. New York: Quill.

Hartmann, H. (1951), Technical implications of ego psychology. *Psychoanal. Quart.*, 20: 31–43.

———, Kris, E., & Loewenstein, R. M. (1953), The function of theory in psychoanalysis. In: *Drives, Affects, and Behavior*, ed. R. M. Loewenstein. New York: International Universities Press, pp. 13–37.

Hexter, J. H. (1971), *The History Primer*. New York: Basic Books.

Hoffman, R. R., & Nead, J. M. (1983), General contextualism, ecological science and cognitive research. *J. Mind Beh.*, 4: 507–559.

Hoffmann, B. (1983), *Relativity and its Roots*. New York: Scientific American Books.

Holt, R. R. (1961). Clinical judgement as a disciplined inquiry. *Journal of Nervous and Mental Disease*, 133: 369–382.

——— (1981), The death and transfiguration of metapsychology. *Internat. Rev. Psycho-Anal.*, 8: 129–143.

Holton, G. (1968), Mach, Einstein, and the search for reality. *Daedalus*, 97: 636–673.

Horowitz, M. J. (1979), *States of Mind*. New York: Plenum.

References

Horwitz, L. (1974), *Clinical Prediction in Psychotherapy*. New York: Aronson.
Hughes, R. I. G. (1981), Quantum logic. *Scientific American*, 248: 202–213.
Hunter, G. (1971), *Metalogic: An Introduction to the Metatheory of Standard First-Order Logic*. Berkeley: University of California Press.
Ingleby, D. (Ed.) (1980), *Critical Psychiatry: The Politics of Mental Health*. New York: Pantheon.
Jacobson, E. (1971), *Depression*. New York: International Universities Press.
Jacoby, R. (1983), *The Repression of Psychoanalysis: Otto Fenichel and the Political Freudians*. New York: Basic Books.
Jameson, F. (1972), *The Prison-House of Language*. Princeton: Princeton University Press.
Janik, A., & Toulmin, S. (1973), *Wittgenstein's Vienna*. New York: Simon & Schuster.
Jaynes, J. (1966), The routes of science. *American Scientist*, 54: 94–102.
―――― (1976), *The Origins of Consciousness in the Breakdown of the Bicameral Mind*. Boston: Houghton Miflin.
Jordan, N. (1968), *Themes in Speculative Psychology*. London: Tavistock.
Kahn, J., & Wright, S. E. (1980), *Human Growth and the Development of Personality*. Oxford: Pergamon.
Kaiser, H. (1965), *Effective Psychotherapy*. New York: Free Press.
Kaplan, D. M. (1977), Differences in the clinical and academic points of view on metapsychology. *Bull. Menn. Clinic*, 41: 207–228.
Kaufmann, W. (1980), *Discovering the Mind* (Vol. 1). New York: McGraw-Hill.
Keat, R. (1981), *The Politics of Social Theory: Habermas, Freud and the Critique of Positivism*. Chicago: University of Chicago Press.
Kernberg, O. (1975), *Borderline Conditions and Pathological Narcissism*. New York: Aronson.
―――― (1976), *Object Relations Theory and Clinical Psychoanalysis*. New York: Aronson.
―――― (1977), The structural diagnosis of borderline personality organization. In: *Borderline Personality Disorders: The Concept, the Syndrome, the Patient*, ed. P. Hartocollis. New York: International Universities Press, pp. 87–121.
―――― (1979), Some implications of object relations theory for psychoanalytic technique. *J. Amer. Psychoanal. Assn.*, 27 (Supp.): 207–239.
Klein, G. S. (1973), Two theories or one? Perspectives to change in psychoanalytic theory. *Bull. Menn. Clinic*, 37: 101–136.
―――― (1976), *Psychoanalytic Theory: An Exploration of Essentials*. New York: International Universities Press.
Klein, M. (1948), On the theory of anxiety and guilt. *Internat. J. Psycho-Anal.*, 29: 114–123. (Reprinted in *Envy and Gratitude and Other Works, 1946–1963*. 1977, pp. 25–42. New York: Delta.)
Koch, S. (1961). Psychological science versus the science-humanism antinomy: Intimations of a significant science of man. *Amer. Psychol.*, 16: 629–639.

Kohut, H. (1971), *The Analysis of the Self*. New York: International Universities Press.
────── (1977). *The Restoration of the Self*. New York: International Universities Press.
────── (1979). The two analyses of Mr Z. *Internat. J. of Psycho-Anal.*, 60: 3–27.
────── (1984), *How Does Analysis Cure?* (Eds. A. Goldberg & P. E. Stepansky.) Chicago: University of Chicago Press.
──────, & Wolf, E. S. (1978), The disorders of the self and their treatment: An outline. *Internat. J. Psycho-Anal.*, 59: 413–425.
Kovel, J. (1974), Erik Erikson's psychohistory. *Social Policy*, 4: 60–64.
────── (1978), Things and words. *Psychoanal. Contemp. Thought*, 1: 21–88.
────── (1981), *The Age of Desire: Reflections of a Radical Psychoanalyst*. New York: Pantheon.
Kubie, L. S. (1975), The language tools of psychoanalysis: A search for better tools drawn from better models. *Internat. Rev. Psycho-Anal.*, 2: 11–24.
Kuhn, T. S. (1970), *The Structure of Scientific Revolutions*. Chicago: University of Chicago Press.
Kumar, S. (Ed.) (1981). *The Schumacher Lectures*. New York: Harper Colophon.
Kwawer, J. S., Lerner, H. D., Lerner, P. M., & Sugarman, A. (1980), *Borderline Phenomena and the Rorschach Test*. New York: International Universities Press.
Lacan, J. (1968), *The Four Fundamental Concepts of Psycho-Analysis*. (J. A. Miller, Ed.; A. Sheridan, Trans.). New York: Norton.
Laing, R. D. (1982), *The Voice of Experience*. New York: Pantheon.
Landau, M. (1984), Human evolution as narrative. *American Scientist*, 72: 262–267.
Langer, S. (1967), *Mind: An Essay on Human Feeling*. (Vol. 1). Baltimore: Johns Hopkins University Press.
────── (1982), *Mind: An Essay on Human Feeling*. (Vol. 3). Baltimore: Johns Hopkins University Press.
Laplanche, J. (1976), *Life and Death in Psychoanalysis*. (J. Mehlman, Trans.). Baltimore: Johns Hopkins University Press.
──────, & Pontalis, J-B. (1973), *The Language of Psychoanalysis*. (D. Nicholson-Smith, Trans.) New York: Norton.
Leavy, S. A. (1980), *The Psychoanalytic Dialogue*. New Haven: Yale University Press.
Lecky, P. (1961), *Self-consistency: A theory of Personality*. (2nd Ed.). New York: Shoe String Press.
Leites, N. (1971), *The New Ego*. New York: Science House.
────── (1977), Transference interpretations *only*? *Internat. J. Psycho-Anal.*, 58: 275–286.
Levenson, E. (1972), *The Fallacy of Understanding*. New York: Basic Books.
────── (1975), A holographic model of psychoanalytic change. *Contemp. Psychoanal.*, 12: 1–20.

References

——— (1983), *The Ambiguity of Change: An Inquiry into the Nature of Psychoanalytic Reality.* New York: Basic Books.

Lewontin, R. C., Rose, S., & Kamin, L. J. (1984), *Not in our Genes: Biology, Ideology, and Human Nature.* New York: Pantheon.

Lichtenberg, J. D. (1983). *Psychoanalysis and Infant Research.* Hillsdale, NJ: The Analytic Press.

Linge, D. E. (1976), Editor's Introduction. In: H-G. Gadamer, *Philosophical Hermeneutics.* Berkeley: University of California Press, pp. xi–lviii.

Loevinger, J. (1966), Three principles for a psychoanalytic psychology. *J. Abnormal Psych.,* 71: 432–443.

Loewald, H. W. (1960), On the therapeutic action of psycho-analysis. *Internat. J. Psycho-Anal.,* 24: 16–33.

——— (1962), Internalization, separation, mourning, and the superego. *Psychoanal. Quart.,* 31: 483–504.

——— (1975), Psychoanalysis as an art and the fantasy character of the psychoanalytic situation. *J. Amer. Psychoanal. Assn.,* 23: 277–299.

——— (1981), Reflections on the psychoanalytic process and its therapeutic potential. In: *Papers on Psychoanalysis.* New Haven: Yale University Press, pp. 372–383.

Loewenstein, R. M. (1956), Some remarks on the role of speech in psychoanalytic technique. *Internat. J. Psycho-Anal.,* 37: 460–468.

London, I. D. (1944), Psychologists' misuse of the auxiliary concepts of physics and mathematics. *Psychol. Rev.,* 51: 266–291.

Louch, A. R. (1966), *Explanation and Human Action.* Berkeley: University of California Press.

Malcolm, N. (1971), The myth of cognitive processes and structures. In: *Cognitive Development and Epistemology,* ed. T. Michel. New York: Academic Press, pp. 385–392.

——— (1977), *Memory and Mind.* Ithaca: Cornell University Press.

Margenau, H. (1934), Meaning and scientific status of causality. *Philosophy of Science,* 1: 133–148.

Matson, W. I. (1976), *Sentience.* Berkeley: University of California Press.

Matte Blanco, I. (1975), *The Unconscious as Infinite Sets.* London: Duckworth.

McGill, V. J. (1962), Pragmatism. In: *Dictionary of Philosophy,* ed. D. D. Runes. Totowa, NJ: Littlefield Adams, pp. 245–247.

McIntosh, D. (1979), The empirical bearing of psychoanalytic theory. *Internat. J. Psycho-Anal.,* 60: 405–431.

Mehan, H., & Wood, H. (1975), *The Reality of Ethnomethodology.* New York: Wiley.

Merleau-Ponty, M. (1962), *The Phenomenology of Perception.* London: Routledge & Kegan Paul.

——— (1963), *The Structure of Behavior.* Boston: Beacon Press.

Milner, M. (1973), *On Not Being Able to Paint.* New York: International Universities Press.

Mitchell, W. J. T. (Ed.) (1981), *On Narrative*. Chicago: University of Chicago Press.

Modell, A. (1976), The holding environment and the therapeutic action of psychoanalysis. *J. Amer. Psychoanal. Assn.*, 24: 285–307.

Nagel, E., Bromberger, S., & Grunbaum, A. (1969), *Observation and Theory in Science*. Baltimore: Johns Hopkins University Press.

Needles, W. (1962), Eros and the repetition compulsion. *Psychoanal. Quart.*, 31: 505–526.

Nozick, R. (1981), *Philosophical Explanation*. Cambridge: Belknap/Harvard University Press.

Nunberg, H. (1937), On the theory of therapeutic results of psycho-analysis. *Internat. J. Psycho-Anal.*, 18: 161–169.

O'Manique, J. T. (1976), Scientific objectivity and the mind-body problem. In: *Basic Issues in the Philosophy of Science*, ed. W. R. Shea. New York: Science History Publications, pp. 107–126.

Ornston, D. G. (in press a), Review of *Freud and Man's Soul*.

―――― (in press b), Freud's conception is different from Strachey's.

Osgood, C. E. (1952), The nature and measurement of meaning. *Psychol. Bull.*, 49: 197–237.

――――, Suci, G. J., & Tannenbaum, P. H. (1957), *The Measurement of Meaning*. Urbana: University of Illinois Press.

Overton, W. F. (1975), General systems, structure, and development. In: *Structure and Transformation: Developmental and Historical Perspectives*, eds. F. Riegel & G. C. Rosenwald. New York: Wiley-Interscience, pp. 61–82.

Palazzoli, M. S., Cecchin, G., Prata, G., & Boscolo, L. (1978), *Paradox and Counterparadox: A New Model in the Theory of the Family in Schizophrenic Transaction*. (E. V. Burt, Trans.). New York: Aronson.

Paris, B. J. (1981), Letter to the Editor. *The New York Times Book Review*, 86, 3; Jan 18, p. 28.

Paul, I. H. (1973), *Letters to Simon*. New York: International Universities Press.

―――― (1978), *The Form and Technique of Psychotherapy*. Chicago: University of Chicago Press.

Pepper, S. C. (1961), *World Hypotheses: A Study in Evidence*. Berkeley: University of California Press.

Peterfreund, E. (1971), Information, Systems, and Psychoanalysis. *Psychological Issues*, Monogr. 25/26. New York: International Universities Press.

Pittenger, R. E., Hockett, C. F., & Danehy, J. J. (1960), *The First Five Minutes: A Sample of Microscopic Interview Analysis*. Ithaca, NY: Martineau.

Polanyi, M. (1972), *The Study of Man*. Chicago: University of Chicago Press.

Pollio, H. (1972), Existential-Phenomenology and the science of psychology. Unpublished paper.

Popper, K. R., & Eccles, J. C. (1977), *The Self and its Brain*. London: Routledge & Kegan Paul.

References

Powers, J. (1982), *Philosophy and the New Physics*. London: Methuen.
Pruyser, P. (1975), What splits in "splitting"? *Bull. Menn. Clinic*, 39: 1–46.
Quine, W. V. (1970), *Philosophy of Logic*. Englewood Cliffs, NJ: Prentice-Hall.
Rabil, A. (1967), *Merleau-Ponty: Existentialist of the Social World*. New York: Columbia University Press.
Rapaport, D. (1953), On the psychoanalytic theory of affects. *Internat. J. Psycho-Anal.*, 34: 177–198. (Reprinted in: *Collected Papers of David Rapaport*, ed. M. M. Gill. New York: Basic Books, 1967, pp. 476–512.)
—— (1958), The theory of ego autonomy. *Bull. Menn. Clinic*, 22: 13–35. (Reprinted in: *Collected Papers of David Rapaport*, ed. M. M. Gill. New York: Basic Books, 1967, pp. 722–744.)
—— (1960), The structure of psychoanalytic theory: A systematizing attempt. *Psychological Issues, Monogr.* 6. New York: International Universities Press.
——, & Gill, M. M. (1959), The points of view and assumptions of metapsychology. *Internat. J. Psycho-Anal.*, 40: 153–162.
Rapoport, A. (1983), *Mathematical Models in the Social and Behavioral Sciences*. New York: Wiley-Interscience.
Reich, W. (1933–1934), *Character Analysis*. New York: Touchstone Books, 1974.
Robbins, M. (1980), Current controversy of object relations theory as outgrowth of a schism between Klein and Fairbairn. *Internat. J. Psycho-Anal.*, 6: 477–492.
Robinson, I. (1975), *The New Grammarians' Funeral: A Critique of Noam Chomsky's Linguistics*. Cambridge: Cambridge University Press.
Rogers, C. (1977), *On Personal Power: Inner Strength and its Revolutionary Impact*. New York: Dell.
Rommetveit, R. (1974), *On Message Structure*. New York: Wiley.
Rorty, R. (Ed.) (1967), *The Linguistic Turn: Recent Essays in Philosophical Method*. Chicago: Univ. Chicago Press.
—— (1979), *Philosophy and the Mirror of Nature*. Princeton: Princeton University Press.
Rosen, V. H. (1974), The nature of verbal interventions in psychoanalysis. In: *Psychoanalysis and Contemporary Science*, Vol. 3, eds. L. Goldberger & V. H. Rosen. New York: International Universities Press, pp. 190–209.
Rosenthal, R. (1966), *Experimenter Effects in Behavioral Research*. New York: Appleton Century Croft.
——, & Rosnow, R. L. (1969), *Artifact in Behavioral Research*. New York: Academic Press.
Royce, J. R. (1983), The importance of Langer's philosophy of mind for a science of psychology. *Journal of Mind and Behavior*, 1: 491–506.
Rubinstein, B. B. (1965), Psychoanalytic theory and the mind-body problem. In: *Psychoanalysis and Current Biological Thought*, eds. N. S. Greenfield & W. C. Lewis. Madison: University of Wisconsin Press, pp. 35–56.
—— (1976), On the possibility of a strictly psychoanalytic theory: An

essay in the philosophy of psychoanalysis. *Psychological Issues, 36,* 229–264. New York: International Universities Press.

Ryle, G. (1964), Ordinary language. In: *Ordinary Language,* ed. V. C. Chappell. Englewood Cliffs, NJ: Prentice-Hall, pp. 24–40.

Sandler, J., & Rosenblatt, B. (1962), The concept of the representational world. *Psychoanalytic Study of the Child,* 17: 128–145.

Schafer, R. (1972), Internalization: Process or fantasy? *Psychoanalytic Study of the Child,* 27: 411–436.

——— (1976), *A New Language for Psychoanalysis.* New Haven: Yale University Press.

——— (1978), *Language and Insight.* New Haven: Yale University Press.

——— (1983), *The Analytic Attitude.* New York: Basic Books.

Schimek, J. G. (1975). The interpretation of the past: Childhood trauma, psychological reality, and historical truth. *J. Amer. Psychoanal. Assn.,* 23: 845–865.

Schumacher, E. F. (1973), *Small is Beautiful.* New York: Harper & Row.

——— (1977), *A Guide for the Perplexed.* New York: Harper & Row.

Searle, J. R. (1969), *Speech Acts: An Essay in the Philosophy of Language.* Cambridge: Cambridge University Press.

Seeman, J. (1965), Perspectives in client-centered therapy. In: *Handbook of Clinical Psychology,* ed. B. B. Wolman. New York: McGraw-Hill, pp. 1215–1229.

Settle, T. (1976), Is scientific knowledge really justified? In: *Basic Issues in the Philosophy of Science,* ed. W. R. Shea. New York: Science History Publications, pp. 15–35.

Shea, W. R. (1976), Introduction: Contemporary philosophy of science. In: *Basic Issues in the Philosophy of Science,* ed. W. R. Shea. New York: Science History Publications, pp. 1–14.

Sherwood, M. (1969), *The Logic of Explanation in Psychoanalysis.* New York: Academic Press.

——— (1973), Another look at the logic of explanation in psychoanalysis. In: *Psychoanalysis and Contemporary Science, vol. 2,* ed. B. B. Rubinstein. New York: Macmillan, pp. 359–366.

Slap, J. W., & Levine, F. J. (1978), On hybrid concepts in psychoanalysis. *Psychoanal. Quart.,* 47: 499–523.

Spence, D. P. (1982), Narrative truth and theoretical truth. *Psychoanal. Quart.,* 51: 43–69.

Spiro, A. (1979). Philosophical appraisal of Roy Schafer's *A New Language for Psychoanalysis. Psychoanal. Contemp. Thought,* 2: 253–291.

Stein, A. (1972), Causes of failure in psychoanalytic psychotherapy. In: *Success and Failure in Psychoanalysis and Psychotherapy,* ed. B. B. Wolman. New York: Macmillan, pp. 37–52.

Steiner, G. (1976), A note on language and psychoanalysis. *Internat. Rev. Psycho-Anal.,* 3: 253–267.

Stoller, R. (1971). Introduction. In: N. Leites, *The New Ego.* New York: Science House, pp. 3–37.

——— (1975), *Perversion: The Erotic Form of Hatred.* New York: Pantheon.

References

Storr, A. (1967), *Psychoanalysis Observed.* London: Rycroft, Constable & Co.

Strachey, J. (1934), The nature of the therapeutic action of psycho-analysis. *Internat. J. Psycho-Anal.,* 15: 127–159.

Straus, E. W. (1969), Embodiment and excarnation. In: Toward a unity of knowledge, ed. M. Grene. *Psychological Issues,* 22. New York: International Universities Press, pp. 212–236.

Strupp, H. H. (1972), Ferment in psychoanalysis and psychoanalytic psychotherapy. In: *Success and Failure in Psychoanalysis and Psychotherapy,* ed. B. B. Wolman. New York: Macmillan, pp. 71–103.

―――, Hadley, S. W., & Gomez-Schwartz, B. (1977), *Psychotherapy for Better or Worse: The Problem of Negative Effects.* New York: Aronson.

Sutherland, J. D. (1963), Object-relations theory and the conceptual model of psychoanalysis. *British Journal of Medical Psychology,* 36: 109–124.

Thayer, H. S. (1967), Pragmatism. In: *The Encyclopedia of Philosophy,* ed. P. Edwards. New York: Macmillan & Free Press, pp. 430–436.

Thoma, H., & Kachele, H. (1975), Problems of metascience and methodology in clinical psychoanalytic research. *Annual of Psychoanalysis,* 3: 49–119.

Turner, M. B. (1971), *Realism and the Explanation of Behavior.* New York: Appleton-Century-Crofts.

Urmson, J. O. (1956), *Philosophical Analysis.* Oxford: Oxford University Press.

von Neumann, J. (1958), *The Computer and the Brain.* New Haven: Yale University Press.

von Wright, G. H. (1971), *Explanation and Understanding.* Ithaca: Cornell University Press.

Waelder, R. (1962), Psychoanalysis, scientific method, and philosophy. *J. Amer. Psychoanal. Assn.,* 10: 617–637.

Wallerstein, R. S. (1976), Psychoanalysis as a science: Its present status and its future tasks. *Psychological Issues,* 36, 198–228. New York: International Universities Press.

Wartofsky, M. W. (1968), *Conceptual Foundations of Scientific Thought.* London: Collier-Macmillan.

Watson, W. H. (1960), On methods of representation. In: *Philosophy of Science,* eds. A. Danto & S. Morgenbesser. Cleveland: Meridian, pp. 226–244.

Weber, R. (1982). The enfolding-unfolding universe: A conversation with David Bohm. In: *The Holographic Paradigm and other Paradoxes: Exploring the Leading Edge of Science,* ed. K. Wilber. Boulder, CO: Shambala, pp. 44–104.

Weil, A. (1972), *The Natural Mind: A New Way of Looking at Drugs and the Higher Consciousness.* Boston: Houghton Mifflin.

――― (1983), *Health and Healing: Understanding Conventional and Alternative Medicine.* Boston: Houghton Mifflin.

Weizenbaum, J. (1976), *Computer Power and Human Reason: From Judgment to Calculation.* San Francisco: Freeman.

Wiggins, D. (1971), On sentence-sense, word-sense, and difference of word-

sense: Towards a philosophical theory of dictionaries. In: *Semantics: An Interdisciplinary Reader in Philosophy, Linguistics and Psychology*, eds. D. D. Steinberg & L. A. Jakobovits. London: Cambridge University Press, pp. 14–34.
Wigner, E. (1982), The limitations of the validity of present-day physics. In: *Mind in Nature*, ed. R. Q. Elvee. San Francisco: Harper & Row, pp. 118–133.
Wilber, K. (Ed.) (1982), *The Holographic Paradigm and other Paradoxes: Exploring the Leading Edge of Science*. Boulder, CO: Shambala.
────── (1983), *Eye to Eye: The Quest for the New Paradigm*. New York: Anchor Doubleday.
────── (Ed.) (1984), *Quantum Questions: Mystical Writings of the Great Physicists*. Boulder, CO: Shambala.
Winch, P. (1958), *The Idea of a Social Science*. New York: Humanities Press.
Winnicott, D. W. (1965), *The Maturational Processes and the Facilitating Environment*. New York: International Universities Press.
────── (1971), *Playing and Reality*. New York: Basic Books.
────── (1975), *Through Paediatrics to Psycho-analysis*. New York: Basic Books.
Wolman, B. B. (1971), Does psychology need its own philosophy of science? *American Psychologist*, 26: 877–886.
────── (Ed.) (1972), *Success and Failure in Psychoanalysis and Psychotherapy*. New York: Macmillan.
Yankelovich, D., & Barrett, W. (1970), *Ego and Instinct: The Psychoanalytic View of Nature—Revised*. New York: Random House.

Author Index

A

Abelson, R., 43
Arnold, M. B., 92
Austin, J. L., 48, 69, 121
Axelrod, C. D., 155

B

Barker, S. F., 49
Barrett, W., 3, 32, 36, 45, 47, 49, 51, 57, 58, 62, 63, 67, 74, 75, 76, 77, 80, 82, 83, 92, 105, 116, 126, 130, 132, 151
Bartley, W. W., 89
Basch, M. F., 115, 188, 189
Bateson, G., 157
Bellman, R., 57, 62, 88
Berger, L. S., 4, 36, 42, 137, 177, 189
Bergson, H., 62, 77, 172
Bettelheim, B., 5, 18, 69, 107, 108, 126, 162, 164
Black, M., 75, 77, 80, 92
Bohm, D., 51, 85, 119, 131, 155, 157
Boring, E., 43
Boscolo, L., 171, 172
Bowlby, J., 12, 59
Braginsky, B. M., 69, 156, 172, 178
Braginsky, D. D., 69, 156, 172, 178
Brenner, C., 109, 188
Bromberger, S., 45, 47
Bronowski, J., 41, 43, 45, 54, 57, 68, 88, 90, 93, 94
Buber, M., 80
Bunge, M., 41, 172

C

Campbell, K., 22
Capra, F., 86
Cecchin, G., 171, 172
Chao, Y. R., 72, 74
Chappell, V. C., 74, 125
Chessick, R. D., 21, 22, 26
Chomsky, N., 68, 72
Church, A., 89

D

Danehy, J. J., 86
Danto, A. C., 80, 94, 184
Davis, P. J., 41, 46, 56, 69, 101
de Bono, E., 134
Deese, J., 189

Deikman, A. J., 57, 63
d'Espagnat, B., 57
Dorpat, T. L., 68
Dreyfus, H. L., 41, 43, 55, 57, 61, 69, 74, 84, 88, 96, 176, 182

E

Eccles, J. C., 183
Edelson, M., 78
Eissler, K. R., 9
Engelmann, P., 62, 75, 76, 77, 89
Erickson, S. A., 76
Ezorsky, G., 130

F

Fairbairn, W. R. D., 10, 19
Feffer, M., 66, 180, 183, 185
Fenichel, O., 9, 10, 12, 13, 19, 22, 23, 26, 27, 30, 32, 71, 102, 107, 150
Feyerabend, P., 84
Feynman, R. P., 158
Fliess, R., 71
Fodor, J. A., 47
Freud, A., 169
Freud, S., 10, 13, 14, 19, 21, 22, 104
Friedman, L., 10, 20, 29, 32, 42, 79, 137, 159, 160, 162, 164
Friedman, L. J., 10, 164
Furlong, F. W., 62

G

Gadamer, H-G., 47, 56, 57, 58, 81, 84, 93, 98, 182
Gedo, J. E., 1, 9, 12, 16, 17, 20, 28, 29, 31, 32, 59, 86, 115, 146, 160, 162, 163, 164, 165

Gill, M. M., 3, 9, 11, 12, 86, 143, 188
Giorgi, A., 172
Gitelson, M., 102
Glover, E., 2, 9, 11, 12, 20, 21, 22, 32, 102, 150, 162
Goldberg, A., 9, 20, 28, 29, 31, 32, 86, 160, 164
Goldstein, H., 40
Gomez-Schwartz, B., 21
Goodman, N., 84, 88, 90
Goodstein, R. L., 182, 183
Graves, J. C., 19, 37, 39, 49, 82, 101, 106, 111, 112, 116, 117, 129, 133, 152, 182
Greenson, R. R., 2, 20, 27
Grene, M., 59, 63
Grunbaum, A., 45, 47
Guntrip, H., 11, 22, 24, 33, 59, 150, 189

H

Hacking, I., 43, 45, 50, 72, 76, 77, 90, 94, 179, 189
Hadley, S. W., 21
Hanson, N., 47
Hardwick, C. S., 179
Harth, E., 172
Hartmann, H., 10, 12, 15, 24, 42
Hersh, R., 41, 46, 56, 69, 101
Hexter, J. H., 63, 69, 81, 98, 118, 120, 122, 125, 128, 131, 151, 156
Hockett, C. F., 86
Hoffman, R. R., 37, 83
Hoffmann, B., 156
Holt, R. R., 3, 31, 35, 36, 72, 78
Holton, G., 57
Horowitz, M. J., 43
Horwitz, L., 21, 26

Author Index

Hughes, R. I. G., 57
Hunter, G., 41, 72

I, J

Ingleby, D., 47, 57, 62, 68, 107, 121, 177
Jacobson, E., 92
Jacoby, R., 107
Jameson, F., 68, 72, 89
Janik, A., 40, 45, 54, 57, 61, 66, 74, 76, 77, 82, 88, 89, 93, 130
Jaynes, J., 58, 69, 85, 92, 121, 152
Jordan, N., 62, 172, 178

K

Kachele, H., 10, 31, 36, 61, 79, 86, 98, 116, 137, 138, 142
Kahn, J., 130
Kaiser, H., 143
Kamin, L. J., 67, 69, 187
Kaplan, D. M., 10, 63
Kaufmann, W., 63
Keat, R., 11, 62, 108, 115, 142, 143, 185
Kernberg, O., 14, 17, 23, 26, 109, 146, 147, 181, 188
Klein, G. S., 3, 5, 11, 30, 31, 32, 36, 59, 86, 109, 143, 144, 188
Klein, M., 122
Koch, S., 85, 173
Kohut, H., 15, 16, 17, 18, 20, 26, 30, 47, 62, 86, 102, 109, 128, 147, 150, 161, 162, 165, 167
Kovel, J., 10, 63, 67, 71, 93, 145, 146, 150, 163
Kris, E., 10
Kubie, L. S., 5, 34, 79
Kuhn, T. S., 37
Kumar, S., 57, 191
Kwawer, J. S., 26

L

Lacan, J., 150
Laing, R. D., 55, 57, 63
Langer, S., 43, 47, 171, 172, 174, 175
Laplanche, J., 14, 71, 97, 161, 181, 190
Leavy, S. A., 11, 36
Lecky, P., 172
Leighton, R. B., 158
Leites, N., 20, 34, 161
Lerner, H. D., 26
Lerner, P. M., 26
Levenson, E., 1, 12, 23, 24, 34, 87, 102, 151
Levine, F. J., 79
Lewontin, R. C., 67, 69, 187
Lichtenberg, J. D., 92, 159, 164, 170
Linge, D. E., 59, 98
Loevinger, J., 151
Loewald, H. W., 12, 47, 63, 69, 102, 103, 108, 160, 183
Loewenstein, R. M., 10, 71
London, I. D., 172
Louch, A. R., 47, 92, 172, 176

M

Malcolm, N., 43, 48, 84, 88, 92
Margenau, H., 185
Matson, W. I., 66, 172
Matte Blanco, I., 12, 20, 24, 34, 36, 61, 83, 109, 150
McGill, V. J., 130, 131
McIntosh, D., 30, 59, 138
Mehan, H., 59, 69, 84, 88
Merleau-Ponty, M., 48, 57, 172
Milner, M., 69
Modell, A., 10, 12, 20, 28, 164
Morgenbesser, S., 184

N

Nagel, E., 45, 47
Nead, J. M., 37, 83
Needles, W., 13
Nozick, R., 47
Nunberg, H., 19

O

O'Manique, J. T., 77
Ornston, D. G., 5, 126, 127
Osgood, C. E., 43
Overton, W. F., 81

P,Q

Palazzoli, M. S., 171, 172
Paris, B. J., 157
Paul, I. H., 143
Pepper, S. C., 45, 47, 69
Peterfreund, E., 34, 116
Pittenger, R. E., 86
Polanyi, M., 111
Pollio, H., 54, 58
Pollock, G. H., 59
Pontalis, J-B., 14, 71, 97, 161, 181
Popper, K. R., 183
Powers, J., 50, 51, 129
Prata, G., 171, 172
Pruyser, P., 79
Quine, W. V., 76, 90

R

Rabil, A., 56
Rapaport, D., 30, 32, 86, 188
Rapoport, A., 43
Reich, W., 106
Robinson, I., 57, 75, 76, 80, 83, 84, 88, 89, 184
Rogers, C., 163
Rommetveit, R., 74, 80, 82, 88, 96, 126, 175
Rorty, R., 36, 41, 42, 43, 44, 45, 47, 48, 49, 51, 57, 63, 69, 74, 76, 77, 92, 93, 98, 125, 130, 131, 132, 154, 174, 185, 187
Rose, S., 67, 69, 182
Rosen, V. H., 78, 79, 137
Rosenblatt, B., 12
Rosenthal, R., 48, 178
Rosnow, R. L., 48, 178
Royce, J. R., 119, 172
Rubinstein, B. B., 30, 32, 35, 59, 116
Ryle, G., 95, 126

S

Sandler, J., 12
Sands, M., 158
Schafer, R., 5, 11, 18, 26, 31, 48, 59, 70, 78, 79, 102, 103, 109, 140, 144, 145, 150, 159, 160, 161, 162, 163
Schimek, J. G., 20, 162
Schumacher, E. F., 57, 61, 63, 177, 181, 185, 191
Searle, J. R., 75, 84, 88
Seeman, J., 108
Settle, T., 45, 47, 76, 172
Shea, W. R., 45
Sherwood, M., 95, 102, 129, 138
Slap, J. W., 79
Spence, D. P., 79, 86, 162
Spiro, A., 146
Stein, A., 1, 20
Steiner, G., 34, 71, 78
Stoller, R., 59, 79, 181
Storr, A., 20
Strachey, J., 19, 102
Straus, E. W., 92

Author Index

Strupp, H. H., 1, 20
Succi, G. J., 43
Sugarman, A., 26
Sutherland, J. D., 11, 12, 102

T,U,V

Tannenbaum, P. H., 43
Thayer, H. S., 130
Thoma, H., 10, 31, 36, 61, 79, 86, 98, 116, 137, 138, 142
Toulmin, S., 40, 45, 57, 61, 66, 74, 76, 77, 82, 88, 89, 93, 130
Turner, M. B., 45
Urmson, J. O., 77
von Neumann, J., 88
von Wright, G. H., 43, 47, 118, 119, 185, 186

W

Waelder, R., 12, 30
Wallerstein, R. S., 1, 34, 59, 146

Wartofsky, M. W., 42
Weber, R., 51, 131, 157
Weil, A., 54, 57
Weizenbaum, J., 41, 43, 57, 59, 63, 69, 72, 75, 89, 90, 151
Wigner, E., 40
Wilber, K., 51, 119
Winch, P., 172
Winnicott, D. W., 11, 28, 84, 135, 162, 164, 168, 183
Wolf, E. S., 15, 16, 18, 30
Wolman, B. B., 21, 41, 42, 43, 47, 48, 69
Wood, H., 59, 69, 84, 88
Wright, S. E., 130

Y

Yankelovich, D., 3, 32, 36, 45, 47, 51, 58, 83, 92, 105, 116, 143, 151

Subject Index

A

Action, therapeutic; see Theory, clinical
Affects, 42, 91–92, 188–191
Alienation, 62–64, 68, 87–90
Artifact, 54, 84
Attributes, as states, 42–44, 74–77, 90–92, 174

B

Biology, 54, 67, 88, 187
Boundary, 64–67, 84, 179–181, 183–184

C

Certainty, 38, 45–50, 68–69, 116, 130
Cheshire Cat phenomenon, 55–56, 59, 83, 89
Clinical theory; see Theory, clinical
Computers, 43, 55–56, 60–61, 66, 75, 88, 96
Construction, psychoanalytic, 161–162
Correlation, 28–30, 164–172

D

Data, theory and, 31, 38–39, 42–43, 45–49, 55–56, 61, 72, 74–77, 90–92, 116, 118–124, 131, 173
Descartes, R.; see Frameworks, Cartesian
Determinism, 40–42, 60, 151, 184–188
Development, human
 and language, 179–184
 and psychotherapy, 27–30, 163–170
Diagnosis, 26, 104, 134–135
Discourse, processive, 118–129, 132; see also Language, scientific; Narrative, psychoanalytic

E

Enfolded order; see Implicate order
Entailment, logical, 3–4, 9–12, 16–19, 115
Explanation, 25, 79, 91, 94–98, 102, 123–126, 133

210

Subject Index

F

Family therapy, 171–172
Focus, 4–6, 100–110, 119, 178
Formalism, definition of, 4
Frameworks, Cartesian
   criticisms of, 52–67, 69–70, 80–99, 118–129, 154–155, 172–177
   in psychoanalysis, 63, 143–146
   see also State process
Free will; *see* Determinism

G,H

Grammar, 73–76, 83
Habermas, J., 141–143
Hierarchies
   in language, 48–49, 85–87, 124–125, 128
   in psychoanalysis, 30–33, 86–87, 115–118, 142, 148
   in psychology, 85
   in theories, 39–40, 46, 48–49, 58–59, 112–115
History, 56, 81, 118, 126
Hologram, 34, 97

I

Implicate order, 51–53, 85–86
Interpretation
   of scientific formalisms, 39, 41–44, 72
   psychoanalytic, 17, 19, 137, 161–162, 168

K,L

Kaiser, H., 143
Knowledge, 12, 41, 55–56, 62–67, 100, 177

Language, acquisition of, 179–184
Language, ordinary, 78–79, 94–98, 125–129, 140, 175
Language, scientific
   in psychoanalysis, 71–72, 77–80, 95, 137–141
   referential function of, 48–49, 72, 74–77, 79–80, 90–92
   structure of, 48–49, 61–62, 72–77, 83–87, 175
   see also Logic
Language, transparency of, 90–91, 94–98, 122–128, 137–140
Language, unorthodox conceptions of, 80–98, 118–129, 133, 140, 177
Level, cognitive, 112–118
Life world, 56–67, 81, 95–97, 187
Limitative theorems; *see* Paradox, logical
Linearity, 82
Logic, 37–39, 43, 45–46, 61–64, 72–79, 81–87, 95, 112, 121, 138–140
   language and, 73–77, 78, 90–98
   limitations of, 60–64, 76, 81–99, 120, 123, 129–130, 151

M

Mathematics, 40–42, 45–46, 56, 60–61, 77, 173
   and psychology, 172–177
   pure versus applied, 101–102
Medicine, 54, 103–110, 177
Metapsychology, 11–12, 71, 79–80, 86, 115–116; *see also* Hierarchies; Theory,

clinical; Theory,
    psychoanalytic
Models
    general scientific, 26, 36, 39–40, 43, 61, 112–114, 127, 176
    psychoanalytic, 26–28, 34, 69–70, 127, 140–141

N,O

Narrative, process; see Discourse, processive
Narrative, psychoanalytic, 70, 95, 138–140
"Normal science," 34, 37–45, 89–90, 101, 173
Observation, 29, 46–50, 52–53, 64–67, 74–77, 79, 85–87, 175
Operationalization, 49–50, 82, 130
Overkill, 23–25, 105–106, 146, 171

P

Paradigm, pure knowledge medical; see Pure knowledge medical paradigm
Paradox, logical, 46, 64–67, 75, 93–94, 180–181, 183
Physics, 15, 40–42, 51–55, 106, 119, 149, 156, 158, 185
Positivism, 36, 45, 46, 62–64
Pragmatism, 97, 111, 125, 129–136, 178–179
    clinical, 115–118, 129, 159–170
Proposals, psychoanalytic, 136–149

Psychology
    criticisms of, 172–179
    and psychoanalysis, 102–103
    and state representations, 42–44, 69–70, 91–92, 172–179
Psychopathology, conceptions of, 23, 104–106, 159–160
Pure knowledge medical paradigm, 5, 100–110, 144, 166, 171

Q,R

Questions, significance of, 6, 60–61, 131, 155–157
Reflexivity; see Paradox, logical
Relevance, clinical, 2–4, 5, 9–12, 102–109, 132–149, 159–172
Representation; see State process
Russell, B., 74, 90, 94, 95

S

Self-reference; see Paradox, logical
Science
    technology and, 33, 101, 131, 178
    unity of, 111, 152
State process
    analysis, 176–177, 182–184, 187
    criticism of, 44–69, 80–99, 155, 172–191
    description of, 37–40
    and language, 44, 70, 74–77, 80–98
    and psychology, 42–44, 57, 62–67, 69–70, 174, 177, 185

Subject Index

and representation, 36, 47–48, 60–64, 67–70, 174–177, 187

T

Technique, psychoanalytic
 origins of, 13–19, 104–105
 and theory, 10–20, 21–34, 102–107, 115–118, 141–149
 theory of; see Theory, clinical
Teleology, 185–187
Theory, clinical, 30–33, 111, 115–118, 136, 141–149, 159–172
Theory, psychoanalytic
 and diagnosis, 26, 104
 and observation, 23, 25, 47–48
 structure of, 30, 39, 59, 61, 115–129, 159; see also Discourse, processive; Hierarchies; Metapsychology
Theory, scientific
 commensurability, 50–51
 derivative status of, 59–60, 83
 and practice, 15, 33–34
 referents of, 38–39, 46–51, 112–113
 reinterpretation of, 19–20, 106–107
 structure of, 37–40, 85, 112–115
Therapy, theory of; see Theory, clinical
Thought experiment, 134–136
Translation
 of Freud, 127, 140–141; see also Language, ordinary
 from infant to adult needs, 29, 163–170
Turing machine, 43, 75, 88, 176; see also Computers

U,V,W

Undifferentiated phase, 167, 180–183
Verification principle, 49–50
Wittgenstein, L., 61–62, 65, 72, 89, 111, 119, 126, 179